Partners

Partners

AN ANTHOLOGY OF READINGS

Selected by Jane Syburg

FIDES PUBLISHERS, INC.
NOTRE DAME, INDIANA

Preface

concerned w marriage [handwritten]

The literature in *Partners* is concerned with marriage. The selections begin with a story showing the effects of an unsuccessful marriage; the main body of the anthology explores various sides of the one man-one woman relationship: a comparison of the male and female viewpoints, expectation and reality, independence and interdependence, compromise, money, sex and various crises; the selections end on a hopeful, joyous note.

The purpose of the anthology is to show, through emotionally involving literary experiences, truths of the marital relationship. There is no attempt to glamorize or sentimentalize the subject, as that type of indoctrination only leads to disillusionment when it is found to be false. The truth of a good marriage is both attractive and challenging, and this literature concerned with it should contain insights for married and unmarried alike.

As an aid to group discussion of the material collected here, a companion volume, PARTNERS DISCUSSION GUIDE, has been prepared which suggests themes to explore, additional resources to tap, and discussion questions.

[handwritten notes:]
- unsuccessful marriage
- one man - one woman relationship
- ♂ vs. ♀ viewpoints
- expectation and reality
- independence and interdependence

Contents

√SONGS MY FATHER SANG ME 9
Elizabeth Bowen

√HER LOVER 24
Maxim Gorky

√A FATHER-TO-BE 31
Saul Bellow

EXCERPTS FROM THE PEARL 43
John Steinbeck

THE GRAPES OF WRATH, CHAPTER I 52
John Steinbeck

THE TWELVE-POUND LOOK 56
James M. Barrie

√THE STRANGER 76
Katherine Mansfield

MIDCENTURY LOVE LETTER 90
Phyllis McGinley

ON THE SUSSEX DOWNS 91
Sara Teasdale

THE SLEEPING BEAUTY 92

DO YOU LOVE ME? 98
Sheldon Harnick

√THE CHASER 100
John Collier

LOVE POEM 104
John Frederick Nims

√THE GIRLS IN THEIR SUMMER DRESSES 105
Irwin Shaw

√A COUPLE OF HAMBURGERS 112
James Thurber

√FOR WORSE IS BETTER AND
SICKNESS IS IN HEALTH 117
Calvin Trillin

THE ELDEST CHILD   125
  Maeve Brennan
THE AMERICAN WIFE   133
  Frank O'Connor
SEA CHEST   148
  Carl Sandburg
THE GIFT OF THE MAGI   149
  O. Henry
THE FUR COAT   156
  Sean O'Faolain
WHEAT CLOSED HIGHER, COTTON WAS MIXED   164
  Seymour Epstein
THE CHEMIST'S WIFE   181
  Anton Chekhov
WIFE-WOOING   188
  John Updike
EXCERPT FROM THE SONG OF SONGS   193
ACE IN THE HOLE   194
  John Updike
GOLDEN WEDDING   204
  Ruth Suckow
THE WIFE   225
  Washington Irving
A DOMESTIC DILEMMA   233
  Carson McCullers
WILL YOU PLEASE BE QUIET, PLEASE?   245
  Raymond Carver
EXCERPTS FROM ROMEO AND JULIET   270
  William Shakespeare
THE LAMP   275
  Sara Teasdale
QUOTE FROM THE BIBLE   276
O MY LOVELY CAROLINE   277
  Hobert Skidmore

ELIZABETH BOWEN

Songs My Father Sang Me

"What's the matter," he asked, "have I said something?"

Not troubling to get him quite into focus, she turned her head and said, "No, why—did you say anything?"

"Or p'r'aps you don't like this place?"

"I don't mind it—why?" she said, looking round the night club, which was not quite as dark as a church, as though for the first time. At some tables you had to look twice, to see who was there; what lights there were were dissolved in a haze of smoke; the walls were rather vault-like, with no mirrors; on the floor dancers drifted like pairs of vertical fish. He, meanwhile, studied her from across their table with neither anxiety nor acute interest, but with a dreamlike caricature of both. Then he raised the bottle between them and said, "Mm-mm?" to which she replied by placing the flat of her hand mutely, mulishly, across the top of her glass. Not annoyed, he shrugged, filled up his own and continued, "Then anything isn't really the matter then?"

"This tune, this song, is the matter."

"Oh—shall we dance?"

"No." Behind her agelessly girlish face, sleekly framed by the cut of her fawn-blonde hair, there passed a wave of genuine trouble for which her features had no vocabulary. "It's what they're playing—this tune."

"It's pre-war," he said knowledgeably.

"It's last war."

"Well, last war's pre-war."

"It's the tune my father remembered he used to dance to; it's the tune I remember him always trying to sing."

"Why, is your father dead?"

"No, I don't suppose so; why?"

"Sorry," he said quickly, "I mean, if . . ."

"Sorry, why are you sorry?" she said, raising her eyebrows. "Didn't I ever tell you about my father? I always thought he made me rather a bore. Wasn't it you I was telling about my father?"

"No. I suppose it must have been someone else. One meets so many people."

"Oh, what," she said, "have I hurt your feelings? But you haven't got any feelings about me."

"Only because you haven't got any feelings about me."

"Haven't I?" she said, as though really wanting to know. "Still, it hasn't seemed all the time as though we were quite a flop."

"Look," he said, "don't be awkward. Tell me about your father."

"He was twenty-six."

"When?"

"How do you mean, 'when'? Twenty-six was my father's age. He was tall and lean and leggy, with a casual sort of way of swinging himself about. He was fair, and the shape of his face was a rather long narrow square. Sometimes his eyes faded in until you could hardly see them; sometimes he seemed to be wearing a blank mask. You really only quite got the plan of his face when it was turned halfway between a light and a shadow—*then* his eyebrows and eyehollows, the dints just over his nostrils, the cut of his upper lip and the cleft of his chin, and the broken in-and-out outline down from his temple past his cheekbone into his jaw all came out at you, like a message you had to read in a single flash."

She paused and lighted a cigarette. He said, "You sound as though you had never got used to him."

She went on, "My father was one of the young men who were not killed in the last war. He was a man in the last war until that stopped; then I don't quite know what he was, and I don't think he ever quite knew either. He got his commission and first went out to France about 1915, I think he said. When he got leaves he got back to London and had good times, by which I mean something larky but quite romantic, in the course of one of which, I don't know which one, he fell in love with my mother and they used to go dancing, and got engaged in that leave and got married the next. My mother was a flapper, if you knew about flappers? They were the pin-ups *de ses jours*, and at the same time inspired idealistic feeling. My mother was dark and fluffy and as slim as a wraith; a great *glacé* ribbon bow tied her hair back and stood out like a calyx behind her face, and her hair itself hung down in a plume so long that it tickled my father's hand while he held her while they were dancing and while she sometimes swam up at him with her violet eyes. Each time he had to go back to the front again she was miserable, and had to put her hair up, because her relations said it was high time. But sometimes when he got back again on leave she returned to being a flapper again, to please him. Between his leaves she had to go back to live with her mother and sisters in West Kensington; and her sisters had a whole pack of business friends who had somehow never had to go near the front, and all these combined in an effort to cheer her up, but, as she always wrote to my father, nothing did any good. I suppose everyone felt it was for the best when they knew there was going to be the patter of little feet. I wasn't actually *born* till the summer of 1918. If you remember, I told you my age last night.

"The first thing *I* remember, upon becoming conscious, was living in one of those bungalows on the flats near Staines. The river must have been somewhere, but I don't think I saw it. The

only point about that region is that it has no point and that it
goes on and on. I think there are floods there sometimes, there
would be nothing to stop them; a forest fire would be what is
needed really, but that would not be possible as there are no
trees. It would have looked better, really, just left as primeval
marsh, but someone had once said, 'Let there be bungalows.' If
you ever motored anywhere near it you probably asked yourself
who lives there, and why. Well, my father and mother and I
did, and why?—because it was cheap, and there was no one to
criticize how you were getting on. Our bungalow was tucked
well away in the middle, got at by a sort of maze of in those days
unmade roads. I'm glad to say I've forgotten which one it was.
Most of our neighbours kept themselves to themselves for, probably, like ours, the best reasons, but most of them kept hens also;
we didn't even do that. All round us, nature ran riot between
corrugated iron, clothes-lines and creosoted lean-to sheds.

"I know that our bungalow had been taken furnished; the
only things we seemed to have of our own were a number of
satin cushions with satin fruits stitched on. In order to dislodge
my biscuit crumbs from the satin apples my mother used to
shake the cushions out of the window on to the lawn. Except for
the prettiness of the dandelions, our lawn got to look and feel
rather like a hearth-rug; I mean, it got covered with threads and
cinders and shreds; once when I was crawling on it I got a pin
in my hand, another time I got sharp glass beads in my knee. The
next-door hens used to slip through and pick about; never, apparently, quite in vain. At the far end, some Dorothy Perkins
roses tried to climb up a pergola that was always falling down.
I remember my father reaching up in his shirt-sleeves, trying to
nail it up. Another thing he had to do in our home was apply the
whole of his strength to the doors, french window and windows,
which warped until they would not open nor shut. I used to
come up behind him and push too.

"The war by now, of course, had been over for some years;
my father was out of the British Army and was what was called

taking his time and looking around. For how long he had been doing so I can't exactly tell you. He not only read all the 'post vacant' advertisements every day but composed and succeeded in getting printed an advertisement of himself, which he read aloud to me: it said he was prepared to go anywhere and try anything. I said, 'But what's an ex-officer?', and he said, 'I am.' Our dining-room table, which was for some reason possibly me, sticky, was always spread with new newspapers he had just brought home, and he used to be leaning over them on his elbows, biting harder and harder on the stem of his pipe. I don't think I discovered for some years later that the principal reason for newspapers is news. My father never looked at them for that reason—just as he always lost interest in any book in which he had lost his place. Or perhaps he was not in the mood for world events. My mother had never cared much for them at the best of times. 'To think of all we expected after the war,' she used to say to my father, from day to day.

"My mother, by this time, had had her hair shingled—in fact, *I* never remember her any other way than with a dark shaved point tapered down the back of her neck. I don't know when she'd begun to be jealous of him and me. Every time he came back from an interview that he hadn't got to or from an interview that hadn't come to anything, he used to bring me back something, to cheer himself up, and the wheels off all the mechanical toys got mixed with the beads and the threads and the cinders into our lawn. What my mother was really most afraid of was that my father would bundle us all off into the great open spaces, in order to start fresh somewhere and grow something. I imagine he knew several chaps who had, or were going to. After one or two starts on the subject he shut up, but I could see she could see he was nursing it. It frustrated her from nagging at him all out about not succeeding in getting a job in England: she was anxious not to provide an opening for him to say, 'Well, there's always one thing we *could* do . . .' The hard glassy look her eyes got made them look like doll's eyes, which may partly have been what kept me from liking dolls. So they practically never talked about anything. I don't think she even knew he minded about her hair.

"You may be going to ask when my father sang. He often *began* to sing—when he hammered away at the pergola, when something he thought of suddenly struck him as good, when the heave he gave at the warped french window sent it flying open into the garden. He was constantly starting to sing, but he never got very far—you see, he had no place where he could sing unheard. The walls were thin and the lawn was tiny and the air round the bungalow was so silent and heavy that my mother was forced to listen to every note. The lordly way my father would burst out singing, like the lordly way he cocked his hat over one eye, had come to annoy her, in view of everything else. But the still more unfortunate thing was that my father only knew, or else only liked, two tunes, which were two tunes out of the bygone years which made him think of the war and being in love. Yes, they were dance tunes; yes, we have just heard one; yes, they also reminded my mother of war and love. So when he had got to the fourth or fifth bar of either, she would call out to know if he wanted to drive her mad. He would say and say, 'Sorry,' but if he was in the mood he'd be well away, the next minute, with the alternative tune, and she would be put to the trouble of stopping that.

"Mother did not know what to look like now she was not a flapper. Mostly she looked like nothing—I wonder whether she knew. Perhaps that was what she saw in the satin cushions: they looked like something—at least, to her. The day she and I so suddenly went to London to call on her sister's friend she did certainly manage, however, to look like something. My father, watching us down the garden path, ventured no comment on her or my appearance. However, which ought to have cheered me up, we created quite a furore in the train. We went sailing into the richly-appointed office of mother's sister's friend, who was one of those who, during the war, had felt mother should be cheered up. Can I, need I, describe him? The usual kind of business pudge, in a suit. He looked in a reluctant way at my mother, and reluctantly, slightly morbidly, at me. I don't know how I got the impression mother held all the cards. The conversation, of course, flowed over my head—I just cruised round and round the room, knocking objects over. But the outcome—as I gathered when we got home—was that mother's sister's friend said he'd give my father a job. He had said he could use an ex-officer, provided it was an ex-officer with charm. What my father would have to do was to interest housewives, not in himself but in vacuum cleaners. If it helped to interest some housewives in vacuum cleaners, he could interest them just a little bit in himself. Mother's sister's friend called this, using judgment of character.

"When my mother, that evening, put all this to my father, he did not say anything but simply stood and stared. *She* said, 'Then I suppose you want us to starve?'

"So my father stopped being a problem and became a travelling salesman. The best part was that the firm allowed him a car.

"I must say for my mother that she did not ask my father how he was getting on. At least she had much less trouble about the singing: sometimes he'd be away for two or three days together; when he was home he simply sprawled in his chair, now and then asking when there'd be something to eat, as unmusical as a gramophone with the spring broken. When I came filtering in he sometimes opened one eye and said, 'And what have *you* been doing?'—as though he'd just finished telling me what he'd been doing himself. He garaged the car some way down the next road, and in the mornings when he was starting off I used to walk with him to the garage. He used to get into the car, start up the engine, back out, then look round at me and say, 'Like to come out on the job?—yes, I bet you would,' then let the clutch in and whizz off. Something about this always made me feel sick.

"I don't of course clearly remember when this began, or how long it went on for; but I know when it stopped. The night before my seventh birthday was a June night, because my birthdays are in June. The people who lived all round us were sitting

out, on the verandas or on their lawns, but my mother had sent
me to bed early because she was having a party for me next day
and did not want to get me over-excited. My birthday cake
which had arrived from the shop was on the dining-room side-
board, with a teacloth over it to keep the flies off, and my father
and mother were in the lounge with the french window shut,
because she had several things to say to him that she did not want
the people all round to hear. The heat travelled through the roof
into all the rooms, so that I could not sleep; also, my bed was
against the wall of my room, and the lounge was the other side
of the wall. My mother went on like someone who has been
saving up—just some touch, I suppose, had been needed to set
her off. She said she would like to know why there was not more
money—my father's job, I suppose now, was on a commission
basis. Or, she said, was he keeping another woman?—a thing she
had heard that most travelling salesmen did. She said she really
felt quite ashamed of having foisted my father on to her sister's
friend, and that she only wondered how long the firm would
stand for it. She said her sisters pitied her, though she had tried
to conceal from them that her life was hell. My father, who had
as usual got home late and as usual had not yet had any supper,
could not be heard saying anything. My mother then said she
wished she knew why she had married him, and would like still
more to know why he had married her.

"My father said, 'You were so lovely—you've no idea.'

"Next morning there was a heat-haze over everything. I
bustled into the dining-room to see if there was anything on my
plate. I forget what my mother had given me, but her richest
sister had sent me a manicure-set in a purple box: all the objects
had purple handles and lay in grooves on white velvet. While I
was taking them out and putting them back again, my father
suddenly looked up from his coffee and said *his* present for me
was in the car, and that I'd have to come out and fetch it. My
mother could hardly say no to this, though of course I saw her
opening her mouth. So out we set, I gripping the manicure-set.

I don't think my father seemed odder than usual, though he was
on the point of doing an unexpected thing—when he had got the
car started and backed out he suddenly held open the other door
and said, 'Come on, nip in, look sharp; my present to you is a
day trip.' So then I nipped in and we drove off, as though this
were the most natural thing in the world.

"The car was a two-seater, with a let-down hood . . . No, of
course I cannot remember what make it was. That morning, the
hood was down. Locked up in the dickie behind my father kept
the specimen vacuum cleaner he interested women in. He drove
fast, and as we hit the bumps in the road I heard the parts of the
cleaner clonking about. As we drove, the sun began to burn its
way through the haze, making the roses in some of the grander
gardens look almost impossibly large and bright. My bare knees
began to grill on the leather cushion, and the crumples eased out
of the front of my cotton frock.

"I had never been with my father when he was driving a car—
it felt as though speed and power were streaming out of him, and
as if he and I were devouring everything that we passed. I sat
slumped round with my cheek against the hot cushion and sometimes stared at his profile, sometimes stared at his wrists, till he
squinted round and said, 'Anything wrong with *me?*' Later on,
he added, 'Why not look at the scenery?' By that time there *was*
some scenery, if that means grass and trees; in fact, these had
been going on for some time, in a green band streaming behind
my father's face. When I said, 'Where are we going?' he said,
'Well, where *are* we going?' At that point I saw quite a large hill,
in fact a whole party of them, lapping into each other as though
they would never stop, and never having seen anything of the
kind before I could not help saying, 'Oh, I say, look!'

"My father gave a nod, without stopping singing—I told you
he had begun to sing? He had not only started but gone on:
when he came to the end of his first tune he said, 'Pom-*pom*,' like
a drum, then started through it again; after that he worked
around to the second, which he sang two or three times, with me

joining in. We both liked the second still better, and how right we were—and it's worn well, hasn't it? That's what this band's just played."

"Oh, what they've just played?" he said, and looked narrowly at the band; while, reaching round for the bottle on the table between them he lifted it to replenish her glass and his. This time she did not see or did not bother to stop him: she looked at her full glass vaguely, then vaguely drank. After a minute she went on:

"Ginger beer, sausage rolls, chocolate—that was what we bought when we stopped at the village shop. Also my father bought a blue comb off a card of combs, with which he attempted to do my hair, which had blown into tags and ratstails over my eyes and face. He looked at me while he combed in a puzzled way, as though something about me that hadn't struck him became a problem to him for the first time. I said, 'Aren't we going to sell any vacuum cleaners?' and he said, 'We'll try and interest the Berkshire Downs.' I thought that meant, meet a family; but all we did was turn out of the village and start up a rough track, to where there could not be any people at all. The car climbed with a slow but exciting roar; from the heat of the engine and the heat of the sun the chocolate in the paper bag in my hands was melting by the time we came to the top.

"From the top, where we lay on our stomachs in the shade of the car, we could see—oh well, can't you imagine, can't you? It was an outsize June day. The country below us looked all colours, and was washed over in the most reckless way with light; going on and on into the distance the clumps of trees and the roofs of villages and the church towers had quivering glimmers round them; but most of all there was space, sort of moulded space, and the blue of earth ran into the blue of sky.

"My father's face was turned away from me, propped up on his hand. I finally said to him, 'What's that?'

" 'What's what?' he said, startled.

" 'What we're looking at.'

" 'England,' he said, 'that's England. I thought I'd like to see her again.'

" 'But don't we live in England?'

"He took no notice. 'How I loved her,' he said.

" 'Oh, but don't you now?'

" 'I've lost her,' he said, 'or she's lost me; I don't quite know which; I don't understand what's happened.' He rolled round and looked at me and said, 'But *you* like it, don't you? I thought I'd like you to see, if just once, what I once saw.'

"I was well into the third of my sausage rolls: my mouth was full, I could only stare at my father. He said, 'And there's something else down there—see it?' I screwed my eyes up but still only saw the distance. 'Peace,' he said. 'Look hard at it; don't forget it.'

" 'What's peace?' I said.

" 'An idea you have when there's a war on, to make you fight well. An idea that gets lost when there isn't a war.'

"I licked pastry-crumbs off my chin and began on chocolate. By this time my father lay on his back, with his fingers thatched together over his eyes: he talked, but more to the sky than me. None of the things he was saying now went anywhere near my brain—a child's brain, how could they?—his actual words are gone as though I had never heard them, but his meaning lodged itself in some part of my inside, and is still there and has grown up with me. He talked about war and how he had once felt, and about leaves and love and dancing and going back to the war, then the birth of me—'Seven years ago to-day,' he said, 'seven years; I remember how they brought me the telegram.'

"Something else, on top of the sausage and heat and chocolate suddenly made me feel sick and begin to cry. 'Oh please, oh please don't,' I said, 'it's my birthday.'

" 'Don't what?' he said. I, naturally, didn't know. My father again looked at me, with the same expression he had worn when attempting to comb my hair. Something about me—my age?—was a proposition. Then he shut his eyes, like—I saw later, not at the time—somebody finally banishing an idea. 'No; it wouldn't work,' he said. 'It simply couldn't be done. You can wait for me if you want. I can't wait for you.'

"Then he began acting like somebody very sleepy: he yawned and yawned at me till I yawned at him. I didn't feel sick any more, but the heat of the afternoon came down like a grey-blue blanket over my head. 'What you and I want,' my father said, watching me, 'is a good sleep.'

"I wish I could tell you at *which* moment I fell asleep, and stopped blurrily looking at him between my eyelids, because *that* was the moment when I last saw my father.

"When I woke, there was no more shadow on my side of the car; the light had changed and everything looked bright yellow. I called to my father but he did not answer, for the adequate reason that he was not there. He was gone. For some reason I wasn't at all frightened; I thought he must have gone to look for something for us for tea. I remembered that I was not at my birthday party, and I must say I thought twice about that pink cake. I was more bored than anything, till I remembered my manicure-set, which owing to the funniness of the day I had not been able to open a second time. I took the objects out of their velvet bedding and began to prod at my nails, as I'd seen my mother do. Then I got up and walked, once more, all the way round the car. It was then that I noticed what I had missed before: a piece of white paper twisted into the radiator. I couldn't read handwriting very well, but did at last make out what my father had put. '*The car and the vacuum cleaner are the property of Messrs. X and X*' (the firm of my mother's sister's friend), '*the child is the property of Mrs. So-and-so, of Such-and-such*' (I needn't bother to give you my mother's name and the name of our bungalow), '*the manicure-set, the comb and anything still left in the paper bags are the property of the child. Signed——*' It was signed with my father's name.

"The two dots I saw starting zigzag up the side of the down turned out to be two sweating policemen. What happened when they came to where I was was interesting at the moment but is not interesting now. They checked up on the message on the front of the car, then told me my father had telephoned to the police station, and that I was to be a good girl and come with them. When they had checked up on the cleaner, we all drove down. I remember the constable's knobby, sticky red hands looked queer on the wheel where my father's had lately been . . . At the police station, someone or other's wife made quite a fuss about me and gave me tea, then we piled into another car and drove on again. I was soon dead asleep; and I only woke when we stopped in the dark at the gate of the bungalow.

"Having tottered down the path, in the light from the front door, my mother clawed me out of the car, sobbing. I noticed her breath smelt unusual. We and the policeman then trooped into the lounge, where the policeman kept nodding and jotting things on a pad. To cheer up my mother he said that England was very small—'And he's not, so far as you know, in possession of a passport?' I sucked blobs of chocolate off the front of my frock while my mother described my father to the policeman. 'But no doubt,' the policeman said, 'he'll be thinking better of this. A man's home is a man's home, I always say.'

"When my mother and I were left alone in the lounge, we stared at each other in the electric light. While she asked if I knew how unnatural my father was, she kept pouring out a little more from the bottle: she said she had to have medicine to settle her nerves, but it seemed to act on her nerves just the opposite way. That I wouldn't say what my father had said and done set her off fairly raving against my father. To put it mildly, she lost all kind of control. She finished up with: 'And such a fool, too— a fool, a fool!'

" 'He is not a fool,' I said, 'he's my father.'

" 'He is not your father,' she screamed, 'and he is a fool.'

"That made me stare at her, and her stare at me.

" 'How do you mean,' I said, 'my father is not my father?'

"My mother's reaction to this was exactly like as if someone had suddenly pitched a pail of cold water over her. She pulled herself up and something jumped in her eyes. She said she had not said anything of the sort, and that if I ever said she had I was a wicked girl. I said I hadn't said she had, but she had said so. She put on a worried look and put a hand on my forehead and said she could feel I'd got a touch of the sun. A touch of the sun, she said, would make me imagine things—and no wonder, after the day I'd had.

"All next day I was kept in bed; not as a punishment but as a kind of treat. My mother was ever so nice to me; she kept coming in to put a hand on my forehead. The one thing she did not do was get the doctor. And afterwards, when I was let get up, nothing was good enough for me; until really anyone would have thought that my mother felt she was in my power. Shortly after, her rich sister came down, and my mother then had a fine time, crying, talking and crying; the sister then took us back with her to London, where my mother talked and cried even more. Of course I asked my aunt about what my mother had said, but my aunt said that if I imagined such wicked things they would have to think there was something wrong with my brain. So I did not re-open the subject, and am not doing so now. In the course of time my mother succeeded in divorcing my father for desertion; she was unable to marry her sister's friend because he was married and apparently always had been, but she did marry a friend of her sister's friend's, and was soon respectably settled in Bermuda, where as far as I know she still is."

"But your father?" he said.

"Well, what about my father?"

"You don't mean you never heard anything more of him?"

"I never said so—he sent me two picture postcards. The last"
—she counted back—"arrived fourteen years ago. But there probably have been others that went astray. The way I've always lived, I'm not long at any address."

He essayed, rashly, "Been a bit of a waif?"

The look he got back for this was halfway between glass and ice. "A waif's the first thing I learned not to be. No, more likely my father decided, better leave it at that. People don't, on the whole, come back, and I've never blamed them. No, why should he be dead? Why should not he be—any place?"

"Here, for instance?"

"To-night, you mean?"

"Why not?" he said. "Why not—as you say?"

"Here?" She looked round the tables, as though she hardly knew where she was herself. She looked round the tables, over which smoke thickened, round which khaki melted into the khaki gloom. Then her eyes returned, to fix, with unsparing attention, an addled trio of men round the fifty-five mark. "Here?" she repeated, "my father?—I hope not."

"But I thought," he said, watching her watching the old buffers, "I thought we were looking for someone of twenty-six?"

"Give me a cigarette," she said, "and, also, don't be cruel."

"I wouldn't be," he said, as he lighted the cigarette, "if you had any feeling for me."

MAXIM GORKY

Her Lover

An acquaintance of mine once told me the following story.

When I was a student at Moscow I happened to live alongside one of those ladies who—you know what I mean. She was a Pole, and they called her Teresa. She was a tallish, powerfully-built brunette, with black, bushy eyebrows and a large coarse face as if carved out by a hatchet—the bestial gleam of her dark eyes, her thick bass voice, her cabman-like gait and her immense muscular vigour, worthy of a fishwife, inspired me with horror. I lived on the top flight and her garret was opposite to mine. I never left my door open when I knew her to be at home. But this, after all, was a very rare occurrence. Sometimes I chanced to meet her on the staircase or in the yard, and she would smile upon me with a smile which seemed to me to be sly and cynical. Occasionally, I saw her drunk, with bleary eyes, touzled hair, and a particularly hideous smile. On such occasions she would speak to me:

"How d'ye do, Mr. Student!" and her stupid laugh would still further intensify my loathing of her. I should have liked to have changed my quarters in order to have avoided such encounters and greetings; but my little chamber was a nice one, and there was such a wide view from the window, and it was always so quiet in the street below—so I endured.

From CHELKASH AND OTHER STORIES, copyright 1915, Alfred A. Knopf, Inc.

And one morning I was sprawling on my couch, trying to find some sort of excuse for not attending my class, when the door opened, and the bass voice of Teresa the loathsome, resounded from my threshold:

"Good health to you, Mr. Student!"

"What do you want?" I said. I saw that her face was confused and supplicatory . . . It was a very unusual sort of face for her.

"Look ye, sir! I want to beg a favour of you. Will you grant it me?"

I lay there silent, and thought to myself:

"Gracious! An assault upon my virtue, neither more nor less. —Courage, my boy!"

"I want to send a letter home, that's what it is," she said, her voice was beseeching, soft, timid.

"Deuce take you!" I thought; but up I jumped, sat down at my table, took a sheet of paper, and said:

"Come here, sit down, and dictate!"

She came, sat down very gingerly on a chair, and looked at me with a guilty look.

"Well, to whom do you want to write?"

"To Boleslav Kashput, at the town of Svyeptsyana, on the Warsaw Road. . . ."

"Well, fire away!"

"My dear Boles . . . my darling . . . my faithful lover. May the Mother of God protect thee! Thou heart of gold, why hast thou not written for such a long time to thy sorrowing little dove, Teresa?"

I very nearly burst out laughing. "A sorrowing little dove!" more than five feet high, with fists a stone and more in weight, and as black a face as if the little dove had lived all its life in a chimney, and had never once washed itself! Restraining myself somehow, I asked:

"Who is this Bolest?"

"Boles, Mr. Student," she said, as if offended with me for blundering over the name, "he is Boles—my young man."

"Young man!"

"Why are you so surprised, sir? Cannot I, a girl, have a young man?"

She? A girl? Well!

"Oh, why not?" I said, "all things are possible. And has he been your young man long?"

"Six years."

"Oh, ho!" I thought. "Well, let us write your letter. . . ."

And I tell you plainly that I would willingly have changed places with this Boles if his fair correspondent had been not Teresa, but something less than she.

"I thank you most heartily, sir, for your kind services," said Teresa to me, with a curtsey. "Perhaps *I* can show *you* some service, eh?"

"No, I most humbly thank you all the same."

"Perhaps, sir, your shirts or your trousers may want a little mending?"

I felt that this mastodon in petticoats had made me grow quite red with shame, and I told her pretty sharply that I had no need whatever of her services.

She departed.

A week or two passed away. It was evening. I was sitting at my window whistling and thinking of some expedient for enabling me to get away from myself. I was bored, the weather was dirty. I didn't want to go out, and out of sheer ennui I began a course of self-analysis and reflection. This also was dull enough work, but I didn't care about doing anything else. Then the door opened. Heaven be praised, someone came in.

"Oh, Mr. Student, you have no pressing business, I hope?"

It was Teresa. Humph!

"No. What is it?"

"I was going to ask you, sir, to write me another letter."

"Very well! To Boles, eh?"

"No, this time it is from him."

"What?"

"Stupid that I am! It is not for me, Mr. Student, I beg your pardon. It is for a friend of mine, that is to say, not a friend but an acquaintance—a man acquaintance. He has a sweetheart just like me here, Teresa. That's how it is. Will you, sir, write a letter to this Teresa?"

I looked at her—her face was troubled, her fingers were trembling. I was a bit fogged at first—and then I guessed how it was.

"Look here, my lady," I said, "there are no Boleses or Teresas at all, and you've been telling me a pack of lies. Don't you come sneaking about me any longer. I have no wish whatever to cultivate your acquaintance. Do you understand?"

And suddenly she grew strangely terrified and distaught; she began to shift from foot to foot without moving from the place, and spluttered comically, as if she wanted to say something and couldn't. I waited to see what would come of all this, and I saw and felt that, apparently, I had made a great mistake in suspecting her of wishing to draw me from the path of righteousness. It was evidently something very different.

"Mr. Student!" she began, and suddenly, waving her hand, she turned abruptly towards the door and went out. I remained with a very unpleasant feeling in my mind. I listened. Her door was flung violently to—plainly the poor wench was very angry. . . . I thought it over, and resolved to go to her, and, inviting her to come in here, write everything she wanted.

I entered her apartment. I looked round. She was sitting at the table, leaning on her elbows, with her head in her hands.

"Listen to me," I said.

Now, whenever I come to this point in my story, I always feel horribly awkward and idiotic. Well, well!

"Listen to me," I said.

She leaped from her seat, came towards me with flashing eyes, and laying her hands on my shoulders, began to whisper, or rather to hum in her peculiar bass voice:

"Look you, now! It's like this. There's no Boles at all, and there's no Teresa either. But what's that to you? Is it a hard thing for you to draw your pen over paper? Eh? Ah, and *you,* too! Still such a little fair-haired boy! There's nobody at all, neither Boles, nor Teresa, only me. There you have it, and much good may it do you!"

"Pardon me!" said I, altogether flabbergasted by such a reception, "what is it all about? There's no Boles, you say?"

"No. So it is."

"And no Teresa either?"

"And no Teresa. I'm Teresa."

I didn't understand it at all. I fixed my eyes upon her, and tried to make out which of us was taking leave of his or her senses. But she went again to the table, searching about for something, came back to me, and said in an offended tone:

"If it was so hard for you to write to Boles, look, there's your letter, take it! Others will write for me."

I looked. In her hand was my letter to Boles. Phew!

"Listen, Teresa! What is the meaning of all this? Why must you get others to write for you when I have already written it, and you haven't sent it?"

"Sent it where?"

"Why, to this—Boles."

"There's no such person."

I absolutely did not understand it. There was nothing for me but to spit and go. Then she explained.

"What is it?" she said, still offended. "There's no such person, I tell you," and she extended her arms as if she herself did not understand why there should be no such person. "But I wanted him to be . . . Am I then not a human creature like the rest of them? Yes, yes, I know, I know, of course. . . . Yet no harm was done to anyone by my writing to him that I can see. . . ."

"Pardon me—to whom?"

"To Boles, of course."

"But he doesn't exist."

"Alas! alas! But what if he doesn't? He doesn't exist, but he *might!* I write to him, and it looks as if he did exist. And Teresa —that's me, and he replies to me, and then I write to him again. . . ."

I understood at last. And I felt so sick, so miserable, so ashamed, somehow. Alongside of me, not three yards away, lived a human creature who had nobody in the world to treat her kindly, affectionately, and this human being had invented a friend for herself!

"Look, now! you wrote me a letter to Boles, and I gave it to someone else to read it to me; and when they read it to me I listened and fancied that Boles was there. And I asked you to write me a letter from Boles to Teresa—that is to me. When they write such a letter for me, and read it to me, I feel quite sure that Boles is there. And life grows easier for me in consequence."

"Deuce take thee for a blockhead!" said I to myself when I heard this.

And from thenceforth, regularly, twice a week, I wrote a letter to Boles, and an answer from Boles to Teresa. I wrote those answers well. . . . She, of course, listened to them, and wept like anything, roared, I should say, with her bass voice. And in return for my thus moving her to tears by real letters from the imaginary Boles, she began to mend the holes I had in my socks, shirts, and other articles of clothing. Subsequently, about three months after this history began, they put her in prison for something or other. No doubt by this time she is dead.

My acquaintance shook the ash from his cigarette, looked pensively at the sky, and thus concluded:

Well, well, the more a human creature has tasted of better things the more it hungers after the sweet things of life. And we, wrapped round in the rags of our virtues, and regarding others through the mist of our self-sufficiency, and persuaded of our universal impeccability, do not understand this.

And the whole thing turns out pretty stupidly—and very cruelly. The fallen classes, we say. And who are the fallen classes, I should like to know? They are, first of all, people with the same bones, flesh, and blood and nerves as ourselves. We have been told this day after day for ages. And we actually listen—and the Devil only knows how hideous the whole thing is. Or are we completely depraved by the loud sermonizing of humanism? In reality, we also are fallen folks, and so far as I can see, very deeply fallen into the abyss of self-sufficiency and the conviction of our own superiority. But enough of this. It is all as old as the hills—so old that it is a shame to speak of it. Very old indeed—yes, that's where it is!

SAUL BELLOW

A Father-To-Be

The strangest notions had a way of forcing themselves into Rogin's mind. Just thirty-one and passable-looking, with short black hair, small eyes, but a high, open forehead, he was a research chemist, and his mind was generally serious and dependable. But on a snowy Sunday evening while this stocky man, buttoned to the chin in a Burberry coat and walking in his preposterous gait—feet turned outward—was going toward the subway, he fell into a peculiar state.

He was on his way to have supper with his fiancee. She had phoned him a short while ago and said, "You'd better pick up a few things on the way."

"What do we need?"

"Some roast beef, for one thing. I bought a quarter of a pound coming home from my aunt's."

"Why a quarter of a pound, Joan?" said Rogin, deeply annoyed. "That's just about enough for one good sandwich."

"So you have to stop at a delicatessen. I had no more money."

He was about to ask, "What happened to the thirty dollars I gave you on Wednesday?" but he knew that would not be right.

"I had to give Phyllis money for the cleaning woman," said Joan.

From MOSBY'S MEMOIRS AND OTHER STORIES by Saul Bellow. Copyright © 1955 by Saul Bellow. Originally appeared in The New Yorker. Reprinted by permission of The Viking Press, Inc.

Phyllis, Joan's cousin, was a young divorcee, extremely wealthy. The two women shared an apartment.

"Roast beef," he said, "and what else?"

"Some shampoo, sweetheart. We've used up all the shampoo. And hurry, darling, I've missed you all day."

"And I've missed you," said Rogin, but to tell the truth he had been worrying most of the time. He had a younger brother whom he was putting through college. And his mother, whose annuity wasn't quite enough in these days of inflation and high taxes, needed money, too. Joan had debts he was helping her to pay, for she wasn't working. She was looking for something suitable to do. Beautiful, well-educated, aristocratic in her attitude, she couldn't clerk in a dime store; she couldn't model clothes (Rogin thought this made girls vain and stiff, and he didn't want her to); she couldn't be a waitress or a cashier. What could she be? Well, something would turn up, and meantime Rogin hesitated to complain. He paid her bills—the dentist, the department store, the osteopath, the doctor, the psychiatrist. At Christmas, Rogin almost went mad. Joan bought him a velvet smoking jacket with frog fasteners, a beautiful pipe, and a pouch. She bought Phyllis a garnet brooch, an Italian silk umbrella, and a gold cigarette holder. For other friends, she bought Dutch pewter and Swedish glassware. Before she was through, she had spent five hundred dollars of Rogin's money. He loved her too much to show his suffering. He believed she had a far better nature than his. She didn't worry about money. She had a marvelous character, always cheerful, and she really didn't need a psychiatrist at all. She went to one because Phyllis did and it made her curious. She tried too much to keep up with her cousin, whose father had made millions in the rug business.

While the woman in the drugstore was wrapping the shampoo bottle a clear idea suddenly arose in Rogin's thoughts. Money surrounds you in life as the earth does in death. Superimposition is the universal law. Who is free? No one is free. Who has no burdens? Everyone is under pressure. The very rocks, the waters of the earth, beasts, men, children—everyone has some weight to carry. This idea was extremely clear to him at first. Soon it became rather vague, but it had a great effect nevertheless, as if someone had given him a valuable gift. (Not like the velvet smoking jacket he couldn't bring himself to wear, or the pipe it choked him to smoke.) The notion that all were under pressure and affliction, instead of saddening him, had the opposite influence. It put him in a wonderful mood. It was extraordinary how happy he became and, in addition, clear-sighted. His eyes all at once were opened to what was around him. He saw with delight how the druggist and the woman who wrapped the shampoo bottle were smiling and flirting, how the lines of worry in her face went over into lines of cheer and the druggist's receding gums did not hinder his kidding and friend-liness. And in the delicatessen, also, it was amazing how much Rogin noted and what happiness it gave him simply to be there.

Delicatessens on Sunday night, when all other stores are shut, will overcharge you ferociously, and Rogin would normally have been on guard, but he was not tonight, or scarcely so. Smells of pickle, sausage, mustard, and smoked fish overjoyed him. He pitied the people who would buy the chicken salad and chopped herring; they could do it only because their sight was too dim to see what they were getting—the fat flakes of pepper on the chicken, the soppy herring, mostly vinegar-soaked stale bread. Who would buy them? Late risers, people living alone, waking up in the darkness of the afternoon, finding their re-frigerators empty, or people whose gaze was turned inward. The roast beef looked not bad, and Rogin ordered a pound.

While the storekeeper was slicing the meat, he yelled at a Puerto Rican kid who was reaching for a bag of chocolate cookies, "Hey, you want to pull me down the whole display on yourself? You, *chico*, wait a half a minute." This storekeeper, though he looked like one of Pancho Villa's bandits, the kind that smeared their enemies with syrup and staked them down on anthills, a man with toadlike eyes and stout hands made to clasp pistols hung around his belly, was not so bad. He was a New York man, thought Rogin—who was from Albany himself

—a New York man toughened by every abuse of the city, trained to suspect everyone. But in his own realm, on the board behind the counter, there was justice. Even clemency.

The Puerto Rican kid wore a complete cowboy outfit—a green hat with white braid, guns, chaps, spurs, boots, and gauntlets—but he couldn't speak any English. Rogin unhooked the cellophane bag of hard circular cookies and gave it to him. The boy tore the cellophane with his teeth and began to chew one of those dry chocolate discs. Rogin recognized his state—the energetic dream of childhood. Once, he, too, had found these dry biscuits delicious. It would have bored him now to eat one.

What else would Joan like? Rogin thought fondly. Some strawberries? "Give me some frozen strawberries. No, raspberries, she likes those better. And heavy cream. And some rolls, cream cheese, and some of those rubber-looking gherkins."

"What rubber?"

"Those, deep green, with eyes. Some ice cream might be in order, too."

He tried to think of a compliment, a good comparison, an endearment, for Joan when she'd open the door. What about her complexion? There was really nothing to compare her sweet, small, daring, shapely, timid, defiant, loving face to. How difficult she was, and how beautiful!

As Rogin went down into the stony, odorous, metallic, captive air of the subway, he was diverted by an unusual confession made by a man to his friend. These were two very tall men, shapeless in their winter clothes, as if their coats concealed suits of chain mail.

"So, how long have you known me?" said one.

"Twelve years."

"Well, I have an admission to make," he said. "I've decided that I might as well. For years I've been a heavy drinker. You didn't know. Practically an alcoholic."

But his friend was not surprised, and he answered immediately, "Yes, I did know."

"You knew? Impossible! How could you?"

Why, thought Rogin, as if it could be a secret! Look at that long, austere, alcohol-washed face, that drink-ruined nose, the skin by his ears like turkey wattles, and those whiskey-saddened eyes.

"Well, I did know, though."

"You couldn't have. I can't believe it." He was upset, and his friend didn't seem to want to soothe him. "But it's all right now," he said. "I've been going to a doctor and taking pills, a new revolutionary Danish discovery. It's a miracle. I'm beginning to believe they can cure you of anything and everything. You can't beat the Danes in science. They do everything. They turned a man into a woman."

"That isn't how they stop you from drinking, is it?"

"No. I hope not. This is only like aspirin. It's super-aspirin. They call it the aspirin of the future. But if you use it, you have to stop drinking."

Rogin's illuminated mind asked of itself while the human tides of the subway swayed back and forth, and cars linked and transparent like fish bladders raced under the streets: How come he thought nobody would know what everybody couldn't help knowing? And, as a chemist, he asked himself what kind of compound this new Danish drug might be, and started thinking about various inventions of his own, synthetic albumen, a cigarette that lit itself, a cheaper motor fuel. Ye gods, but he needed money! As never before. What was to be done? His mother was growing more and more difficult. On Friday night, she had neglected to cut up his meat for him, and he was hurt. She had sat at the table motionless, with her long-suffering face, severe, and let him cut his own meat, a thing she almost never did. She had always spoiled him and made his brother envy him. But what she expected now! Oh, Lord, how he had to pay, and it had never even occurred to him formerly that these things might have a price.

Seated, one of the passengers, Rogin recovered his calm, happy, even clairvoyant state of mind. To think of money was to think as the world wanted you to think; then you'd never be your own master. When people said they wouldn't do something for love or money, they meant that love and money were opposite passions and one the enemy of the other. He went on to reflect how little people knew about this, how they slept through life, how small a light the light of consciousness was. Rogin's clean, snub-nosed face shone while his heart was torn with joy at these deeper thoughts of our ignorance. You might take this drunkard as an example, who for long years thought his closest friends never suspected he drank. Rogin looked up and down the aisle for this remarkable knightly symbol, but he was gone.

However, there was no lack of things to see. There was a small girl with a new white muff; into the muff a doll's head was sewn, and the child was happy and affectionately vain of it, while her old man, stout and grim, with a huge scowling nose, kept picking her up and resettling her in the seat, as if he were trying to change her into something else. Then another child, led by her mother, boarded the car, and this other child carried the very same doll-faced muff, and this greatly annoyed both parents. The woman, who looked like a difficult, contentious woman, took her daughter away. It seemed to Rogin that each child was in love with its own muff and didn't even see the other, but it was one of his foibles to think he understood the hearts of little children.

A foreign family next engaged his attention. They looked like Central Americans to him. On one side the mother, quite old, dark-faced, white-haired, and worn out; on the other a son with the whitened, porous hands of a dishwasher. But what was the dwarf who sat between them—a son or a daughter? The hair was long and wavy and the cheeks smooth, but the shirt and tie were masculine. The overcoat was feminine, but the shoes—the shoes were a puzzle. A pair of brown oxfords with an outer seam like a man's, but Baby Louis heels like a woman's—a plain toe like a man's, but a strap across the instep like a woman's. No stockings. That didn't help much. The dwarf's fingers were beringed, but without a wedding band. There were small grim dents in the cheeks. The eyes were puffy and concealed, but Rogin did not doubt that they could reveal strange things if they chose and that this was a creature of remarkable understanding. He had for many years owned De la Mare's *Memoirs of a Midget*. Now he took a resolve; he woud read it. As soon as he had decided, he was free from his consuming curiosity as to the drawf's sex and was able to look at the person who sat beside him.

Thoughts very often grow fertile in the subway, because of the motion, the great company, the subtlety of the rider's state as he rattles under streets and rivers, under the foundations of great buildings, and Rogin's mind had already been strangely stimulated. Clasping the bag of groceries from which there rose odors of bread and pickle spice, he was following a train of reflections, first about the chemistry of sex determination, the X and Y chromosomes, hereditary linkages, the uterus, afterward about his brother as a tax exemption. He recalled two dreams of the night before. In one, an undertaker had offered to cut his hair, and he had refused. In another, he had been carrying a woman on his head. Sad dreams, both! Very sad! Which was the woman—Joan or Mother? And the undertaker—his lawyer? He gave a deep sigh, and by force of habit began to put together his synthetic albumen that was to revolutionize the entire egg industry.

Meanwhile, he had not interrupted his examination of the passengers and had fallen into a study of the man next to him. This was a man whom he had never in his life seen before but with whom he now suddenly felt linked through all existence. He was middle-aged, sturdy, with clear skin and blue eyes. His hands were clean, well formed, but Rogin did not approve of them. The coat he wore was a fairly expensive blue check such as Rogin would never have chosen for himself. He would not have worn blue suède shoes, either, or such a faultless hat, a cumbersome felt animal of a hat encircled by a high, fat ribbon. There are all kinds of dandies, not all of them are of the flaunting kind; some are dandies of respectability, and Rogin's fellow passenger was one of these. His straight-nosed profile was handsome, yet he had betrayed his gift, for he was flat-looking. But in his flat way he seemed to warn people that he wanted no difficulties with them, he wanted nothing to do with them. Wearing such blue suède shoes, he could not afford to have people treading on his feet, and he seemed to draw about himself a circle of privilege, notifying all others to mind their own business and let him read his paper. He was holding a *Tribune*, and perhaps it would be overstatement to say that he was reading. He was holding it.

His clear skin and blue eyes, his straight and purely Roman nose—even the way he sat—all strongly suggested one person to Rogin: Joan. He tried to escape the comparison, but it couldn't be helped. This man not only looked like Joan's father, whom Rogin detested; he looked like Joan herself. Forty years hence, a son of hers, provided she had one, might be like this. A son of hers? Of such a son, he himself, Rogin, would be the father. Lacking in dominant traits as compared with Joan, his heritage would not appear. Probably the children would resemble her. Yes, think forty years ahead, and a man like this, who sat by him knee to knee in the hurtling car among their fellow creatures, unconscious participants in a sort of great carnival of transit—such a man would carry forward what had been Rogin.

This was why he felt bound to him through all existence. What were forty years reckoned against eternity! Forty years were gone, and he was gazing at his own son. Here he was. Rogin was frightened and moved. "My son! My son!" he said to himself, and the pity of it almost made him burst into tears. The holy and frightful work of the masters of life and death brought this about. We were their instruments. We worked toward ends we thought were our own. But no! The whole thing was so unjust. To suffer, to labor, to toil and force your way through the spikes of life, to crawl through its darkest caverns, to push through the worst, to struggle under the weight of economy, to make money—only to become the father of a fourth-rate man of the world like this, so flat-looking, with his ordinary, clean, rosy, uninteresting, self-satisfied, fundamentally bourgeois face. What a curse to have a dull son! A son like this, who could never understand his father. They had absolutely nothing, but nothing, in common, he and this neat, chubby, blue-eyed man. He was so pleased, thought Rogin, with all he owned and all he did and all he was that he could hardly unfasten his lip. Look at that lip, sticking up at the tip like a little thorn or egg tooth. He wouldn't give anyone the time of day. Would this perhaps be general forty years from now? Would personalities be chillier as the world aged and grew colder? The inhumanity of the next generation incensed Rogin. Father and son had no sign to make to each other. Terrible! Inhuman! What a vision of existence it gave him. Man's personal aims were nothing, illusion. The life force occupied each of us in turn in its progress toward its own fulfillment, trampling on our individual humanity, using us for its own ends like mere dinosaurs or bees, exploiting love heartlessly, making us engage in the social process, labor, struggle for money, and submit to the law of pressure, the universal law of layers, superimposition!

What the blazes am I getting into? Rogin thought. To be the father of a throwback to *her* father. The image of this white-haired, gross, peevish old man with his ugly selfish blue eyes revolted Rogin. This was how his grandson would look. Joan, with whom Rogin was now more and more displeased, could not help that. For her, it was inevitable. But did it have to be inevitable for him? Well, then, Rogin, you fool, don't be a damned instrument. Get out of the way!

But it was too late for this, because he had already experienced the sensation of sitting next to his own son, his son and Joan's. He kept staring at him, waiting for him to say something, but the presumptive son remained coldly silent though he must have been aware of Rogin's scrutiny. They even got out at the same stop—Sheridan Square. When they stepped to the platform, the man, without even looking at Rogin, went away in a different direction in his detestable blue-checked coat, with his rosy, nasty face.

The whole thing upset Rogin very badly. When he approached Joan's door and heard Phyllis's little dog Henri barking even before he could knock, his face was very tense. "I won't be used," he declared to himself. "I have my own right to exist." Joan had better watch out. She had a light way of bypassing grave questions he had given earnest thought to. She always assumed no really disturbing thing would happen. He could not afford the luxury of such a carefree, debonair attitude himself, because he had to work hard and earn money so that disturbing things would *not* happen. Well, at the moment this situation could not be helped, and he really did not mind the money if he could feel that she was not necessarily the mother of such a son as his subway son or entirely the daughter of that awful, obscene father of hers. After all, Rogin was not himself so much like either of his parents, and quite different from his brother.

Joan came to the door, wearing one of Phyllis's expensive housecoats. It suited her very well. At first sight of her happy face, Rogin was brushed by the shadow of resemblance; the touch of it was extremely light, almost figmentary, but it made his flesh tremble.

She began to kiss him, saying, "Oh, my baby. You're covered with snow. Why didn't you wear your hat? It's all over its little head"—her favorite third-person endearment.

"Well, let me put down this bag of stuff. Let me take off my coat," grumbled Rogin, and escaped from her embrace. Why couldn't she wait making up to him? "It's so hot in here. My face is burning. Why do you keep this place at this temperature? And that damned dog keeps barking. If you didn't keep it cooped up, it wouldn't be so spoiled and noisy. Why doesn't anybody ever walk him?"

"Oh, it's not really so hot here! You've just come in from the cold. Don't you think this housecoat fits me better than Phyllis? Especially across the hips. She thinks so, too. She may sell it to me."

"I hope not," Rogin almost exclaimed.

She brought a towel to dry the melting snow from his short black hair. The flurry of rubbing excited Henri intolerably, and Joan locked him up in the bedroom, where he jumped persistently against the door with a rhythmic sound of claws on the wood.

Joan said, "Did you bring the shampoo?"

"Here it is."

"Then I'll wash your hair before dinner. Come."

"I don't want it washed."

"Oh, come on," she said, laughing.

Her lack of consciousness of guilt amazed him. He did not see how it could be. And the carpeted, furnished, lamplit, curtained room seemed to stand against his vision. So that he felt accusing and angry, his spirit sore and bitter, but it did not seem fitting to say why. Indeed, he began to worry lest the reason for it all slip away from him.

They took off his coat and his shirt in the bathroom, and she filled the sink. Rogin was full of his troubled emotions; now that his chest was bare he could feel them even more distinctly inside, and he said to himself, I'll have a thing or two to tell her pretty soon. I'm not letting them get away with it. "Do you think," he was going to tell her, "that I alone was made to carry the burden of the whole world on me? Do you think I was born just to be taken advantage of and sacrificed? Do you think I'm just a natural resource, like a coal mine, or oil well, or fishery, or the like? Remember, that I'm a man is no reason why I should be loaded down. I have a soul in me no bigger or stronger than yours.

"Take away the externals, like the muscles, deeper voice, and so forth, and what remains? A pair of spirits, practically alike. So why shouldn't there also be equality? I can't always be the strong one."

"Sit here," said Joan, bringing up a kitchen stool to the sink. "Your hair's gotten all matted."

He sat with his breast against the cool enamel, his chin on the edge of the basin, the green, hot radiant water reflecting the glass and the tile, and the sweet, cool, fragrant juice of the shampoo poured on his head. She began to wash him.

"You have the healthiest-looking scalp," she said. "It's all pink."

He answered, "Well, it should be white. There must be something wrong with me."

"But there's absolutely nothing wrong with you," she said, and pressed against him from behind, surrounding him, pouring the water gently over him until it seemed to him that the water came from within him, it was the warm fluid of his own secret loving spirit overflowing into the sink, green and foaming, and the words he had rehearsed he forgot, and his anger at his son-to-be disappeared altogether, and he sighed, and said to her from the water-filled hollow of the sink, "You always have such wonderful ideas, Joan. You know? You have a kind of instinct, a regular gift."

JOHN STEINBECK

Excerpts from The Pearl

Kino awakened in the near dark. The stars still shone and the day had drawn only a pale wash of light in the lower sky to the east. The roosters had been crowing for some time, and the early pigs were already beginning their ceaseless turning of twigs and bits of wood to see whether anything to eat had been overlooked. Outside the brush house in the tuna clump, a covey of little birds chittered and flurried with their wings.

Kino's eyes opened, and he looked first at the lightening square which was the door and then he looked at the hanging box where Coyotito slept. And last he turned his head to Juana, his wife, who lay beside him on the mat, her blue head shawl over her nose and over her breasts and around the small of her back. Juana's eyes were open too. Kino could never remember seeing them closed when he awakened. Her dark eyes made little reflected stars. She was looking at him as she was always looking at him when he awakened.

Kino heard the little splash of morning waves on the beach. It was very good—Kino closed his eyes again to listen to his music. Perhaps he alone did this and perhaps all of his people did

it. His people had once been great makers of songs so that everything they saw or thought or did or heard became a song. That
was very long ago. The songs remained; Kino knew them, but
no new songs were added. That does not mean that there were
no personal songs. In Kino's head there was a song now, clear
and soft, and if he had been able to speak of it, he would have
called it the Song of the Family.

His blanket was over his nose to protect him from the dank
air. His eyes flicked to a rustle beside him. It was Juana arising,
almost soundlessly. On her hard bare feet she went to the hanging box where Coyotito slept, and she leaned over and said a
little reassuring word. Coyotito looked up for a moment and
closed his eyes and slept again.

Juana went to the fire pit and uncovered a coal and fanned it
alive while she broke little pieces of brush over it.

Now Kino got up and wrapped his blanket about his head
and nose and shoulders. He slipped his feet into his sandals and
went outside to watch the dawn.

Outside the door he squatted down and gathered the blanket
ends about his knees. He saw the specks of Gulf clouds flame
high in the air. And a goat came near and sniffed at him and
stared with its cold yellow eyes. Behind him Juana's fire leaped
into flame and threw spears of light through the chinks of the
brushhouse wall and threw a wavering square of light out the
door. A late moth blustered in to find the fire. The Song of the
Family came now from behind Kino. And the rhythm of the
family song was the grinding stone where Juana worked the
corn for the morning cakes.

The dawn came quickly now, a wash, a glow, a lightness,
and then an explosion of fire as the sun arose out of the Gulf.
Kino looked down to cover his eyes from the glare. He could
hear the pat of the corncakes in the house and the rich smell of
them on the cooking plate. The ants were busy on the ground,
big black ones with shiny bodies, and little dusty quick ants.
Kino watched with the detachment of God while a dusty ant

frantically tried to escape the sand trap an ant lion had dug for him. A thin, timid dog came close and, at a soft word from Kino, curled up, arranged its tail neatly over its feet, and laid its chin delicately on the pile. It was a black dog with yellow-gold spots where its eyebrows should have been. It was a morning like other mornings and yet perfect among mornings.

Kino heard the creak of the rope when Juana took Coyotito out of his hanging box and cleaned him and hammocked him in her shawl in a loop that placed him close to her breast. Kino could see these things without looking at them. Juana sang softly an ancient song that had only three notes and yet endless variety of interval. And this was part of the family song too. It was all part. Sometimes it rose to an aching chord that caught the throat, saying this is safety, this is warmth, this is the *Whole*.

. . . . . .

2. . . . In the afternoon, when the sun had gone over the mountains of the Peninsula to sink in the outward sea, Kino squatted in his house with Juana beside him. And the brush house was crowded with neighbors. Kino held the great pearl in his hand, and it was warm and alive in his hand. And the music of the pearl had merged with the music of the family so that one beautified the other. The neighbors looked at the pearl in Kino's hand and they wondered how such luck could come to any man.

And Juan Tomás, who squatted on Kino's right hand because he was his brother, asked, "What will you do now that you have become a rich man?"

Kino looked into his pearl, and Juana cast her eyelashes down and arranged her shawl to cover her face so that her excitement could not be seen. And in the incandescence of the pearl the pictures formed of the things Kino's mind had considered in the past and had given up as impossible. In the pearl he saw Juana and Coyotito and himself standing and kneeling at the high altar, and they were being married now that they could pay. He spoke softly, "We will be married—in the church."

In the pearl he saw how they were dressed—Juana in a shawl stiff with newness and a new skirt, and from under the long skirt Kino could see that she wore shoes. It was in the pearl—the picture glowing there. He himself was dressed in new white clothes, and he carried a new hat—not of straw but of fine black felt— and he too wore shoes—not sandals but shoes that laced. But Coyotito—he was the one—he wore a blue sailor suit from the United States and a little yachting cap such as Kino had seen once when a pleasure boat put into the estuary. All of these things Kino saw in the lucent pearl and he said, "We will have new clothes."

And the music of the pearl rose like a chorus of trumpets in his ears.

Then to the lovely gray surface of the pearl came the little things Kino wanted: a harpoon to take the place of one lost a year ago, a new harpoon of iron with a ring in the end of the shaft; and—his mind could hardly make the leap—a rifle—but why not, since he was so rich. And Kino saw Kino in the pearl, Kino holding a Winchester carbine. It was the wildest daydreaming and very pleasant. His lips moved hesitantly over this—"A rifle," he said. "Perhaps a rifle."

It was the rifle that broke down the barriers. This was an impossibility, and if he could think of having a rifle whole horizons were burst and he could rush on. For it is said that humans are never satisfied, that you give them one thing and they want something more. And this is said in disparagement, whereas it is one of the greatest talents the species has and one that has made it superior to animals that are satisfied with what they have.

The neighbors, close pressed and silent in the house, nodded their heads at his wild imaginings. And a man in the rear murmured, "A rifle. He will have a rifle."

But the music of the pearl was shrilling with triumph in Kino. Juana looked up, and her eyes were wide at Kino's courage and at his imagination. And electric strength had come to him now the horizons were kicked out. In the pearl he saw Coyotito sitting at a little desk in a school, just as Kino had once seen it through an open door. And Coyotito was dressed in a jacket, and he had on a white collar and a broad silken tie. Moreover, Coyotito was writing on a big piece of paper. Kino looked at his neighbors fiercely. "My son will go to school," he said, and the neighbors were hushed. Juana caught her breath sharply. Her eyes were bright as she watched him, and she looked quickly down at Coyotito in her arms to see whether this might be possible.

But Kino's face shone with prophecy. "My son will read and open the books, and my son will write and will know writing. And my son will make numbers, and these things will make us free because he will know—he will know and through him we will know." And in the pearl Kino saw himself and Juana squatting by the little fire in the brush hut while Coyotito read from a great book. "This is what the pearl will do," said Kino. And he had never said so many words together in his life. And suddenly he was afraid of his talking. His hand closed down over the pearl and cut the light away from it. Kino was afraid as a man is afraid who says, "I will," without knowing.

. . . . . .

3. Now the tension which had been growing in Juana boiled up to the surface and her lips were thin. "This thing is evil," she cried harshly. "This pearl is like a sin! It will destroy us," and her voice rose shrilly. "Throw it away, Kino. Let us break it between stones. Let us bury it and forget the place. Let us throw it back into the sea. It has brought evil. Kino, my husband, it will destroy us." And in the firelight her lips and her eyes were alive with her fear.

But Kino's face was set, and his mind and his will were set. "This is our one chance," he said. "Our son must go to school. He must break out of the pot that holds us in."

"It will destroy us all," Juana cried. "Even our son."

"Hush," said Kino. "Do not speak any more. In the morning

we will sell the pearl, and then the evil will be gone, and only
the good remain.

. . . . . .

4. "Kino, my husband," she cried, and his eyes stared past her.
"Kino, can you hear me?"

"I hear you," he said dully.

"Kino, this pearl is evil. Let us destroy it before it destroys
us. Let us crush it between two stones. Let us—let us throw it
back in the sea where it belongs. Kino, it is evil, it is evil!"

And as she spoke the light came back in Kino's eyes so that
they glowed fiercely and his muscles hardened and his will
hardened.

"No," he said. "I will fight this thing. I will win over it. We
will have our chance." His fist pounded the sleeping mat. "No
one shall take our good fortune from us," he said. His eyes
softened then and he raised a gentle hand to Juana's shoulder.
"Believe me," he said. "I am a man." And his face grew crafty.

"In the morning we will take our canoe and we will go over
the sea and over the mountains to the capital, you and I. We will
not be cheated. I am a man."

"Kino," she said huskily, "I am afraid. A man can be killed.
Let us throw the pearl back into the sea."

"Hush," he said fiercely. "I am a man. Hush." And she was
silent, for his voice was command. "Let us sleep a little," he said.
"In the first light we will start. You are not afraid to go with
me?"

"No, my husband."

His eyes were soft and warm on her then, his hand touched
her cheek. "Let us sleep a little," he said.

. . . . . .

5. . . . There was no anger in her for Kino. He had said, "I am
a man," and that meant certain things to Juana. It meant that he
was half insane and half god. It meant that Kino would drive
his strength against a mountain and plunge his strength against

the sea. Juana, in her woman's soul, knew that the mountain would stand while the man broke himself; that the sea would surge while the man drowned in it. And yet it was this thing that made him a man, half insane and half god, and Juana had need of a man; she could not live without a man. Although she might be puzzled by these differences between man and woman, she knew them and accepted them and needed them. Of course she would follow him, there was no question of that. Sometimes the quality of woman, the reason, the caution, the sense of preservation, could cut through Kino's manness and save them all.

. . . . . .

6. Everyone in La Paz remembers the return of the family; there may be some old ones who saw it, but those whose fathers and whose grandfathers told it to them remember it nevertheless. It is an event that happened to everyone.

It was late in the golden afternoon when the first little boys ran hysterically in the town and spread the word that Kino and Juana were coming back. And everyone hurried to see them. The sun was settling toward the western mountains and the shadows on the ground were long. And perhaps that was what left the deep impression on those who saw them.

The two came from the rutted country road into the city, and they were not walking in single file, Kino ahead and Juana behind, as usual, but side by side. The sun was behind them and their long shadows stalked ahead, and they seemed to carry two towers of darkness with them. Kino had a rifle across his arm and Juana carried her shawl like a sack over her shoulder. And in it was a small limp heavy bundle. The shawl was crusted with dried blood, and the bundle swayed a little as she walked. Her face was hard and lined and leathery with fatigue and with the tightness with which she fought fatigue. And her wide eyes stared inward on herself. She was as remote and as removed as Heaven. Kino's lips were thin and his jaws tight, and the people say that he carried fear with him, that he was as dangerous as a rising storm. The people say that the two seemed to be removed from human experience; that they had gone through pain and had come out on the other side; that there was almost a magical protection about them. And those people who had rushed to see them crowded back and let them pass and did not speak to them.

Kino and Juana walked through the city as though it were not there. Their eyes glanced neither right nor left nor up nor down, but stared only straight ahead. Their legs moved a little jerkily, like well-made wooden dolls, and they carried pillars of black fear about them. And as they walked through the stone and plaster city brokers peered at them from barred windows and servants put one eye to a slitted gate and mothers turned the faces of their youngest children inward against their skirts. Kino and Juana strode side by side through the stone and plaster city and down among the brush houses, and the neighbors stood back and let them pass. Juan Tomas raised his hand in greeting and did not say the greeting and left his hand in the air for a moment uncertainly.

In Kino's ears the Song of the Family was as fierce as a cry. He was immune and terrible, and his song had become a battle cry. They trudged past the burned square where their house had been without even looking at it. They cleared the brush that edged the beach and picked their way down the shore toward the water. And they did not look toward Kino's broken canoe.

And when they came to the water's edge they stopped and stared out over the Gulf. And then Kino laid the rifle down, and he dug among his clothes, and then he held the great pearl in his hand. He looked into its surface and it was gray and ulcerous. Evil faces peered from it into his eyes, and he saw the light of burning. And in the surface of the pearl he saw the frantic eyes of the man in the pool. And in the surface of the pearl he saw Coyotito lying in the little cave with the top of his head shot away. And the pearl was ugly; it was gray, like a malignant growth. And Kino heard the music of the pearl, distorted and insane. Kino's hand shook a little, and he turned slowly to Juana and held the pearl out to her. She stood beside him, still holding her dead bundle over her shoulder. She looked at the pearl in his hand for a moment and then she looked into Kino's eyes and said softly, "No, you."

And Kino drew back his arm and flung the pearl with all his might. Kino and Juana watched it go, winking and glimmering under the setting sun. They saw the little splash in the distance, and they stood side by side watching the place for a long time.

And the pearl settled into the lovely green water and dropped toward the bottom. The waving branches of the algae called to it and beckoned to it. The lights on its surface were green and lovely. It settled down to the sand bottom among the fern-like plants. Above, the surface of the water was a green mirror. And the pearl lay on the floor of the sea. A crab scampering over the bottom raised a little cloud of sand, and when it settled the pearl was gone.

And the music of the pearl drifted to a whisper and disappeared.

JOHN STEINBECK

The Grapes
of Wrath

CHAPTER I

To the red country and part of the gray country of Oklahoma,
the last rains came gently, and they did not cut the scarred earth.
The plows crossed and recrossed the rivulet marks. The last rains
lifted the corn quickly and scattered weed colonies and grass
along the sides of the roads so that the gray country and the
dark red country began to disappear under a green cover. In the
last part of May the sky grew pale and the clouds that had hung
in high puffs for so long in the spring were dissipated. The sun
flared down on the growing corn day after day until a line of
brown spread along the edge of each green bayonet. The clouds
appeared, and went away, and in a while they did not try any
more. The weeds grew darker green to protect themselves, and
they did not spread any more. The surface of the earth crusted,
a thin hard crust, and as the sky became pale, so the earth became
pale, pink in the red country and white in the gray country.

In the water-cut gullies the earth dusted down in dry little
streams. Gophers and ant lions started small avalanches. And as
the sharp sun struck day after day, the leaves of the young corn

became less stiff and erect; they bent in a curve at first, and then, as the central ribs of strength grew weak, each leaf tilted downward. Then it was June, and the sun shone more fiercely. The brown lines on the corn leaves widened and moved in on the central ribs. The weeds frayed and edged back toward their roots. The air was thin and the sky more pale; and every day the earth paled.

In the roads where the teams moved, where the wheels milled the ground and the hooves of the horses beat the ground, the dirt crust broke and the dust formed. Every moving thing lifted the dust into the air: a walking man lifted a thin layer as high as his waist, and a wagon lifted the dust as high as the fence tops, and an automobile boiled a cloud behind it. The dust was long in settling back again.

When June was half gone, the big clouds moved up out of Texas and the Gulf, high heavy clouds, rain-heads. The men in the fields looked up at the clouds and sniffed at them and held wet fingers up to sense the wind. And the horses were nervous while the clouds were up. The rain-heads dropped a little spattering and hurried on to some other country. Behind them the sky was pale again and the sun flared In the dust there were drop craters where the rain had falle , and there were clean splashes on the corn, and that was all.

A gentle wind followed the rain clouds, driving them on northward, a wind that softly clashed the drying corn. A day went by and the wind increased, steady, unbroken by gusts. The dust from the roads fluffed up and spread out and fell on the weeds beside the fields, and fell into the fields a little way. Now the wind grew strong and hard and it worked at the rain crust in the corn fields. Little by little the sky was darkened by the mixing dust, and the wind felt over the earth, loosened the dust, and carried it away. The wind grew stronger. The rain crust broke and the dust lifted up out of the fields and drove gray plumes into the air like sluggish smoke. The corn threshed the wind and made a dry, rushing sound. The finest dust did not settle back to earth now, but disappeared into the darkening sky.

The wind grew stronger, whisked under stones, carried up straws and old leaves, and even little clods, marking its course as it sailed across the fields. The air and the sky darkened and through them the sun shone redly, and there was a raw sting in the air. During a night the wind raced faster over the land, dug cunningly among the rootlets of the corn, and the corn fought the wind with its weakened leaves until the roots were freed by the prying wind and then each stalk settled wearily sideways toward the earth and pointed the direction of the wind.

The dawn came, but no day. In the gray sky a red sun appeared, a dim red circle that gave a little light, like dusk; and as that day advanced, the dusk slipped back toward darkness, and the wind cried and whimpered over the fallen corn.

Men and women huddled in their houses, and they tied handkerchiefs over their noses when they went out, and wore goggles to protect their eyes.

When the night came again it was black night, for the stars could not pierce the dust to get down, and the window lights could not even spread beyond their own yards. Now the dust was evenly mixed with the air, an emulsion of dust and air. Houses were shut tight, and cloth wedged around doors and windows, but the dust came in so thinly that it could not be seen in the air, and it settled like pollen on the chairs and tables, on the dishes. The people brushed it from their shoulders. Little lines of dust lay at the door sills.

In the middle of that night the wind passed on and left the land quiet. The dust-filled air muffled sound more completely than fog does. The people, lying in their beds, heard the wind stop. They awakened when the rushing wind was gone. They lay quietly and listened deep into the stillness. Then the roosters crowed, and their voices were muffled, and the people stirred restlessly in their beds and wanted the morning. They knew it would take a long time for the dust to settle out of the air. In the morning the dust hung like fog, and the sun was as red as ripe new blood. All day the dust sifted down from the sky, and the next day it sifted down. An even blanket covered the earth. It settled on the corn, piled up on the tops of the fence posts, piled up on the wires; it settled on roofs, blanketed the weeds and trees.

The people came out of their houses and smelled the hot stinging air and covered their noses from it. And the children came out of the houses, but they did not run or shout as they would have done after a rain. Men stood by their fences and looked at the ruined corn, drying fast now, only a little green showing through the film of dust. The men were silent and they did not move often. And the women came out of the houses to stand beside their men—to feel whether this time the men would break. The women studied the men's faces secretly, for the corn could go, as long as something else remained. The children stood near by, drawing figures in the dust with bare toes, and the children sent exploring senses out to see whether men and women would break. The children peeked at the faces of the men and women, and then drew careful lines in the dust with their toes. Horses came to the watering troughs and nuzzled the water to clear the surface dust. After a while the faces of the watching men lost their bemused perplexity and became hard and angry and resistant. Then the women knew that they were safe and that there was no break. Then they asked, What'll we do? And the men replied, I don't know. But it was all right. The women knew it was all right, and the watching children knew it was all right. Women and children knew deep in themselves that no misfortune was too great to bear if their men were whole. The women went into the houses to their work, and the children began to play, but cautiously at first. As the day went forward the sun became less red. It flared down on the dust-blanketed land. The men sat in the doorways of their houses; their hands were busy with sticks and little rocks. The men sat still—thinking—figuring.

JAMES M. BARRIE

The Twelve-Pound Look

If quite convenient (as they say about cheques) you are to conceive that the scene is laid in your own house, and that HARRY SIMS *is you. Perhaps the ornamentation of the house is a trifle ostentatious, but if you cavil at that we are willing to re-decorate: you don't get out of being* HARRY SIMS *on a mere matter of plush and dados. It pleases us to make him a city man, but (rather than lose you) he can be turned with a scrape of the pen into a K.C., fashionable doctor, Secretary of State, or what you will. We conceive him of a pleasant rotundity with a thick red neck, but we shall waive that point if you know him to be thin.*

It is that day in your career when everything went wrong just when everything seemed to be superlatively right.

In HARRY'S *case it was a woman who did the mischief. She came to him in his great hour and told him she did not admire him. Of course he turned her out of the house and was soon himself again, but it spoilt the morning for him. This is the subject of the play, and quite enough too.*

HARRY *is to receive the honour of knighthood in a few days, and we discover him in the sumptuous 'snuggery' of his home in Kensington (or is it Westminster?), rehearsing the ceremony with his wife. They have been at it all the morning, a pleasing occupation.* MRS. SIMS (*as we may call her for the last time, as it were, and strictly as a good-natured joke*) *is wearing her presentation gown, and personates the august one who is about to dub her* HARRY *knight. She is seated regally. Her jewelled shoulders proclaim aloud her husband's generosity. She must be an extraordinarily proud and happy woman, yet she has a drawn face and shrinking ways as if there were some one near her of whom she is afraid. She claps her hands, as the signal to* HARRY. *He enters bowing, and with a graceful swerve of the leg. He is only partly in costume, the sword and the real stockings not having arrived yet. With a gliding motion that is only delayed while one leg makes up on the other, he reaches his wife, and, going on one knee, raises her hand superbly to his lips. She taps him on the shoulder with a paper-knife and says huskily, 'Rise, Sir Harry.' He rises, bows, and glides about the room, going on his knees to various articles of furniture, and rises from each a knight. It is a radiant domestic scene, and* HARRY *is as dignified as if he knew that royalty was rehearsing it at the other end.*

SIR HARRY (*complacently*). Did that seem all right, eh?

LADY SIMS (*much relieved*). I think perfect.

SIR HARRY. But was it dignified?

LADY SIMS. Oh, very. And it will be still more so when you have the sword.

SIR HARRY. The sword will lend it an air. There are really the five moments—(*suiting the action to the word*)—the glide—the dip—the kiss—the tap—and you back out a knight. It's short, but it's a very beautiful ceremony. (*Kindly*) Anything you can suggest?

LADY SIMS. No—oh no. (*Nervously, seeing him pause to kiss the tassel of a cushion*). You don't think you have practised till you know what to do almost too well?

(*He has been in a blissful temper, but such niggling criticism would try any man.*)

SIR HARRY. I do not. Don't talk nonsense. Wait till your opinion is asked for.

LADY SIMS (*abashed*). I'm sorry, Harry. (*A perfect butler appears and presents a card.*) 'The Flora Type-Writing Agency.'

SIR HARRY. Ah, yes. I telephoned them to send some one. A woman, I suppose, Tombes?

TOMBES. Yes, Sir Harry.

SIR HARRY. Show her in here. (*He has very lately become a stickler for etiquette.*) And, Tombes, strictly speaking, you know, I am not Sir Harry till Thursday.

TOMBES. Beg pardon, sir, but it is such a satisfaction to us.

SIR HARRY (*good-naturedly*). Ah, they like it downstairs, do they?

TOMBES (*unbending*). Especially the females, Sir Harry.

SIR HARRY. Exactly. You can show her in, Tombes. (*The butler departs on his mighty task.*) You can tell the woman what she is wanted for, Emmy, while I change. (*He is too modest to boast about himself, and prefers to keep a wife in the house for that purpose.*) You can tell her the sort of things about me that will come better from you. (*Smiling happily*) You heard what Tombes said, 'Especially the females.' And he is right. Success! The women like it even better than the men. And rightly. For they share. *You* share, *Lady* Sims. Not a woman will see that gown without being sick with envy of it. I know them. Have all our lady friends in to see it. It will make them ill for a week.

(*These sentiments carry him off lightheartedly, and presently the disturbing element is shown in. She is a mere typist, dressed in uncommonly good taste, but at contemptibly small expense, and she is carrying her typewriter in a friendly way rather than as a badge of slavery, as of course it is. Her eye is clear; and in odd contrast to* LADY SIMS, *she is self-reliant and serene.*)

KATE (*respectfully, but she should have waited to be spoken to*). Good morning, madam.

LADY SIMS (*in her nervous way, and scarcely noticing that the typist is a little too ready with her tongue*). Good morning. (*As a first impression she rather likes the woman, and the woman, though it is scarcely worth mentioning, rather likes her.* LADY SIMS *has a maid for buttoning and unbuttoning her, and probably another for waiting on the maid, and she gazes with a little envy perhaps at a woman who does things for herself.*) Is that the type-writing machine?

KATE (*who is getting it ready for use*). Yes (*not 'Yes, madam,' as it ought to be*). I suppose if I am to work here I may take this off. I get on better without it. (*She is referring to her hat.*)

LADY SIMS. Certainly. (*But the hat is already off.*) I ought to apologise for my gown. I am to be presented this week, and I was trying it on. (*Her tone is not really apologetic. She is rather clinging to the glory of her gown, wistfully, as if not absolutely certain, you know, that it is a glory.*)

KATE. It is beautiful, if I may presume to say so. (*She frankly admires it. She probably has a best, and a second best of her own: that sort of thing.*)

LADY SIMS (*with a flush of pride in the gown*). Yes, it is very beautiful. (*The beauty of it gives her courage.*) Sit down, please.

KATE (*the sort of woman who would have sat down in any case*). I suppose it is some copying you want done? I got no particulars. I was told to come to this address, but that was all.

LADY SIMS (*almost with the humility of a servant*). Oh, it is not work for me, it is for my husband, and what he needs is not exactly copying. (*Swelling, for she is proud of* HARRY.) He wants a number of letters answered—hundreds of them—letters and telegrams of congratulation.

KATE (*as if it were all in the day's work*). Yes?

LADY SIMS (*remembering that* HARRY *expects every wife to do her duty*). My husband is a remarkable man. He is about to be knighted. (*Pause, but* KATE *does not fall to the floor.*) He is to be knighted for his services to—(*on reflection*)—for his services. (*She is conscious that she is not doing* HARRY *justice.*) He can explain it so much better than I can.

KATE (*in her business-like way*). And I am to answer the congratulations?

LADY SIMS (*afraid that it will be a hard task*). Yes.

KATE (*blithely*). It is work I have had some experience of. (*She proceeds to type.*)

LADY SIMS. But you can't begin till you know what he wants to say.

KATE. Only a specimen letter. Won't it be the usual thing?

LADY SIMS (*to whom this is a new idea*). Is there a usual thing?

KATE. Oh, yes.

> (*She continues to type, and* LADY SIMS, *half-mesmerised, gazes at her nimble fingers. The useless woman watches the useful one, and she sighs, she could not tell why.*)

LADY SIMS. How quickly you do it! It must be delightful to be able to do something, and to do it well.

KATE (*thankfully*). Yes, it is delightful.

LADY SIMS (*again remembering the source of all her greatness*). But, excuse me, I don't think that will be any use. My husband wants me to explain to you that his is an exceptional case. He did not try to get this honour in any way. It was a complete surprise to him——

KATE (*who is a practical Kate and no dealer in sarcasm*). That is what I have written.

LADY SIMS (*in whom sarcasm would meet a dead wall*). But how could you know?

KATE. I only guessed.

LADY SIMS. Is that the usual thing?

KATE. Oh, yes.

LADY SIMS. They don't try to get it?

KATE. I don't know. That is what we are told to say in the letters.

> (*To her at present the only important thing about the letters is that they are ten shillings the hundred.*)

LADY SIMS (*returning to surer ground*). I should explain that my husband is not a man who cares for honours. So long as he does his duty——

KATE. Yes, I have been putting that in.

LADY SIMS. Have you? But he particularly wants it to be known that he would have declined a title were it not——

KATE. I have got it here.

LADY SIMS. What have you got?

KATE (*reading*). 'Indeed, I would have asked to be allowed to decline had it not been that I want to please my wife.'

LADY SIMS (*heavily*). But how could you know it was that?

KATE. Is it?

LADY SIMS (*who after all is the one with the right to ask questions*). Do they all accept it for that reason?

KATE. That is what we are told to say in the letters.

LADY SIMS (*thoughtlessly*). It is quite as if you knew my husband.

KATE. I assure you, I don't even know his name.

LADY SIMS (*suddenly showing that she knows him*). Oh, he wouldn't like that!

> (*And it is here that* HARRY *re-enters in his city garments, looking so gay, feeling so jolly that we bleed for him. However, the annoying* KATHERINE *is to get a shock also.*)

LADY SIMS. This is the lady, Harry.

SIR HARRY (*shooting his cuffs*). Yes, yes. Good morning, my dear.

> (*Then they see each other, and their mouths open, but not for words. After the first surprise* KATE *seems to find some humour in the situation, but* HARRY *lowers like a thundercloud.*)

LADY SIMS (*who has seen nothing*). I have been trying to explain to her——

SIR HARRY. Eh—what? (*He controls himself.*) Leave it to me, Emmy; I'll attend to her.

> (LADY SIMS *goes, with a dread fear that somehow she has vexed her lord, and then* HARRY *attends to the intruder.*)

SIR HARRY (*with concentrated scorn*). You!

KATE (*as if agreeing with him*). Yes, it's funny.

SIR HARRY. The shamelessness of your daring to come here.

KATE. Believe me, it is not less a surprise to me than it is to you. I was sent here in the ordinary way of business. I was given only the number of the house. I was not told the name.

SIR HARRY (*withering her*). The ordinary way of business! This is what you have fallen to—a typist!

KATE (*unwithered*). Think of it!

SIR HARRY. After going through worse straits, I'll be bound.

KATE (*with some grim memories*). Much worse straits.

SIR HARRY (*alas, laughing coarsely*). My congratulations!

KATE. Thank you, Harry.

SIR HARRY (*who is annoyed, as any man would be, not to find her abject*). Eh? What was that you called me, madam?

KATE. Isn't it Harry? On my soul, I almost forget.

SIR HARRY. It isn't Harry to you. My name is Sims, if you please.

KATE. Yes, I had not forgotten that. It was my name, too, you see.

SIR HARRY (*in his best manner*). It was your name till you forfeited the right to bear it.

KATE. Exactly.

SIR HARRY (*gloating*). I was furious to find you here, but on second thoughts it pleases me. (*From the depths of his moral nature*) There is a grim justice in this.

KATE (*sympathetically*). Tell me?

SIR HARRY. Do you know what you were brought here to do?

KATE. I have just been learning. You have been made a knight, and I was summoned to answer the messages of congratulation.

SIR HARRY. That's it, that's it. You come on this day as my servant!

KATE. I, who might have been Lady Sims.

SIR HARRY. And you are her typist instead. And she has four men-servants. Oh, I am glad you saw her in her presentation gown.

KATE. I wonder if she would let me do her washing, Sir Harry? (*Her want of taste disgusts him.*)

Sɪʀ Hᴀʀʀʏ (*with dignity*). You can go. The mere thought that only a few flights of stairs separates such as you from my innocent children—

(*He will never know why a new light has come into her face.*)

Kᴀᴛᴇ (*slowly*). You have children?

Sɪʀ Hᴀʀʀʏ (*inflated*). Two.

(*He wonders why she is so long in answering.*)

Kᴀᴛᴇ (*resorting to impertinence*). Such a nice number.

Sɪʀ Hᴀʀʀʏ (*with an extra turn of the screw*). Both boys.

Kᴀᴛᴇ. Successful in everything. Are they like you, Sir Harry?

Sɪʀ Hᴀʀʀʏ (*expanding*). They are very like me.

Kᴀᴛᴇ. That's nice.

(*Even on such a subject as this she can be ribald.*)

Sɪʀ Hᴀʀʀʏ. Will you please to go.

Kᴀᴛᴇ. Heigho! What shall I say to my employer?

Sɪʀ Hᴀʀʀʏ. That is no affair of mine.

Kᴀᴛᴇ. What will you say to Lady Sims?

Sɪʀ Hᴀʀʀʏ. I flatter myself that whatever I say, Lady Sims will accept without comment.

(*She smiles, heaven knows why, unless her next remark explains it.*)

Kᴀᴛᴇ. Still the same Harry.

Sɪʀ Hᴀʀʀʏ. What do you mean?

Kᴀᴛᴇ. Only that you have the old confidence in your profound knowledge of the sex.

Sɪʀ Hᴀʀʀʏ (*beginning to think as little of her intellect as of her morals*). I suppose I know my wife.

Kᴀᴛᴇ (*hopelessly dense*). I suppose so. I was only remembering that you used to think you knew her in the days when I was the lady. (*He is merely wasting his time on her, and he indicates the door. She is not sufficiently the lady to retire worsted.*) Well, good-bye, Sir Harry. Won't you ring, and the four men-servants will show me out?

(*But he hesitates.*)

SIR HARRY (*in spite of himself*). As you are here, there is something I want to get out of you. (*Wishing he could ask it less eagerly.*) Tell me, who was the man?

   (*The strange woman—it is evident now that she has always been strange to him—smiles tolerantly.*)

KATE. You never found out?

SIR HARRY. I could never be sure.

KATE (*reflectively*). I thought that would worry you.

SIR HARRY (*sneering*). It's plain that he soon left you.

KATE. Very soon.

SIR HARRY. As I could have told you. (*But still she surveys him with the smile of Mona Lisa. The badgered man has to entreat.*) Who was he? It was fourteen years ago, and cannot matter to any of us now. Kate, tell me who he was?

   (*It is his first youthful moment, and perhaps because of that she does not wish to hurt him.*)

KATE (*shaking a motherly head*). Better not ask.

SIR HARRY. I do ask. Tell me.

KATE. It is kinder not to tell you.

SIR HARRY (*violently*). Then, by James, it was one of my own pals. Was it Bernard Roche? (*She shakes her head.*) It may have been some one who comes to my house still.

KATE. I think not. (*Reflecting*) Fourteen years! You found my letter that night when you went home?

SIR HARRY (*impatient*). Yes.

KATE. I propped it against the decanters. I thought you would be sure to see it there. It was a room not unlike this, and the furniture was arranged in the same attractive way. How it all comes back to me. Don't you see me, Harry, in hat and cloak, putting the letter there, taking a last look round, and then stealing out into the night to meet—

SIR HARRY. Whom?

KATE. Him. Hours pass, no sound in the room but the tick-tack of the clock, and then about midnight you return alone. You take—

SIR HENRY (*gruffly*). I wasn't alone.

KATE (*the picture spoilt*). No? oh. (*Plaintively*) Here have I all these years been conceiving it wrongly. (*She studies his face.*) I believe something interesting happened?

SIR HARRY (*growling*). Something confoundedly annoying.

KATE (*coaxing*). Do tell me.

SIR HARRY. We won't go into that. Who was the man? Surely a husband has a right to know with whom his wife bolted.

KATE (*who is detestably ready with her tongue*). Surely the wife has a right to know how he took it. (*The woman's love of bargaining comes to her aid.*) A fair exchange. You tell me what happened, and I will tell you who he was.

SIR HARRY. You will? Very well. (*It is the first point on which they have agreed, and, forgetting himself, he takes a place beside her on the fire-seat. He is thinking only of what he is to tell her, but she, woman-like, is conscious of their proximity.*)

KATE (*tastelessly*). Quite like old times. (*He moves away from her indignantly.*) Go on, Harry.

SIR HARRY (*who has a manful shrinking from saying anything that is to his disadvantage*). Well, as you know, I was dining at the club that night.

KATE. Yes.

SIR HARRY. Jack Lamb drove me home. Mabbett Green was with us, and I asked them to come in for a few minutes.

KATE. Jack Lamb, Mabbett Green? I think I remember them. Jack was in Parliament.

SIR HARRY. No, that was Mabbett. They came into the house with me and—(*with sudden horror*)—was it him?

KATE (*bewildered*). Who?

SIR HARRY. Mabbett?

KATE. What?

SIR HARRY. The man?

KATE. What man? (*understanding*) Oh no. I thought you said he came into the house with you.

SIR HARRY. It might have been a blind.

KATE. Well, it wasn't. Go on.

SIR HARRY. They came in to finish a talk we had been having at the club.

KATE. An interesting talk, evidently.

SIR HARRY. The papers had been full that evening of the elopement of some countess woman with a fiddler. What was her name?

KATE. Does it matter?

SIR HARRY. No. (*Thus ends the countess.*) We had been discussing the thing and—(*he pulls a wry face*)—and I had been rather warm—

KATE (*with horrid relish*). I begin to see. You had been saying it served the husband right, that the man who could not look after his wife deserved to lose her. It was one of your favourite subjects. Oh, Harry, say it was that!

SIR HARRY (*sourly*). It may have been something like that.

KATE. And all the time the letter was there, waiting; and none of you knew except the clock. Harry, it is sweet of you to tell me. (*His face is not sweet. The illiterate woman has used the wrong adjective.*) I forget what I said precisely in the letter.

SIR HARRY (*pulverising her*). So do I. But I have it still.

KATE (*not pulverised*). Do let me see it again. (*She has observed his eye wandering to the desk.*)

SIR HARRY. You are welcome to it as a gift. (*The fateful letter, a poor little dead thing, is brought to light from a locked drawer.*)

KATE (*taking it*). Yes, this is it. Harry, how you did crumple it! (*She reads, not without curiosity.*) 'Dear husband—I call you that for the last time—I am off. I am what you call making a bolt of it. I won't try to excuse myself nor to explain, for you would not accept the excuses nor understand the explanation. It will be a little shock to you, but only to your pride; what will astound you is that any woman could be such a fool as to leave such a man as you. I am taking nothing with me that belongs to you. May you be very happy.—Your ungrateful KATE. P.S.—You need not try to find out who he is. You will try, but you won't succeed.' (*She folds the nasty little thing up.*) I may really have it for my very own?

SIR HARRY. You really may.

KATE (*impudently*). If you would care for a typed copy——?

SIR HARRY (*in a voice with which he used to frighten his grand-mother*). None of your sauce! (*Wincing*) I had to let them see it in the end.

KATE. I can picture Jack Lamb eating it.

SIR HARRY. A penniless parson's daughter.

KATE. That is all I was.

SIR HARRY. We searched for the two of you high and low.

KATE. Private detectives?

SIR HARRY. They couldn't get on the track of you.

KATE (*smiling*). No?

SIR HARRY. But at last the courts let me serve the papers by ad-vertisement on a man unknown, and I got my freedom.

KATE. So I saw. It was the last I heard of you.

SIR HARRY (*each word a blow for her*). And I married again just as soon as ever I could.

KATE. They say that is always a compliment to the first wife.

SIR HARRY (*violently*). I showed them.

KATE. You soon let them see that if one woman was a fool, you still had the pick of the basket to choose from.

SIR HARRY. By James, I did.

KATE (*bringing him to earth again*). But still, you wondered who he was.

SIR HARRY. I suspected everybody—even my pals. I felt like jumping at their throats and crying, 'It's you!'

KATE. You had been so admirable to me, an instinct told you that I was sure to choose another of the same.

SIR HARRY. I thought, it can't be money, so it must be looks. Some dolly face. (*He stares at her in perplexity.*) He must have had something wonderful about him to make you willing to give up all that you had with me.

KATE (*as if he was the stupid one*). Poor Harry.

SIR HARRY. And it couldn't have been going on for long, for I would have noticed the change in you.

KATE. Would you?

SIR HARRY. I knew you so well.

KATE. You amazing man.

SIR HARRY. So who was he? Out with it.

KATE. You are determined to know?

SIR HARRY. Your promise. You gave your word.

KATE. If I must—— (*She is the villain of the piece, but it must be conceded that in this matter she is reluctant to pain him.*) I am sorry I promised. (*Looking at him steadily.*) There was no one, Harry; no one at all.

SIR HARRY (*rising*). If you think you can play with me——

KATE. I told you that you wouldn't like it.

SIR HARRY (*rasping*). It is unbelievable.

KATE. I suppose it is; but it is true.

SIR HARRY. Your letter itself gives you the lie.

KATE. That was intentional. I saw that if the truth were known you might have a difficulty in getting your freedom; and as I was getting mine it seemed fair that you should have yours also. So I wrote my good-bye in words that would be taken to mean what you thought they meant, and I knew the law would back you in your opinion. For the law, like you, Harry, has a profound understanding of women.

SIR HARRY (*trying to straighten himself*). I don't believe you yet.

KATE (*looking not unkindly into the soul of this man*). Perhaps that is the best way to take it. It is less unflattering than the truth. But you were the only one. (*Summing up her life.*) You sufficed.

SIR HARRY. Then what mad impulse——

KATE. It was no impulse, Harry. I had thought it out for a year.

SIR HARRY. A year? (*dazed*). One would think to hear you that I hadn't been a good husband to you.

KATE (*with a sad smile*). You were a good husband according to your lights.

Sir Harry (*stoutly*). I think so.

Kate. And a moral man, and chatty, and quite the philanthropist.

Sir Harry (*on sure ground*). All women envied you.

Kate. How you loved me to be envied.

Sir Harry. I swaddled you in luxury.

Kate (*making her great revelation*). That was it.

Sir Harry (*blankly*). What?

Kate (*who can be serene because it is all over*). How you beamed at me when I sat at the head of your fat dinners in my fat jewellery, surrounded by our fat friends.

Sir Harry (*aggrieved*). They weren't so fat.

Kate (*a side issue*). All except those who were so thin. Have you ever noticed, Harry, that many jewels make women either incredibly fat or incredibly thin?

Sir Harry (*shouting*). I have not. (*Is it worth while to argue with her any longer?*) We had all the most interesting society of the day. It wasn't only business men. There were politicians, painters, writers———

Kate. Only the glorious, dazzling successes. Oh, the fat talk while we ate too much—about who had made a hit and who was slipping back, and what the noo house cost and the noo motor and the gold soup-plates, and who was to be the noo knight.

Sir Harry (*who it will be observed is unanswerable from first to last*). Was anybody getting on better than me, and consequently you?

Kate. Consequently me! Oh, Harry, you and your sublime religion.

Sir Harry (*honest heart*). My religion? I never was one to talk about religion, but—

Kate. Pooh, Harry, you don't even know what your religion was and is and will be till the day of your expensive funeral. (*And here is the lesson that life has taught her.*) One's religion is whatever he is most interested in, and yours is Success.

Sir Harry (*quoting from his morning paper*). Ambition—it is the last infirmity of noble minds.

KATE. Noble minds!

SIR HARRY (*at last grasping what she is talking about*). You are not saying that you left me because of my success?

KATE. Yes, that was it. (*And now she stands revealed to him.*) I couldn't endure it. If a failure had come now and then—but your success was suffocating me. (*She is rigid with emotion.*) The passionate craving I had to be done with it, to find myself among people who had not got on.

SIR HARRY (*with proper spirit*). There are plenty of them.

KATE. There were none in our set. When they began to go down-hill they rolled out of our sight.

SIR HARRY (*clenching it*). I tell you I am worth a quarter of a million.

KATE (*unabashed*). That is what you are worth to yourself. I'll tell you what you are worth to me: exactly twelve pounds. For I made up my mind that I could launch myself on the world alone if I first proved my mettle by earning twelve pounds; and as soon as I had earned it I left you.

SIR HARRY (*in the scales*). Twelve pounds!

KATE. That is your value to a woman. If she can't make it she has to stick to you.

SIR HARRY (*remembering perhaps a rectory garden*). You valued me at more than that when you married me.

KATE (*seeing it also*). Ah, I didn't know you then. If only you had been a man, Harry.

SIR HARRY. A man? What do you mean by a man?

KATE (*leaving the garden*). Haven't you heard of them? They are something fine; and every woman is loathe to admit to herself that her husband is not one. When she marries, even though she has been a very trivial person, there is in her some vague stirring toward a worthy life, as well as a fear of her capacity for evil. She knows her chance lies in him. If there is something good in him, what is good in her finds it, and they join forces against the baser parts. So I didn't give you up willingly, Harry. I invented all sorts of theories to explain you.

Your hardness—I said it was a fine want of maukishness. Your coarseness—I said it goes with strength. Your contempt for the weak—I called it virility. Your want of ideals was clear-sightedness. Your ignoble views of women—I tried to think them funny. Oh, I clung to you to save myself. But I had to let go; you had only the one quality, Harry, success; you had it so strong that it swallowed all the others.

SIR HARRY (*not to be diverted from the main issue*). How did you earn that twelve pounds?

KATE. It took me nearly six months; but I earned it fairly. (*She presses her hand on the typewriter as lovingly as many a woman has pressed a rose.*) I learned this. I hired it and taught myself. I got some work through a friend, and with my first twelve pounds I paid for my machine. Then I considered that I was free to go, and I went.

SIR HARRY. All this going on in my house while you were living in the lap of luxury! (*She nods.*) By God, you were determined.

KATE (*briefly*). By God, I was.

SIR HARRY (*staring.*) How you must have hated me.

KATE (*smiling at the childish word*). Not a bit—after I saw that there was a way out. From that hour you amused me, Harry; I was even sorry for you, for I saw that you couldn't help yourself. Success is just a fatal gift.

SIR HARRY. Oh, thank you.

KATE (*thinking, dear friends in front, of you and me perhaps*). Yes, and some of your most successful friends knew it. One or two of them used to look very sad at times, as if they thought they might have come to something if they hadn't got on.

SIR HARRY (*who has a horror of sacrilege*). The battered crew you live among now—what are they but folk who have tried to succeed and failed?

KATE. That's it; they try, but they fail.

SIR HARRY. And always will fail.

KATE. Always. Poor souls—I say of them. Poor soul—they say of me. It keeps us human. That is why I never tire of them.

SIR HARRY (*comprehensively*). Bah! Kate, I tell you I'll be worth half a million yet.

KATE. I'm sure you will. You're getting stout, Harry.

SIR HARRY. No, I'm not.

KATE. What was the name of that fat old fellow who used to fall asleep at our dinner-parties?

SIR HARRY. If you mean Sir William Crackley——

KATE. That was the man. Sir William was to me a perfect picture of the grand success. He had got on so well that he was very, very stout, and when he sat on a chair it was thus (*her hands meeting in front of her*)—as if he were holding his success together. That is what you are working for, Harry. You will have that and the half million about the same time.

SIR HARRY (*who has surely been very patient*). Will you please to leave my house.

KATE (*putting on her gloves, soiled things*). But don't let us part in anger. How do you think I am looking, Harry, compared to the dull, inert thing that used to roll round in your padded carriages?

SIR HARRY (*in masterly fashion*). I forget what you were like. I'm very sure you never could have held a candle to the present Lady Sims.

KATE. That is a picture of her, is it not?

SIR HARRY (*seizing his chance again*). In her wedding-gown. Painted by an R.A.

KATE (*wickedly*). A knight?

SIR HARRY (*deceived*). Yes.

KATE (*who likes* LADY SIMS: *a piece of presumption on her part*). It is a very pretty face.

SIR HARRY (*with the pride of possession*). Acknowledged to be a beauty everywhere.

KATE. There is a merry look in the eyes, and character in the chin.

SIR HARRY (*like an auctioneer*). Noted for her wit.

KATE. All of her life before her when that was painted. It is a *spirituelle* face too. (*Suddenly she turns on him with anger, for the first and only time in the play.*) Oh, Harry, you brute!

SIR HARRY (*staggered*). Eh? What?

KATE. That dear creature capable of becoming a noble wife and mother—she is the spiritless woman of no account that I saw here a few minutes ago. I forgive you for myself, for I escaped, but that poor lost soul, oh, Harry, Harry.

SIR HARRY (*waving her to the door*). I'll thank you— If ever there was a woman proud of her husband and happy in her married life, that woman is Lady Sims.

KATE. I wonder.

SIR HARRY. Then you needn't wonder.

KATE (*slowly*). If I was a husband—it is my advice to all of them—I would often watch my wife quietly to see whether the twelve-pound look was not coming into her eyes. Two boys, did you say, and both like you?

SIR HARRY. What is that to you?

KATE (*with glistening eyes*). I was only thinking that somewhere there are two little girls who, when they grow up—the dear, pretty girls who are all meant for the men that don't get on! Well, good-bye, Sir Harry.

SIR HARRY (*showing a little human weakness, it is to be feared*). Say first that you're sorry.

KATE. For what?

SIR HARRY. That you left me. Say you regret it bitterly. You know you do. (*She smiles and shakes her head. He is pettish. He makes a terrible announcement.*) You have spoilt the day for me.

KATE (*to hearten him*). I am sorry for that; but it is only a pin-prick, Harry. I suppose it is a little jarring in the moment of your triumph to find that there is—one old friend—who does not think you a success; but you will soon forget it. Who cares what a typist thinks?

SIR HARRY (*heartened*). Nobody. A typist at eighteen shillings a week!

KATE (*proudly*). Not a bit of it, Harry. I double that.

SIR HARRY (*neatly*). Magnificent!
>   (*There is a timid knock at the door.*)

LADY SIMS. May I come in?

SIR HARRY (*rather appealingly*). It is Lady Sims.

KATE. I won't tell. She is afraid to come into her husband's room without knocking!

SIR HARRY. She is not. (*Uxoriously*) Come in, dearest. (*Dearest enters carrying the sword. She might have had the sense not to bring it in while this annoying person is here.*)

LADY SIMS (*thinking she has brought her welcome with her*). Harry, the sword has come.

SIR HARRY (*who will dote on it presently*). Oh, all right.

LADY SIMS. But I thought you were so eager to practise with it.
>   (*The person smiles at this. He wishes he had not looked to see if she was smiling.*)

SIR HARRY (*sharply*). Put it down.
>   (LADY SIMS *flushes a little as she lays the sword aside.*)

KATE (*with her confounded courtesy*). It is a beautiful sword, if I may say so.

LADY SIMS (*helped*). Yes.
>   (*The person thinks she can put him in the wrong, does she? He'll show her.*)

SIR HARRY (*with one eye on* KATE). Emmy, the one thing your neck needs is more jewels.

LADY SIMS (*faltering*). More!

SIR HARRY. Some ropes of pearls. I'll see to it. It's a bagatelle to me. (KATE *conceals her chagrin, so she had better be shown the door. He rings.*) I won't detain you any longer, miss.

KATE. Thank you.

LADY SIMS. Going already? You have been very quick.

SIR HARRY. The person doesn't suit, Emmy.

LADY SIMS. I'm sorry.

KATE. So am I, madam, but it can't be helped. Good-bye, your ladyship—good-bye, Sir Harry. (*There is a suspicion of an impertinent curtsey, and she is escorted off the premises by*

TOMBES. *The air of the room is purified by her going.* SIR HARRY *notices it at once.*)

LADY SIMS (*whose tendency is to say the wrong thing*). She seemed such a capable woman.

SIR HARRY (*on his hearth*). I don't like her style at all.

LADY SIMS (*meekly*). Of course you know best. (*This is the right kind of woman.*)

SIR HARRY (*rather anxious for corroboration*). Lord, how she winced when I said I was to give you those ropes of pearls.

LADY SIMS. Did she? I didn't notice. I suppose so.

SIR HARRY (*frowning*). Suppose? Surely I know enough about women to know that.

LADY SIMS. Yes, oh yes.

SIR HARRY. (*Odd that so confident a man should ask this.*) Emmy, I know you well, don't I? I can read you like a book, eh?

LADY SIMS (*nervously*). Yes, Harry.

SIR HARRY (*jovially, but with an inquiring eye*). What a different existence yours is from that poor lonely wretch's.

LADY SIMS. Yes, but she has a very contented face.

SIR HARRY (*with a stamp of his foot*). All put on. What?

LADY SIMS (*timidly*). I didn't say anything.

SIR HARRY (*snapping*). One would think you envied her.

LADY SIMS. Envied? Oh no—but I thought she looked so alive. It was while she was working the machine.

SIR HARRY. Alive! That's no life. It is you that are alive. (*Curtly*) I'm busy, Emmy. (*He sits at the writing-table.*)

LADY SIMS (*dutifully*). I'm sorry; I'll go, Harry (*inconsequentially*). Are they very expensive?

SIR HARRY. What?

LADY SIMS. Those machines?

(*When she has gone the possible meaning of her question startles him. The curtain hides him from us, but we may be sure that he will soon be bland again. We have a comfortable feeling, you and I, that there is nothing of* HARRY SIMS *in us.*)

KATHERINE MANSFIELD

The Stranger

It seemed to the little crowd on the wharf that she was never going to move again. There she lay, immense, motionless on the grey crinkled water, a loop of smoke above her, an immense flock of gulls screaming and diving after the galley droppings at the stern. You could just see little couples parading—little flies walking up and down the dish on the grey crinkled tablecloth. Other flies clustered and swarmed at the edge. Now there was a gleam of white on the lower deck—the cook's apron or the stewardess perhaps. Now a tiny black spider raced up the ladder on to the bridge.

In the front of the crowd a strong-looking, middle-aged man, dressed very well, very snugly in a grey overcoat, grey silk scarf, thick gloves and dark felt hat, marched up and down, twirling his folded umbrella. He seemed to be the leader of the little crowd on the wharf and at the same time to keep them together. He was something between the sheep-dog and the shepherd.

But what a fool—what a fool he had been not to bring any glasses! There wasn't a pair of glasses between the whole lot of them.

"Curious thing, Mr. Scott, that none of us thought of glasses. We might have been able to stir 'em up a bit. We might have managed a little signalling. *Don't hesitate to land. Natives harmless.* Or: *A welcome awaits you. All is forgiven.* What? Eh?"

Mr. Hammond's quick, eager glance, so nervous and yet so friendly and confiding, took in everybody on the wharf, roped in even those old chaps lounging against the gangways. They knew, every man-jack of them, that Mrs. Hammond was on that boat, and he was so tremendously excited it never entered his head not to believe that this marvelous fact meant something to them too. It warmed his heart towards them. They were, he decided, as decent a crowd of people——— Those old chaps over by the gangways, too—fine, solid old chaps. What chests—by Jove! And he squared his own, plunged his thick-gloved hands into his pockets, rocked from heel to toe.

"Yes, my wife's been in Europe for the last ten months. On a visit to our eldest girl, who was married last year. I brought her up here, as far as Salisbury, myself. So I thought I'd better come and fetch her back. Yes, yes, yes." The shrewd grey eyes narrowed again and searched anxiously, quickly, the motionless liner. Again his overcoat was unbuttoned. Out came the thin, butter-yellow watch again, and for the twentieth—fiftieth—hundredth time he made the calculation.

"Let me see, now. It was two fifteen when the doctor's launch went off. Two fifteen. It is now exactly twenty-eight minutes past four. That is to say, the doctor's been gone two hours and thirteen minutes. Two hours and thirteen minutes! Whee-ooh!" He gave a queer little half-whistle and snapped his watch to again. "But I think we should have been told if there was anything up—don't you, Mr. Gaven?"

"Oh, yes, Mr. Hammond! I don't think there's anything to—anything to worry about," said Mr. Gaven, knocking out his pipe against the heel of his shoe. "At the same time——"

"Quite so! Quite so!" cried Mr. Hammond. "Dashed annoying!" He paced quickly up and down and came back again to his stand between Mr. and Mrs. Scott and Mr. Gaven. "It's getting quite dark, too," and he waved his folded umbrella as though the dusk at least might have had the decency to keep off for a bit. But the dusk came slowly, spreading like a slow stain over the water. Little Jean Scott dragged at her mother's hand.

"I wan' my tea, mammy!" she wailed.

"I expect you do," said Mr. Hammond. "I expect all these ladies want their tea." And his kind, flushed, almost pitiful glance roped them all in again. He wondered whether Janey was having a final cup of tea in the saloon out there. He hoped so; he thought not. It would be just like her not to leave the deck. In that case perhaps the deck steward would bring her up a cup. If he'd been there he'd have got it for her—somehow. And for a moment he was on deck, standing over her, watching her little hand fold round the cup in the way she had, while she drank the only cup of tea to be got on board. . . . But now he was back here, and the Lord only knew when that cursed Captain would stop hanging about in the stream. He took another turn, up and down, up and down. He walked as far as the cab-stand to make sure his driver hadn't disappeared; back he swerved again to the little flock huddled in the shelter of the banana crates. Little Jean Scott was still wanting her tea. Poor little beggar! He wished he had a bit of chocolate on him.

"Here, Jean!" he said. "Like a lift up?" And easily, gently, he swung the little girl on to a higher barrel. The movement of holding her, steadying her, relieved him wonderfully, lightened his heart.

"Hold on," he said, keeping an arm round her.

"Oh, don't worry about *Jean*, Mr. Hammond!" said Mrs. Scott.

"That's all right, Mrs. Scott. No trouble. It's a pleasure. Jean's a little pal of mine, aren't you, Jean?"

"Yes, Mr. Hammond," said Jean, and she ran her finger down the dent of his felt hat.

But suddenly she caught him by the ear and gave a loud scream. "Lo-ok, Mr. Hammond! She's moving! Look, she's coming in!"

By Jove! So she was. At last! She was slowly, slowly turning round. A bell sounded far over the water and a great spout of steam gushed into the air. The gulls rose; they fluttered away like bits of white paper. And whether that deep throbbing was her engines or his heart Mr. Hammond couldn't say. He had to nerve himself to bear it, whatever it was. At that moment old Captain Johnson, the harbor master, came striding down the wharf, a leather portfolio under his arm.

"Jean'll be all right," said Mr. Scott. "I'll hold her." He was just in time. Mr. Hammond had forgotten about Jean. He sprang away to greet old Captain Johnson.

"Well, Captain," the eager, nervous voice rang out again, "you've taken pity on us at last."

"It's no good blaming me, Mr. Hammond," wheezed old Captain Johnson, staring at the liner. "You got Mrs. Hammond on board, ain't yer?"

"Yes, yes!" said Hammond, and he kept by the harbor master's side. "Mrs. Hammond's there. Hul-lo! We shan't be long now!"

With her telephone ring-ringing, the thrum of her screw filling the air, the big liner bore down on them, cutting sharp through the dark water so that big white shavings curled to either side. Hammond and the harbor master kept in front of the rest. Hammond took off his hat; he raked the decks—they were crammed with passengers; he waved his hat and bawled a loud, strange "Hul-lo!" across the water; and then turned round and burst out laughing and said something—nothing—to old Captain Johnson.

"Seen her?" asked the harbor master.

"No, not yet. Steady—wait a bit!" And suddenly, between two great clumsy idiots—"Get out of the way there!" he signed with his umbrella—he saw a hand raised—a white glove shaking a handkerchief. Another moment, and—thank God, thank God! —there she was. There was Janey. There was Mrs. Hammond, yes, yes, yes—standing by the rail and smiling and nodding and waving her handkerchief.

"Well, that's first class—first class! Well, well, well!" He positively stamped. Like lightning he drew out his cigar case and offered it to old Captain Johnson. "Have a cigar, Captain! They're pretty good. Have a couple! Here"—and he pressed all the cigars in the case on the harbor master—"I've a couple of boxes up at the hotel."

"Thenks, Mr. Hammond!" wheezed old Captain Johnson.

Hammond stuffed the cigar-case back. His hands were shaking, but he'd got hold of himself again. He was able to face Janey. There she was, leaning on the rail, talking to some woman and at the same time watching him, ready for him. It struck him, as the gulf of water closed, how small she looked on that huge ship. His heart was wrung with such a spasm that he could have cried out. How little she looked to have come all the long way and back by herself! Just like her, though. Just like Janey. She had the courage of a—— And now the crew had come forward and parted the passengers; they had lowered the rails for the gangways.

The voices on shore and the voices on board flew to greet each other.

"All well?"

"All well."

"How's mother?"

"Much better."

"Hullo, Jean!"

"Hillo, Aun' Emily!"

"Had a good voyage?"

"Splendid!"

"Shan't be long now!"

"Not long now."

The engines stopped. Slowly she edged to the wharf-side.

"Make way there—make way—make way!" And the wharf hands brought the heavy gangways along at a sweeping run. Hammond signed to Janey to stay where she was. The old harbor master stepped forward; he followed. As to "ladies first," or any rot like that, it never entered his head.

"After you, Captain!" he cried genially. And, treading on the old man's heels, he strode up the gangway on to the deck in a bee-line to Janey, and Janey was clasped in his arms.

"Well, well, well! Yes, yes! Here we are at last!" he stammered. It was all he could say. And Janey emerged, and her cool little voice—the only voice in the world for him—said,

"Well, darling! Have you been waiting long?"

No; not long. Or, at any rate, it didn't matter. It was over now. But the point was, he had a cab waiting at the end of the wharf. Was she ready to go off? Was her luggage ready? In that case they could cut off sharp with her cabin luggage and let the rest go hang until tomorrow. He bent over her and she looked up with her familiar half-smile. She was just the same. Not a day changed. Just as he'd always known her. She laid her small hand on his sleeve.

"How are the children, John?" she asked.

(Hang the children!) "Perfectly well. Never better in their lives."

"Haven't they sent me letters?"

"Yes, yes—of course! I've left them at the hotel for you to digest later on."

"We can't go quite so fast," said she. "I've got people to say good-bye to—and then there's the Captain." As his face fell she gave his arm a small understanding squeeze. "If the Captain comes off the bridge I want you to thank him for having looked after your wife so beautifully." Well, he'd got her. If she wanted another ten minutes——— As he gave way she was surrounded. The whole first-class seemed to want to say good-bye to Janey.

"Good-bye, *dear* Mrs. Hammond! And next time you're in Sydney I'll *expect* you."

"Darling Mrs. Hammond! You won't forget to write to me, will you?"

"Well, Mrs. Hammond, what this boat would have been without you!"

It was as plain as a pikestaff that she was by far the most popular woman on board. And she took it all—just as usual.

Absolutely composed. Just her little self—just Janey all over; standing there with her veil thrown back. Hammond never noticed what his wife had on. It was all the same to him whatever she wore. But to-day he did notice that she wore a black "costume"—didn't they call it?—with white frills, trimmings he supposed they were, at the neck and sleeves. All this while Janey handed him round.

"John, dear!" And then: "I want to introduce you to———"

Finally they did escape, and she led the way to her stateroom. To follow Janey down the passage that she knew so well —that was so strange to him; to part the green curtains after her and to step into the cabin that had been hers gave him exquisite happiness. But—confound it!—the stewardess was there on the floor, strapping up the rugs.

"That's the last, Mrs. Hammond," said the stewardess, rising and pulling down her cuffs.

He was introduced again, and then Janey and the stewardess disappeared into the passage. He heard whisperings. She was getting the tipping business over, he supposed. He sat down on the striped sofa and took his hat off. There were the rugs she had taken with her; they looked good as new. All her luggage looked fresh, perfect. The labels were written in her beautiful little clear hand—"Mrs. John Hammond."

"Mrs. John Hammond!" He gave a long sigh of content and leaned back, crossing his arms. The strain was over. He felt he could have sat there forever sighing his relief—the relief at being rid of that horrible tug, pull, grip on his heart. The danger was over. That was the feeling. They were on dry land again.

But at that moment Janey's head came round the corner.

"Darling—do you mind? I just want to go and say good-bye to the doctor."

Hammond started up. "I'll come with you."

"No, no!" she said. "Don't bother. I'd rather not. I'll not be a minute."

And before he could answer she was gone. He had half a mind to run after her; but instead he sat down again.

Would she really not be long? What was the time now? Out came the watch; he stared at nothing. That was rather queer of Janey, wasn't it? Why couldn't she have told the stewardess to say good-bye for her? Why did she have to go chasing after the ship's doctor? She could have sent a note from the hotel even if the affair had been urgent. Urgent? Did it—could it mean that she had been ill on the voyage—she was keeping something from him? That was it! He seized his hat. He was going off to find that fellow to wring the truth out of him at all costs. He thought he'd noticed just something. She was just a touch too calm—too steady. From the very first moment———

The curtains rang. Janey was back. He jumped to his feet.

"Janey, have you been ill on this voyage? You have!"

"Ill?" Her airy little voice mocked him. She stepped over the rugs, and came up close, touched his breast, and looked up at him.

"Darling," she said, "don't frighten me. Of course I haven't! Whatever makes you think I have? Do I look ill?"

But Hammond didn't see her. He only felt that she was looking at him and that there was no need to worry about anything. She was here to look after things. It was all right. Everything was.

The gentle pressure of her hand was so calming that he put his over hers to hold it there. And she said:

"Stand still. I want to look at you. I haven't seen you yet. You've had your beard beautifully trimmed, and you look— younger, I think, and decidedly thinner! Bachelor life agrees with you."

"Agrees with me!" He groaned for love and caught her close again. And again, as always, he had the feeling he was holding something that never was quite his—his. Something too delicate, too precious, that would fly away once he let go.

"For God's sake let's get off to the hotel so that we can be by ourselves!" And he rang the bell hard for someone to look sharp with the luggage.

●   ●   ●

Walking down the wharf together she took his arm. He had
her on his arm again. And the difference it made to get into the
cab after Janey—to throw the red-and-yellow striped blanket
round them both—to tell the driver to hurry because neither of
them had had any tea. No more going without his tea or pouring out his own. She was back. He turned to her, squeezed her
hand, and said gently, teasingly, in the "special" voice he had
for her: "Glad to be home again, dearie?" She smiled; she didn't
even bother to answer, but gently she drew his hand away as
they came to the brighter streets.

"We've got the best room in the hotel," he said. "I wouldn't
be put off with another. And I asked the chambermaid to put
in a bit of a fire in case you felt chilly. She's a nice, attentive
girl. And I thought now we were here we wouldn't bother to go
home tomorrow, but spend the day looking round and leave the
morning after. Does that suit you? There's no hurry, is there?
The children will have you soon enough. . . . I thought a day's
sight-seeing might make a nice break in your journey—eh,
Janey?"

"Have you taken the tickets for the day after?" she asked.

"I should think I have!" He unbuttoned his overcoat and
took out his bulging pocket-book. "Here we are! I reserved a
first-class carriage to Cooktown. There it is—'Mr. *and* Mrs. John
Hammond.' I thought we might as well do ourselves comfort-
ably, and we don't want other people butting in, do we? But if
you'd like to stop here a bit longer———?"

"Oh, no!" said Janey quickly. "Not for the world! The day
after tomorrow, then. And the children———"

But they had reached the hotel. The manager was standing
in the broad, brilliantly lighted porch. He came down to greet
them. A porter ran from the hall for their boxes.

"Well, Mr. Arnold, here's Mrs. Hammond at last!"

The manager led them through the hall himself and pressed
the elevator-bell. Hammond knew there were business pals of
his sitting at the little hall tables having a drink before dinner.

But he wasn't going to risk interruption; he looked neither to the right nor the left. They could think what they pleased. If they didn't understand, the more fools they—and he stepped out of the lift, unlocked the door of their room, and shepherded Janey in. The door shut. Now, at last, they were alone together. He turned up the light. The curtains were drawn; the fire blazed. He flung his hat on to the huge bed and went towards her.

But—would you believe it?—again they were interrupted. This time it was the porter with the luggage. He made two journeys of it, leaving the door open in between, taking his time, whistling through his teeth in the corridor. Hammond paced up and down the room, tearing off his gloves, tearing off his scarf. Finally he flung his overcoat on to the bedside.

At last the fool was gone. The door clicked. Now they *were* alone. Said Hammond: "I feel I'll never have you to myself again. These cursed people! Janey"—and he bent his flushed, eager gaze upon her—"let's have dinner up here. If we go down to the restaurant we'll be interrupted, and then there's the confounded music" (the music he'd praised so highly, applauded so loudly last night!). "We shan't be able to hear each other speak. Let's have something up here in front of the fire. It's too late for tea. I'll order a little supper, shall I? How does that idea strike you?"

"Do, darling!" said Janey. "And while you're away—the children's letters———"

"Oh, later on will do!" said Hammond.

"But then we'd get it over," said Janey. "And I'd first have time to———"

"Oh, I needn't go down!" explained Hammond. "I'll just ring and give the order . . . you don't want to send me away, do you?"

Janey shook her head and smiled.

"But you're thinking of something else. You're worrying about something," said Hammond. "What is it? Come and sit here—come and sit on my knee before the fire."

"I'll just unpin my hat," said Janey, and she went over to the dressing-table. "A-ah!" She gave a little cry.

"What is it?"

"Nothing, darling. I've just found the children's letters. That's all right! They will keep. No hurry now!" She turned to him, clasping them. She tucked them into her frilled blouse. She cried quickly, gaily: "Oh, how typical this dressing table is of you!"

"Why? What's the matter with it?" said Hammond.

"If it were floating in eternity I should say 'John!' " laughed Janey, staring at the big bottle of hair tonic, the wicker bottle of eau-de-Cologne, the two hair-brushes, and a dozen new collars tied with pink tape. "Is this all your luggage?"

"Hang my luggage!" said Hammond; but all the same he liked being laughed at by Janey. "Let's talk. Let's get down to things. Tell me"—and as Janey perched on his knees he leaned back and drew her into the deep, ugly chair—"tell me you're really glad to be back, Janey."

"Yes, darling, I am glad," she said.

But just as when he embraced her he felt she would fly away, so Hammond never knew—never knew for dead certain that she was as glad as he was. How could he know? Would he ever know? Would he always have this craving—this pang like hunger, somehow, to make Janey so much part of him that there wasn't any of her to escape? He wanted to blot out everybody, everything. He wished now he'd turned off the light. That might have brought her nearer. And now those letters from the children rustled in her blouse. He could have chucked them into the fire.

"Janey," he whispered.

"Yes, dear?" She lay on his breast, but so lightly, so remotely. Their breathing rose and fell together.

"Janey!"

"What is it?"

"Turn to me," he whispered. A slow, deep flush flowed into his forehead. "Kiss me, Janey! You kiss me!"

It seemed to him there was a tiny pause—but long enough for him to suffer torture—before her lips touched his, firmly, lightly—kissing them as she always kissed him, as though the kiss—how could he describe it?—confirmed what they were saying, signed the contract. But that wasn't what he wanted; that wasn't at all what he thirsted for. He felt suddenly, horribly tired.

"If you knew," he said, opening his eyes, "what it's been like—waiting today. I thought the boat never would come in. There we were, hanging about. What kept you so long?"

She made no answer. She was looking away from him at the fire. The flames hurried—hurried over the coals, flickered, fell.

"Not asleep, are you?" said Hammond, and he jumped her up and down.

"No," she said. And then: "Don't do that, dear. No, I was thinking. As a matter of fact," she said, "one of the passengers died last night—a man. That's what held us up. We brought him in—I mean, he wasn't buried at sea. So, of course, the ship's doctor and the shore doctor———"

"What was it?" asked Hammond uneasily. He hated to hear of death. He hated this to have happened. It was, in some queer way, as though he and Janey had met a funeral on their way to the hotel.

"Oh, it wasn't anything in the least infectious!" said Janey. She was speaking scarcely above her breath. "It was *heart*." A pause. "Poor fellow!" she said. "Quite young." And she watched the fire flicker and fall. "He died in my arms," said Janey.

The blow was so sudden that Hammond thought he would faint. He couldn't move; he couldn't breathe. He felt all his strength flowing—flowing into the big dark chair, and the big dark chair held him fast, gripped him, forced him to bear it.

"What?" he said dully. "What's that you say?"

"The end was quite peaceful," said the small voice. "He just" —and Hammond saw her lift her gentle hand—"breathed his life away at the end." And her hand fell.

"Who—else was there?" Hammond managed to ask.

"Nobody. I was alone with him."

Ah, my God, what was she saying! What was she doing to him! This would kill him! And all the while she spoke:

"I saw the change coming and I sent the steward for the doctor, but the doctor was too late. He couldn't have done anything anyway."

"But—why *you*, why *you?*" moaned Hammond.

At that Janey turned quickly, quickly searched his face.

"You don't *mind*, John, do you?" she asked. "You don't——— It's nothing to do with you and me."

Somehow or other he managed to shake some sort of smile at her. Somehow or other he stammered: "No—go—on, go on! I want you to tell me."

"But, John darling———"

"Tell me, Janey!"

"There's nothing to tell," she said, wondering. "He was one of the first-class passengers. I saw he was very ill when he came on board. . . . But he seemed to be so much better until yesterday. He had a severe attack in the afternoon—excitement—nervousness, I think, about arriving. And after that he never recovered."

"But why didn't the stewardess———"

"Oh, my dear—the stewardess!" said Janey. "What would he have felt? And besides . . . he might have wanted to leave a message . . . to———"

"Didn't he?" muttered Hammond. "Didn't he say anything?"

"No, darling, not a word!" She shook her head softly. "All the time I was with him he was too weak . . . he was too weak even to move a finger. . . ."

Janey was silent. But her words, so light, so soft, so chill, seemed to hover in the air, to rain into his breast like snow.

The fire had gone red. Now it fell in with a sharp sound and the room was colder. Cold crept up his arms. The room was huge, immense, glittering. It filled his whole world. There was the great blind bed, with his coat flung across it like some headless man saying his prayers. There was the luggage, ready to be carried away again, anywhere, tossed into trains, carted on to boats.

. . . "He was too weak. He was too weak to move a finger." And yet he died in Janey's arms. She—who'd never—never once in all these years———never on one single solitary occasion———

No; he mustn't think of it. Madness lay in thinking of it. No, he wouldn't face it. He couldn't stand it. It was too much to bear!

And now Janey touched his tie with her fingers. She pinched the edges of the tie together.

"You're not—sorry I told you, John darling? It hasn't made you sad? It hasn't spoilt our evening—our being alone together?"

But at that he had to hide his face. He put his face into her bosom and his arms enfolded her.

Spoilt their evening! Spoilt their being alone together! They would never be alone together again.

PHYLLIS McGINLEY ·

Midcentury Love Letter

Stay near me. Speak my name. Oh, do not wander
By a thought's span, heart's impulse, from the light
We kindle here. You are my sole defender
(As I am yours) in this precipitous night,
Which over earth, till common landmarks alter,
Is falling, without stars, and bitter cold.
We two have but our burning selves for shelter.
Huddle against me. Give me your hand to hold.

So might two climbers lost in mountain weather
On a high slope and taken by the storm,
Desperate in the darkness, cling together
Under one cloak and breathe each other warm.
Stay near me. Spirit, perishable as bone,
In no such winter can survive alone.

FROM TIMES THREE BY PHYLLIS McGINLEY. COPYRIGHT 1953 BY
PHYLLIS McGINLEY. ORIGINALLY APPEARED IN THE NEW YORKER. RE-
PRINTED BY PERMISSION OF THE VIKING PRESS, INC.

SARA TEASDALE

On the
Sussex Downs

Over the downs there were birds flying,
　　Far off glittered the sea,
And toward the north the weald of Sussex
　　Lay like a kingdom under me.

I was happier than the larks
　　That nest on the downs and sing to the sky,
Over the downs the birds flying
　　Were not so happy as I.

It was not you, though you were near,
　　Though you were good to hear and see,
It was not earth, it was not heaven
　　It was myself that sang in me.

The Sleeping Beauty

There was once a King and his Queen, who had no children, which grieved them more than can be imagined. They went to all the healing waters in the world; they made vows; they went on pilgrimages; they did everything they could think of: but it was all to no good.

At last, however, the Queen did have a baby—a little girl. There was a fine christening party; and all the fairies in the kingdom (there were seven of them) were made godmothers to the Princess, so that each of them could give her a gift, as was the custom of fairies at that time, and so she was endowed with every good quality imaginable. After the baptism itself, all the guests came back to the King's palace, where there was a great banquet in honour of the fairies. Each of them sat at table, and a rich cloth was spread for her, and on it a golden casket containing a knife, fork, and spoon of fine gold, all studded with diamonds and rubies. But just as every one had sat down, in came an old fairy who had not been invited because for more than fifty years she had not come out of her tower, so that every one thought she must be dead or else under a spell.

The King had a place laid for her; but they could not manage to find a golden casket, such as the others had, because only the set of seven had been made. The old fairy thought she was being slighted, so she grumbled to herself in a threatening way. One of the younger fairies sitting beside her heard this, and fearing that she might be giving the little Princess some unlucky gift, went and hid behind the curtains when the banquet was over, so as to be the last to speak, and thus be able to put right, as far as she could, any harm that the old fairy might do.

Now the fairies began to present their gifts to the Princess. The youngest granted her this boon—that she should be the most beautiful girl in the world; the next, that she should be the wittiest; the third, that whatever she did, she should do most gracefully; the fourth, that she should dance perfectly; the fifth, that she should sing like a nightingale; and the sxith, that she should be able to play sweetly on all kinds of musical instruments.

Now it was the old fairy's turn; wagging her head more in spite than from old age, she said that the Princess would prick herself with a distaff, and that would be the death of her. Everybody shuddered at this terrible gift, and all burst into tears. At that moment the young lady stepped out from behind the curtains and said in a loud voice: "Take courage, Your Majesties; your daughter will not die: true, I have not the power to undo completely what my elder sister has prophesied, and the Princess will indeed prick her hand with a distaff—but, far from dying of it, she will only fall into a deep sleep which shall last a hundred years, at the end of which time a king's son shall come and wake her."

The King tried to avert the ill-fortune promised by the old fairy, by at once having it proclaimed that no one was allowed to spin with a distaff, or to have a distaff in their house, on pain of death.

After fifteen or sixteen years, the King and Queen having gone to stay in one of their country houses, it chanced that the little Princess, roaming about the palace and wandering from room to room and from floor to floor, came to the top of one of the towers, and found a little attic, where a kindly old woman was sitting spinning. For this old woman had never heard of the King's orders against the use of the distaff.

"What are you doing, my good woman?" asked the Princess.

"Why, spinning, my pretty dear," answered the old woman, who did not know who her visitor was.

"How nice it looks!" said the Princess. "How do you do it? Here, let me have it, to see if I can do it as well."

No sooner had she taken hold of the distaff than she pricked her hand, because she was rather hasty and snatched, and because, anyhow, the fairies would have it so; and down she fell in a faint. The kind old woman was in a taking; she shouted for help: people came running from all directions, dashed water over the Princess, undid her stays, chafed her hands, and rubbed her temples with Hungary water; but nothing would bring her round.

Meanwhile the King had come home; hearing the noise he rushed up the tower, and seeing what had happened remembered what the fairies had promised. Rightly guessing that there was no help for it since what the fairies foretell must be, he had the Princess carried to the finest room in the palace, and laid on a bed all hung with gold and silver brocade. She looked like an angel, she was so beautiful; for her faint had not faded the bright colours of her complexion; her cheeks were the colour of pale pink carnations, and her lips like coral; only her eyes were closed; they could still hear her breathing softly, so at any rate she could not be dead. The King ordered his people to leave her in peace, till the hour should come for her to awake.

The good fairy who had saved her life by ordering her to sleep for a hundred years was in the kingdom of Mataquin, twelve thousand leagues away, when the accident happened; but she was told of it within the instant by a little dwarf in seven-league boots (that is, boots in which one can walk seven leagues at a stride). The fairy set out at once, and arrived in an hour, driving a chariot drawn by dragons, all of fire.

The King came out and gave her his arm as she dismounted from the chariot. She said he had done all for the best. But as she thought of everything beforehand, it struck her that the Princess would be very lonely all alone in that great palace when she at last awoke; so this is what she did. She touched everything in the palace with her magic wand, except the King and Queen —the governesses, the maids of honour, the waiting gentlewomen, the gentlemen of the bedchamber, the officers, the stewards, the cooks, the scullions, the grooms, the guards, the ushers, the pages, the footmen; she touched all the horses in the stables, and the stable-boys too, the mastiffs in the yard and Pouffle, the Princess's little lap-dog, who was curled up on her bed. As soon as she touched them they all fell asleep, never to wake until their mistress did, so as to be always ready to serve her when she should have need of them. Even the spit in front of the kitchen fire, on which partridges and pheasants were roasting, stopped turning, and the fire died down. It was all done in a moment; for fairies are fast workers when they choose.

Then the King and Queen, having kissed their dear child without waking her, left the palace and forbade any one to go near it. Indeed it was not necessary to forbid it; for in a matter of minutes there grew up round the borders of the park such a quantity of trees both great and small, of briars and brambles all twined together, that neither man nor beast could get through it: so that nohing was left to sight, even from a great way off, but the tops of the palace towers. No one doubted that the fairy had done this on purpose, so that the Princess would not be bothered with sightseers during her long sleep.

A hundred years went by. Another royal family came to the throne, and the son of the King who was then reigning was out hunting near the old palace. He asked what were the towers he could see above the tops of that great thick wood. Every one answered according to what he had heard tell; some saying that it was an old haunted castle; others that it was the place where the local witches held their meetings; but the most common opinion was that a great ogre lived there, and that he carried off thither all the children he could catch, to eat them at his ease without being followed, for he alone was able to force his way through the wood.

The Prince did not know what to believe; but just then an old countryman up and said: "Your Highness, it's more nor fifty years gone since I heard my old father say that there was a Princess in that castle, the prettiest that ever was seen; and she was bound to sleep there a hundred years, and be awakened by the King's son, who was the one for her."

Hearing this the young Prince felt himself all on fire. In a flash he determined to fulfill the prophecy; and, spurred on by love and glory, he resolved to see for himself how things stood. No sooner had he advanced on the wood than all the briars and brambles and all the great trees bent back to let him pass. He walked towards the palace along a great avenue of trees, surprised to see that none of his servants could follow, because the trees had closed up behind him as soon as he had passed by. None the less he went on, for a young Prince in love is always brave.

He came into a great forecourt, where all that met his eyes at first sight was enough to freeze his blood. There was a frightful silence; the appearance of death was everywhere; bodies of men and animals, seemingly dead, were stretched all round. But he could tell by the red noses and beery complexions of the ushers that they were only asleep. The goblets in their hands still held a few drops of wine to show that they had fallen asleep while drinking.

He went on into a great courtyard paved all in marble, and up a staircase into a guard-room, where the guards were drawn up with their muskets on their shoulders, all snoring away. He passed through room after room full of ladies and gentlemen in waiting, all fast asleep, some sitting and some on their feet. At last he came to a room all over gilt; there on a bed with all its curtains drawn back, he saw the most beautiful sight of his whole life: a Princess who seemed to be about fifteen or sixteen years old who had something mysteriously splendid, and as it were shining, about her. Trembling all over he came nearer to admire her, and fell on his knees beside her. At that moment the spell ceased to work; the Princess awoke, and bending on him what I must call a loving glance indeed, considering it was the first time she had set eyes on him, said: "Is it you, my Prince? You have been a long time coming."

The Prince was overjoyed to hear this, and delighted with the way in which she spoke it, so that he could not think how to express his joy and gratitude; he assured her that he loved her better than he did himself. The other things he told her were rather confusing; they cried a good deal, and were tongue-tied with love. He was in even greater confusion than she was, and no wonder; she had had time to think over what she would say, for it seems (though history tells us nothing of this) that the good fairy had arranged for her to have pleasant dreams during her long sleep. They talked for four hours without getting to the end of half the things they meant to tell each other.

Meanwhile the palace had come to life at the same time as the Princess, and every one bethought himself of going about his business. But as not every one was in love, they felt ravenously hungry. The maid of honor was as hungry as any of them, and losing her patience called out to her mistress that dinner was ready. The Prince helped the Princess to rise: she was already dressed in magnificent clothes, but he had the sense not to tell her that she was wearing his grandmother's fashions, with a high neckline; she was none the less beautiful for that.

They went into the dining-room all hung with mirrors, where dinner was served by the officers of her household, while a band of violins and hautboys played quaint old music most sweetly—tunes that had not been heard for a hundred years. Afterwards the chaplain married them in the palace chapel without delay, and they lived happily ever after.

Do You Love Me?

TEVYE: Golde, do you love me?

GOLDE: Do I *what?*

TEVYE: Do you love me?

GOLDE: Do I love you? With our daughters getting married, and there's trouble in the town—You're upset, you're worn out. Go inside, go lie down. Maybe it's indigestion.

TEVYE: Golde, I'm asking you a question. Do you love me?

GOLDE: You're a fool.

TEVYE: I know, but do you love me?

GOLDE: Do I love you?

TEVYE: Well?

GOLDE: For twenty-five years I've washed your clothes, cooked your meals, cleaned your house, given you children, milked the cow. After twenty-five years why talk about love right now?

TEVYE: Golde, the first time I met you was on our wedding day. I was scared.

GOLDE: I was shy.

TEVYE: I was nervous.

GOLDE: So was I.

TEVYE: But my father and my mother said we'd learn to love each other, and now I'm asking, Golde, do you love me?

GOLDE: I'm your *wife*.

TEVYE: I know, but do you love me?

GOLDE: Do I love him?

TEVYE: Well?

GOLDE: For twenty-five years I've lived with him, fought with him, starved with him. Twenty-five years my bed is his. If that's not love, what is?

TEVYE: Then you love me?

GOLDE: I suppose I do.

TEVYE: And I suppose I love you, too.

GOLDE and TEVYE: It doesn't change a thing, but, even so, after twenty-five years it's nice to know.

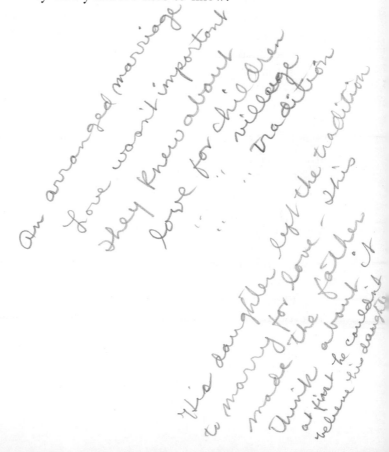

JOHN COLLIER

The Chaser

Alan Austen, as nervous as a kitten, went up certain dark and creaky stairs in the neighborhood of Pell Street, and peered about for a long time on the dim landing before he found the name he wanted written obscurely on one of the doors.

He pushed open this door, as he had been told to do, and found himself in a tiny room, which contained no furniture but a plain kitchen table, a rocking-chair, and an ordinary chair. On one of the dirty buff-coloured walls were a couple of shelves, containing in all perhaps a dozen bottles and jars.

An old man sat in the rocking-chair, reading a newspaper. Alan, without a word, handed him the card he had been given. "Sit down, Mr. Austen," said the old man very politely. "I am glad to make your acquaintance."

"Is it true," asked Alan, "that you have a certain mixture that has—er—quite extraordinary effects?"

"My dear sir," replied the old man, "my stock in trade is not very large—I don't deal in laxatives and teething mixtures —but such as it is, it is varied. I think nothing I sell has effects which could be precisely described as ordinary."

"Well, the fact is . . ." began Alan.

"Here, for example," interrupted the old man, reaching for a bottle from the shelf. "Here is a liquid as colorless as water, almost tasteless, quite imperceptible in coffee, wine, or any other beverage. It is also quite imperceptible to any known method of autopsy."

"Do you mean it is a poison?" cried Alan, very much horrified.

"Call it a glove-cleaner if you like," said the old man indifferently. "Maybe it will clean gloves. I have never tried. One might call it a life-cleaner. Lives need cleaning sometimes."

"I want nothing of that sort," said Alan.

"Probably it is just as well," said the old man. "Do you know the price of this? For one teaspoonful, which is sufficient, I ask five thousand dollars. Never less. Not a penny less."

"I hope all your mixtures are not as expensive," said Alan apprehensively.

"Oh dear, no," said the old man. "It would be no good charging that sort of price for a love potion, for example. Young people who need a love potion very seldom have five thousand dollars. Otherwise they would not need a love potion."

"I am glad to hear that," said Alan.

"I look at it like this," said the old man. "Please a customer with one article, and he will come back when he needs another. Even if it *is* more costly. He will save up for it, if necessary."

"So," said Alan, "you really do sell love potions?"

"If I did not sell love potions," said the old man, reaching for another bottle, "I should not have mentioned the other matter to you. It is only when one is in a position to oblige that one can afford to be so confidential."

"And these potions," said Alan. "They are not just—just— er—"

"Oh, no," said the old man. "Their effects are permanent, and extend far beyond the mere casual impulse. But they include it. Oh, yes, they include it. Bountifully, insistently. Everlastingly."

"Dear me!" said Alan, attempting a look of scientific detachment. "How very interesting!"

"But consider the spiritual side," said the old man.

"I do, indeed," said Alan.

"For indifference," said the old man, "they substitute devotion. For scorn, adoration. Give one tiny measure of this to the young lady—its flavor is imperceptible in orange juice, soup, or cocktails—and however gay and giddy she is, she will change altogether. She will want nothing but solitude and you."

"I can hardly believe it," said Alan. "She is so fond of parties."

"She will not like them any more," said the old man. "She will be afraid of the pretty girls you may meet."

"She will actually be jealous?" cried Alan in a rapture. "Of me?"

"Yes, she will want to be everything to you."

"She is, already. Only she doesn't care about it."

"She will, when she has taken this. She will care intensely. You will be her sole interest in life."

"Wonderful!" cried Alan.

"She will want to know all you do," said the old man. "All that has happened to you during the day. Every word of it. She will want to know what you are thinking about, why you smile suddenly, why you are looking sad."

"That is love!" cried Alan.

"Yes," said the old man. "How carefully she will look after you! She will never allow you to be tired, to sit in a draught, to neglect your food. If you are an hour late, she will be terrified. She will think you are killed, or that some siren has caught you."

"I can hardly imagine Diana like that!" cried Alan, overwhelmed with joy.

"You will not have to use your imagination," said the old man. "And, by the way, since there are always sirens, if by any chance you *should*, later on, slip a little, you need not worry. She will forgive you, in the end. She will be terribly hurt, of course, but she will forgive you—in the end."

"That will not happen," said Alan fervently.

"Of course not," said the old man. "But, if it did, you need not worry. She would never divorce you. Oh, no! And, of course,

she will never give you the least, the very least, grounds for—
uneasiness."

"And how much," said Alan, "is this wonderful mixture?"

"It is not as dear," said the old man, "as the glove-cleaner, or
life-cleaner, as I sometimes call it. No. That is five thousand dollars, never a penny less. One has to be older than you are, to in-
dulge in that sort of thing. One has to save up for it."

"But the love potion?" said Alan.

"Oh, that," said the old man, opening the drawer in the kitchen table, and taking out a tiny, rather dirty-looking phial.
"That is just a dollar."

"I can't tell you how grateful I am," said Alan, watching him
fill it.

"I like to oblige," said the old man. "Then customers come
back, later in life, when they are better off, and want more expensive things. Here you are. You will find it very effective."

"Thank you again," said Alan. "Good-bye."

"Au revoir," said the old man.

JOHN FREDERICK NIMS

Love Poem

My clumsiest dear, whose hands shipwreck vases,
At whose quick touch all glasses chip and ring,
Whose palms are bulls in china, burs in linen,
And have no cunning with any soft thing

Except all ill-at-ease fidgeting people:
The refugee uncertain at the door
You make at home; deftly you steady
The drunk clambering on his undulant floor.

Unpredictable dear, the taxi drivers' terror,
Shrinking from far headlights pale as a dime
Yet leaping before red apoplectic streetcars—
Misfit in any space. And never on time.

A wrench in clocks and the solar system. Only
With words and people and love you move at ease.
In traffic of wit expertly maneuver
And keep us, all devotion, at your knees.

Forgetting your coffee spreading on our flannel,
Your lipstick grinning on our coat,
So gayly in love's unbreakable heaven
Our souls on glory of split bourbon float.

Be with me, darling, early and late. Smash glasses—
I will study wry music for your sake.
For should your hands drop white and empty
All the toys of the world would break.

FROM THE IRON PASTORAL BY JOHN FREDERICK NIMS. PUBLISHED
BY WILLIAM SLOANE ASSOCIATES. REPRINTED BY PERMISSION OF WILLIAM
MORROW & CO., INC. COPYRIGHT © 1947 BY JOHN FREDERICK NIMS.

IRWIN SHAW

The Girls in Their Summer Dresses

Fifth Avenue was shining in the sun when they left the Brevoort. The sun was warm, even though it was February, and everything looked like Sunday morning—the buses and the well-dressed people walking slowly in couples and the quiet buildings with the windows closed.

Michael held Frances' arm tightly as they walked toward Washington Square in the sunlight. They walked lightly, almost smiling, because they had slept late and had a good breakfast and it was Sunday. Michael unbuttoned his coat and let it flap around him in the mild wind.

"Look out," Frances said as they crossed Eighth Street. "You'll break your neck." Michael laughed and Frances laughed with him.

"She's not so pretty," Frances said. "Anyway, not pretty enough to take a chance of breaking your neck."

Michael laughed again. "How did you know I was looking at her?"

Frances cocked her head to one side and smiled at her husband under the brim of her hat. "Mike, darling," she said.

"O.K.," he said. "Excuse me."

Frances patted his arm lightly and pulled him along a little faster toward Washington Square. "Let's not see anybody all day," she said. "Let's just hang around with each other. You and me. We're always up to our neck in people, drinking their Scotch or drinking our Scotch; we only see each other in bed. I want to go out with my husband all day long. I want him to talk only to me and listen only to me."

"What's to stop us?" Michael asked.

"The Stevensons. They want us to drop by around one o'clock and they'll drive us into the country."

"The cunning Stevensons," Mike said. "Transparent. They can whistle. They can go driving in the country by themselves."

"Is it a date?"

"It's a date."

Frances leaned over and kissed him on the tip of the ear.

"Darling," Michael said, "this is Fifth Avenue."

"Let me arrange a program," Frances said. "A planned Sunday in New York for a young couple with money to throw away."

"Go easy."

"First let's go to the Metropolitan Museum of Art," Frances suggested, because Michael had said during the week he wanted to go. "I haven't been there in three years and there're at least ten pictures I want to see again. Then we can take the bus down to Radio City and watch them skate. And later we'll go down to Cavanagh's and get a steak as big as a blacksmith's apron, with a bottle of wine, and after that there's a French picture at the Filmarte that everybody says—say, are you listening to me?"

"Sure," he said. He took his eyes off the hatless girl with the dark hair, cut dancer-style like a helmet, who was walking past him.

"That's the program for the day," Frances said flatly. "Or maybe you'd just rather walk up and down Fifth Avenue."

"No," Michael said. "Not at all."

"You always look at other women," Frances said. "Everywhere. Every damned place we go."

"No, darling," Michael said, "I look at everything. God gave me eyes and I look at women and men in subway excavations and moving pictures and the little flowers of the field. I casually inspect the universe."

"You ought to see the look in your eye," Frances said, "as you casually inspect the universe on Fifth Avenue."

"I'm a happily married man." Michael pressed her elbow tenderly. "Example for the whole twentieth century—Mr. and Mrs. Mike Loomis. Hey, let's have a drink," he said, stopping.

"We just had breakfast."

"Now listen, darling," Mike said, choosing his words with care, "it's a nice day and we both feel good and there's no reason why we have to break it up. Let's have a nice Sunday."

"All right. I don't know why I started this. Let's drop it. Let's have a good time."

They joined hands consciously and walked without talking among the baby carriages and the old Italian men in their Sunday clothes and the young women with Scotties in Washington Square Park.

"At least once a year everyone should go to the Metropolitan Museum of Art," Frances said after a while, her tone a good imitation of the tone she had used at breakfast and at the beginning of their walk. "And it's nice on Sunday. There's a lot of people looking at the pictures and you get the feeling maybe Art isn't on the decline in New York City, after all—"

"I want to tell you something," Michael said very seriously. "I have not touched another woman. Not once. In all the five years."

"All right," Frances said.

"You believe that, don't you?"

"All right."

They walked between the crowded benches, under the scrubby city-park trees.

"I try not to notice it," Frances said, "but I feel rotten inside, in my stomach, when we pass a woman and you look at her and I see that look in your eye and that's the way you looked at me the first time. In Alice Maxwell's house. Standing there in the living room, next to the radio, with a green hat on and all those people."

"I remember the hat," Michael said.

"The same look," Frances said. "And it makes me feel bad. It makes me feel terrible."

"Sh-h-h, please, darling, sh-h-h."

"I think I would like a drink now," Frances said.

They walked over to a bar on Eighth Street, not saying anything, Michael automatically helping her over curbstones and guiding her past automobiles. They sat near a window in the bar and the sun streamed in and there was a small, cheerful fire in the fireplace. A little Japanese waiter came over and put down some pretzels and smiled happily at them.

"What do you order after breakfast?" Michael asked.

"Brandy, I suppose," Frances said.

"Courvoisier," Michael told the waiter. "Two Courvoisiers."

The waiter came with the glasses and they sat drinking the brandy in the sunlight. Michael finished half his and drank a little water.

"I look at women," he said. "Correct. I don't say it's wrong or right. I look at them. If I pass them on the street and I don't look at them, I'm fooling you, I'm fooling myself."

"You look at them as though you want them," Frances said, playing with her brandy glass. "Every one of them."

"In a way," Michael said, speaking softly and not to his wife, "in a way that's true. I don't do anything about it, but it's true."

"I know it. That's why I feel bad."

"Another brandy," Michael called. "Waiter, two more brandies."

He sighed and closed his eyes and rubbed them gently with his fingertips. "I love the way women look. One of the things I like best about New York is the battalions of women. When I first came to New York from Ohio that was the first thing I noticed, the million wonderful women, all over the city. I walked around with my heart in my throat."

"A kid," Frances said. "That's a kid's feeling."

"Guess again," Michael said. "Guess again. I'm older now. I'm a man getting near middle age, putting on a little fat, and I still love to walk along Fifth Avenue at three o'clock on the east side of the street between Fiftieth and Fifty-seventh Streets. They're all out then, shopping, in their furs and their crazy hats, everything all concentrated from all over the world into seven blocks—the best furs, the best clothes, the handsomest women, out to spend money and feeling good about it."

The Japanese waiter put the two drinks down, smiling with great happiness.

"Everything is all right?" he asked.

"Everything is wonderful," Michael said.

"If it's just a couple of fur coats," Frances said, "and forty-five dollar hats—"

"It's not the fur coats. Or the hats. That's just the scenery for that particular kind of woman. Understand," he said, "you don't have to listen to this."

"I want to listen."

"I like the girls in the offices. Neat, with their eyeglasses, smart, chipper, knowing what everything is about. I like the girls on Forty-fourth Street at lunchtime, the actresses, all dressed up on nothing a week. I like the salesgirls in the stores, paying attention to you first because you're a man, leaving lady customers waiting. I got all this stuff accumulated in me because I've been thinking about it for ten years and now you've asked for it and here it is."

"Go ahead," Frances said.

"When I think of New York City, I think of all the girls on parade in the city. I don't know whether it's something special with me or whether every man in the city walks around with the same feeling inside him, but I feel as though I'm at a picnic in this city. I like to sit near the women in the theatres, the famous beauties who've taken six hours to get ready and look it. And the young girls at the football games, with the red cheeks, and when the warm weather comes, the girls in their summer dresses." He finished his drink. "That's the story."

Frances finished her drink and swallowed two or three times extra. "You say you love me?"

"I love you."

"I'm pretty, too," Frances said. "As pretty as any of them."

"You're beautiful," Michael said.

"I'm good for you," Frances said, pleading. "I've made a good wife, a good housekeeper, a good friend. I'd do any damn thing for you."

"I know," Michael said. He put his hand out and grasped hers.

"You'd like to be free to—" Frances said.

"Sh-h-h."

"Tell the truth." She took her hand away from under his.

Michael flicked the edge of his glass with his finger. "O.K.," he said gently. "Sometimes I feel I would like to be free."

"Well," Frances said, "any time you say."

"Don't be foolish." Michael swung his chair around to her side of the table and patted her thigh.

She began to cry silently into her handkerchief, bent over just enough so that nobody else in the bar would notice. "Someday," she said, crying, "you're going to make a move."

Michael didn't say anything. He sat watching the bartender slowly peel a lemon.

"Aren't you?" Frances asked harshly. "Come on, tell me. Talk. Aren't you?"

"Maybe," Michael said. He moved his chair back again. "How the hell do I know?"

"You know," Frances persisted. "Don't you know?"

"Yes," Michael said after a while, "I know."

Frances stopped crying then. Two or three snuffles into the handkerchief and she put it away and her face didn't tell anything to anybody. "At least do me one favor," she said.

"Sure."

"Stop talking about how pretty this woman is or that one. Nice eyes, nice breasts, a pretty figure, good voice." She mimicked his voice. "Keep it to yourself. I'm not interested."

Michael waved to the waiter. "I'll keep it to myself," he said.

Frances flicked the corners of her eyes. "Another brandy," she told the waiter.

"Two," Michael said.

"Yes, Ma'am, yes, sir," said the waiter, backing away.

Frances regarded Michael coolly across the table. "Do you want me to call the Stevensons?" she asked. "It'll be nice in the country."

"Sure," Michael said. "Call them."

She got up from the table and walked across the room toward the telephone. Michael watched her walk, thinking what a pretty girl, what nice legs.

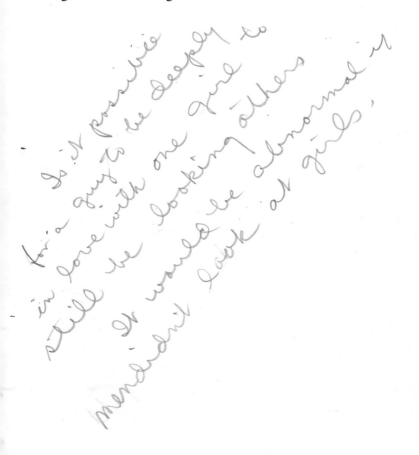

JAMES THURBER

A Couple of Hamburgers

It had been raining for a long time, a slow, cold rain falling out of iron-colored clouds. They had been driving since morning and they still had a hundred and thirty miles to go. It was about three o'clock in the afternoon. "I'm getting hungry," she said. He took his eyes off the wet, winding road for a fraction of a second and said, "We'll stop at a dog-wagon." She shifted her position irritably. "I wish you wouldn't call them *dog*-wagons," she said. He pressed the klaxon button and went around a slow car. "That's what they are," he said. "Dog-wagons." She waited a few seconds. "*Decent* people call them *diners*," she told him, and added, "Even if you call them diners, I don't like them." He speeded up a hill. "They have better stuff than most restaurants," he said. "Anyway, I want to get home before dark and it takes too long in a restaurant. We can stay our stomachs with a couple hamburgers." She lighted a cigarette and he asked her to light one for him. She lighted one deliberately and handed it to him. "I wish you wouldn't say 'stay our stomachs,'" she said. "You know I hate that. It's like 'sticking to your ribs.' You say that all the time." He grinned. "Good old American expressions, both of them," he said. "Like sow belly. Old pioneer term, sow belly." She sniffed. "My ancestors were pioneers, too. You don't have to be vulgar just because you were a pioneer." "Your ancestors never got as far west as mine did," he said. "The real pioneers travelled on their sow belly and got somewhere." He laughed loudly at that. She looked out at the wet trees and signs and telephone poles going by. They drove on for several miles without a word; he kept chortling every now and then.

"What's that funny sound?" she asked, suddenly. It invariably made him angry when she heard a funny sound. "What funny sound?" he demanded. "You're always hearing funny sounds." She laughed briefly. "That's what you said when the bearing burned out," she reminded him. "You'd never have noticed it if it hadn't been for me." "I noticed it, all right," he said. "Yes," she said. "When it was too late." She enjoyed bringing up the subject of the burned-out bearing whenever he got to chortling. "It was too late when *you* noticed it, as far as that goes," he said. Then, after a pause, "Well, what does it sound like *this* time? All engines make a noise running, you know." "I know all about that," she answered. "It sounds like—it sounds like a lot of safety pins being jiggled around in a tumbler." He snorted. "That's your imagination. Nothing gets the matter with a car that sounds like a lot of safety pins. I happen to know that." She tossed away her cigarette. "Oh, sure," she said. "You always happen to know everything." They drove on in silence.

"I want to stop somewhere and get something to *eat!*" she said loudly. "All right, all right!" he said. "I been watching for a dog-wagon, haven't I? There hasn't been any. I can't make you a dog-wagon." The wind blew rain in on her and she put up the window on her side all the way. "I won't stop at just any old diner," she said. "I won't stop unless it's a cute one." He looked around at her. "Unless it's a *what* one?" he shouted. "You know what I mean," she said. "I mean a decent, clean one where they don't slosh things at you. I hate to have a lot of milky coffee sloshed at me." "All right," he said. "We'll find a cute one, then. You pick it out. I wouldn't know. I might find one that was cunning but not cute." That struck him as funny and he began to chortle again. "Oh, shut up," she said.

Five miles farther along they came to a place called Sam's
Diner. "Here's one," he said, slowing down. She looked it over.
"I don't want to stop there," she said. "I don't like the ones that
have nicknames." He brought the car to a stop at one side of the
road. "Just what's the matter with the ones that have nicknames?"
he asked with edgy, mock interest. "They're always Greek ones,"
she told him. "They're always Greek ones," he repeated after
her. He set his teeth firmly together and started up again. After
a time, "Good old Sam, the Greek," he said, in a singsong. "Good
old Connecticut Sam Beardsley, the Greek." "You didn't see his
name," she snapped. "Winthrop, then," he said. "Old Samuel
Cabot Winthrop, the Greek dog-wagon man." He was getting
hungry.

On the outskirts of the next town she said, as he slowed down,
"It looks like a factory kind of town." He knew that she meant
she wouldn't stop there. He drove on through the place. She
lighted a cigarette as they pulled out into the open again. He
slowed down and lighted a cigarette for himself. "Factory kind
of town than *I* am!" he snarled. It was ten miles before they came
to another town. "Torrington," he growled. "Happen to know
there's a dog-wagon here because I stopped in it once with Bob
Combs. Damn cute place, too, if you ask me." "I'm not asking
you anything," she said, coldly. "You think you're *so* funny. I
think I know the one you mean," she said, after a moment. "It's
right in the town and it sits at an angle from the road. They're
never so good, for some reason." He glared at her and almost ran
up against the curb. "What the hell do you mean 'sits at an angle
from the road'?" he cried. He was very hungry now. "Well, it
isn't silly," she said, calmly. "I've noticed the ones that sit at an
angle. They're cheaper, because they fitted them into funny little
pieces of ground. The big ones parallel to the road are the best."
He drove right through Torrington, his lips compressed. "Angle
from the *road*, for God's sake!" he snarled, finally. She was looking out her window.

On the outskirts of the next town there was a diner called
The Elite Diner. "This looks—" she began. "I see it, I see it!" he

said. "It doesn't happen to look any cuter to me than any god-dam—" she cut him off. "Don't be such a sorehead, for Lord's sake," she said. He pulled up and stopped beside the diner, and turned on her. "Listen," he said, grittingly, "I'm going to put down a couple of hamburgers in this place even if there isn't one single inch of chintz or cretonne in the whole—" "Oh, be still," she said. "You're just hungry and mean like a child. Eat your old hamburgers, what do I care?" Inside the place they sat down on stools and the counterman walked over to them, wiping up the counter top with a cloth as he did so. "What'll it be, folks?" he said. "Bad day, ain't it? Except for ducks." "I'll have a couple of—" began the husband, but his wife cut in. "I just want a pack of cigarettes," she said. He turned around slowly on his stool and stared at her as she put a dime and a nickel in the cigarette machine and ejected a package of Lucky Strikes. He turned to the counterman again. "I want a couple of hamburgers," he said. "With mustard and lots of onion. *Lots* of onion!" She hated onions. "I'll wait for you in the car," she said. He didn't answer and she went out.

He finished his hamburgers and his coffee slowly. It was terrible coffee. Then he went out to the car and got in and drove off, slowly humming "Who's Afraid of the Big Bad Wolf?" After a mile or so, "Well," he said, "what was the matter with the Elite Diner, milady?" "Didn't you *see* that cloth the man was wiping the counter with?" she demanded. "Ugh!" She shuddered. "I didn't happen to want to eat any of the counter," he said. He laughed at that comeback. "You didn't even notice it," she said. "You never notice anything. It was filthy." "I noticed they had some damn fine coffee in there," he said. "It was swell." He knew she loved good coffee. He began to hum his tune again; then he whistled it; then he began to sing it. She did not show her annoyance, but she knew that he knew she was annoyed. "Will you be kind enough to tell me what time it is?" she asked. "Big *bad* wolf, big *bad* wolf—five minutes o' five—tum-dee-*doo*-dee-dum-m-m." She settled back in her seat and took a cigarette from her case and tapped it on the case. "I'll wait till we get home,"

she said. "If you'll be kind enough to speed up a little." He drove
on at the same speed. After a time he gave up the "Big Bad Wolf"
and there was deep silence for two miles. Then suddenly he began
to sing, very loudly, *H-A*-double-*R-I-G-A-N spells Harrr*-i-
gan—" She gritted her teeth. She hated that worse than any of
his songs except "Barney Google." He would go on to "Barney
Google" pretty soon, she knew. Suddenly she leaned slightly
forward. The straight line of her lips began to curve up ever so
slightly. She heard the safety pins in the tumbler again. Only
now they were louder, more insistent, ominous. He was singing
too loud to hear them. "Is a *name* that *shame* has never been
con-*nec*-ted with—*Harrr*-i-gan, that's *me!*" She relaxed against
the back of the seat, content to wait.

CALVIN TRILLIN

For Worse Is Better and Sickness Is in Health

From their wedding day two years ago, a Kansas City couple, both educators, have recorded every argument they've had with each other. [Joseph] Edwards and his wife, Dr. Diane Edwards, began marriage with pencil, graph paper and a beanbag among their household goods. By noting every argument and recording it on a graph, the couple discovered a pattern to their conflicts. . . . The couple used the beanbag as a signal that what began as a simple debate was becoming an attack on personalities. Whenever the situation became heated, one of them would grab the beanbag from its place in the living room and toss it to the floor, a kind of throwing in of the towel. A beanbag was selected so that no other activity might be associated with it.—*Kansas City Star*.

Mary Beth and I would never have known about the beanbag-and-graph method if it hadn't been for Harvey Feldspar, who reads the Kansas City *Star* regularly in the belief that it may someday reveal information valuable to anyone who speculates in wheat futures. Harvey and his wife, Thelma, were over at our house to argue. I don't mean we had invited them to argue; we had invited them to play bridge. But, in the same way that some married couples become devoted to each other, Harvey and

Thelma had become devoted to arguing with each other, and they went about their arguing with such single-mindedness that it always seemed as if arguing was what they had come over to do. What brought the subject up was that Harvey and Thelma had also read about a book by a California psychologist who maintained that arguing was necessary for a healthy marriage—a revelation they had greeted the way a four-Martinis-for-lunch man might greet the discovery that alcohol in large quantities is enormously beneficial to the lymph nodes. They had read about the book in either *Time* or *Newsweek*. In fact, the question of whether it had been *Time* or *Newsweek* started a ten-minute argument about the accuracy of each other's memory and the level of each other's reading tastes, ending on a political note with Harvey calling Thelma a fuzzy-headed bleeding heart and Thelma saying that only a concern for our carpeting prevented her from making Harvey a bleeding-headed fuzzy heart with a poker she happened to be holding. When they stopped, red-faced and winded, they seemed rather refreshed, and in that frame of mind Harvey brought up the experiment of measuring arguments on a graph.

"You two wouldn't have much to measure," he said to Mary Beth and me, with what I thought was a touch of condescension. "Everyone knows the Placid Plovins never fight." Even before that California psychologist prescribed brawling as the way to get along with each other, a lot of people in our set had remarked on how Mary Beth and I managed to avoid domestic warfare; they used the same tone that might be used by people in a small Midwestern town remarking on how some family managed to avoid attending church.

"Oh, we have our little disagreements, don't we, Marvin?" Mary Beth said, tossing me a smile.

I tossed one back at her—my most understanding. "Of course, dear," I said. "Of course we do."

"When was the last one?" Thelma Feldspar demanded.

"Well, I really can't recall the precise moment," I said,

ridiculously embarrassed at not being able to put my finger on the kind of assault with a deadly weapon that was always fresh in the minds of the Feldspars.

"Oh, remember when we disagreed on what color dress I should buy in Jamaica?" Mary Beth said, helpful as always.

"You mean Trinidad," I said.

"Oh, yes, dear, you're right," Mary Beth said. "How stupid of me."

"Well, we did stop in Jamaica, so it was an easy mistake to have made," I said. "Also, three years is a long time to remember which island was which."

"How sweet of you to put it that way, Marvy," Mary Beth said.

"But what happened? What happened?" Thelma said loudly.

"I think you liked the red one with the six wooden buttons and the belt, and I liked the same dress in green," I said to Mary Beth. "Is that the way it happened, sweetheart?"

"That was it exactly," Mary Beth said. "Marvin, you have such an evocative way of recalling details."

"So what happened?" Thelma and Harvey said, almost together.

"Well, naturally I dress to please Marvin," Mary Beth said, looking at me lovingly. "So I took the green. When I thought about it, I realized that the red hadn't been as nice after all. Red isn't really my color."

"Oh," Thelma Feldspar said, looking a bit let down.

"You two are hopeless," Harvey Feldspar said. "Maybe we should try keeping track of *our* arguments, Thelma."

"You must be out of your tiny little mind!" Thelma said.

"That's right," Harvey said. "*I'm* out of my mind! *I'm* the one in this family spending fifty dollars an hour to tell dirty stories to some quack headshrinker!"

"Oh, now it comes out!" Thelma shouted, lowering her voice a bit when she noticed one of our cut-glass vases beginning to tremble. (The Feldspars have always been considerate of spectators.) "Now it comes out that a few dollars to repair the damage inflicted on his wife's mental health by life with a monster is begrudged by the last of the big spenders. Fifty dollars for a custom-made cardigan sweater to hide his spreading paunch—that's O.K., of course."

Mary Beth and I looked at each other helplessly, amazed, as we always were, with the care Harvey and Thelma took in searching out precisely the kind of embarrassing matters that we would have worked to avoid. For instance, Mary Beth herself had recently completed a financial transaction similar to Harvey's fifty-dollar cardigan. But I understood perfectly well that the purchase had been brought on by Mary Beth's kindly feeling toward simple folk and her mild naivete about money—a rather endearing combination that just happened to have resulted in a complicated mail order of handicrafts that left us (in exchange for forty-five dollars and eighty cents, plus mailing charges) with three pot holders shaped like emaciated squirrels and an apron that, judging from its size, had been created especially for President William Howard Taft. I would no more have considered alluding to that little debacle than Mary Beth would have thought of taunting me about what I recognize to be a certain, well, precision on my part about the details of living—a tendency that some women might have ridiculed as "nit-picky" or "compulsive," and that Mary Beth, if pressed for an opinion, would have defended as being preferable to a sloppy mind. Yet here, in our own living room, Thelma was consciously exploiting what had become, I noticed, a significant bulge around Harvey's middle.

"Now wait a minute!" Harvey shouted in reply. "That's below the belt. The book specifically said you should argue but not hit below the belt."

"Below the belt, above the belt, slurping over the belt," Thelma said. "Pushing against the belt, requiring another notch in the belt, hiding the belt."

Harvey stomped out of the living room, muttering about

getting himself some more coffee, but I think Thelma's voice was loud enough to reach him anywhere in the house: "Quietly enveloping the belt, softly enfolding the belt, making the belt entirely unnecessary, mocking the idea of a belt."

After Harvey and Thelma had left, Mary Beth and I had a quiet chat about the evening. If the California psychologist was right, we realized, Harvey and Thelma were in bliss and we were hovering on legal separation. We knew that was silly, but it did occur to us that if we tried the graph-and-beanbag method we might at least document enough little tiffs to take the sting out of that "Placid Plovins" talk. What finally made up our minds to try it, I'm certain, was a sweet remark by Mary Beth. "Oh, Marvy," she said. "It'll be another thing for us to do together."

"You're absolutely right, Mary Beth," I said. "As usual."

"I'll get the graph paper and beanbag downtown tomorrow," Mary Beth said. "That way you won't have to disturb your day."

"Oh, no, dear," I said. "I'll pick them up while I'm at the office. You have such a busy time—keeping the house spick and span, performing your wizardry in the kitchen. Don't think I don't appreciate what you do for me."

"For us, darling," she said. "And I love doing it. But if you'd like to pick up the supplies, why don't you?" She smiled. "You win the first argument," she said.

As it turned out, I did get rather busy that next day, and I had to ask my secretary, Miss Columbine, if she would mind picking up the graph paper and beanbag on her lunch hour. (Miss Columbine, I should add, is considered quite voluptuous by the office woman-fanciers, but Mary Beth had never displayed any jealousy, nor did she have cause to—being correct in her assumption that a man with true respect for his wife and himself need not go to the extreme of having an old and unattractive secretary if a voluptuous one happens to take shorthand at a hundred and twenty words a minute and types like a whiz.) That evening, I was able to present Mary Beth with the package Miss Columbine

had been kind enough to pick up for me, and to announce, with
some of the dry humor Mary Beth so often praises, that we could
begin our experiment whenever she felt the first wave of uncontrollable fury about to possess her.

"This is going to be such fun, Marvy," Mary Beth said. "Just
like our vacation scrapbooks. I'll keep the graph, so you won't
have to bother."

"That's all right, dear," I said. "I'll keep the graph. It's kind
of man's work, really—making all those lines, charting things
out. You have so much work to do around the house anyway."

"I don't mind keeping it," she said. "I think it would be
easier."

"I don't understand," I said. I didn't.

"I just think it would be easier if I kept it, Marvin," she said,
a bit more firmly. "You know."

"I know what?" I asked.

"It would just be easier," she insisted.

"What do you mean, Mary Beth?"

"Well, it's certainly nothing important, dear," Mary Beth
said. "I'm just afraid you might have to spend too much time
getting each dot on the graph exactly just so."

"What makes you think that?"

She sighed—briefly but audibly. "Well," she said. "You do
have a tendency to be a bit persnickety about details, Marvin.
Although, naturally, I love you for it."

"What do you mean—'a bit persnickety'?" I asked.

"Well, Marvin, you're just like that," she said. "I mean, how
many other men are that concerned about what color dress their
wives wear?"

"I thought you dressed for me," I said.

"I do, Marvin. Most wives dress for their husbands, but most
husbands don't take the role seriously enough to inspect the
brand of zippers on every article of clothing."

"I don't see anything reprehensible about taking sensible pre-
cautions against shoddy merchandise," I said.

"What you mean by that is that you don't think I'm sensible about money," Mary Beth said. "Isn't it really that you don't trust me with money at all?"

"It is not that, Mary Beth," I said. "It is merely that I think the decision-making on such matters is better left to your husband than to some slick fairy dress designer."

"Oh, you think I'm being taken advantage of because of my gullibility," she said, in a voice much louder than I had ever heard her use. "Why don't you go ahead and say what you mean—button inspector!"

It was at that moment that I realized the argument was getting out of hand, and before we had even taken out the graph paper. But I also realized that the graph-and-beanbag method includes a device to deal with precisely what was happening. I fumbled into the package Miss Columbine had brought me, grabbed the beanbag, and immediately tossed it out on the floor—a squashy gingham ball with a face formed on one side by scraps of cloth.

I thought Mary Beth would calm down once she saw what had happened, but her face seemed to be growing redder. "The debate is becoming an attack on personalities," I reminded her. "The beanbag is a reminder of that, selected so that no other activity might be associated with it."

She stared at the beanbag. "You have never forgotten that forty-five dollars' worth of handicrafts, have you, you compulsive skinflint?" she shouted.

"Forty-five dollars and eighty cents," I said, without thinking. "Plus postage."

That is the statement that drove her to violence, I'm certain, and, oddly enough, it was pure reflex on my part rather than any desire to quibble over money. She snatched the beanbag from the floor and threw it at me. It hit me on the nose, causing blood to ruin my necktie, which happened to have cost six dollars and fifty-five cents.

Mary Beth and I are divorced now, of course. We probably shouldn't have been married in the first place. We were too compatible. I see now that, as the California psychologist said, our lack of fighting resulted in mere "pseudo-intimacy" that formed no solid foundations for the kind of brouhaha that keeps marriages together. I never had this understanding before, but Harvey and Thelma occasionally invite Peggy—Miss Columbine— and me over to watch them argue, and I'm beginning to see what a real marriage can be like.

MAEVE BRENNAN

The Eldest Child

Mrs. Bagot had lived in the house for fifteen years, ever since her marriage. It was on a narrow street, a dead end, in the suburbs of Dublin. Her three children had been born there, in the upstairs front bedroom, and she was glad of that, because her first child, her son, was dead, and it comforted her to think that she was still familiar with what had been his one glimpse of earth—he had died at three days. At the time he died she said to herself that she would never get used to it, and what she meant by that was that as long as she lived she would never accept what had happened in the mechanical subdued way that the rest of them accepted it. They carried on, they talked and moved about her room as though when they tidied the baby away they had really tidied him away, and it seemed to her that more than anything else they expressed the hope that nothing more would be said about him. They behaved as though what had happened was finished, as though some ordinary event had taken place and come to an end in a natural way. There had not been an ordinary event, and it had not come to an end.

Lying in her bed, Mrs. Bagot thought her husband and the rest of them seemed very strange, or else, she thought fearfully, perhaps it was she herself who was strange, delirious, or even a bit unbalanced. If she was unbalanced she wasn't going to let them know about it—not even Martin, who kept looking at her with frightened eyes and telling her she must try to rest. It might be better not to talk, yet she was very anxious to explain how she felt. Words did no good. Either they did not want to hear her, or they were not able to hear her. What she was trying to tell them seemed very simple to her. What had happened could not come to an end, that was all. It could not come to an end. Without a memory, how was the baby going to find his way? Mrs. Bagot would have liked to ask that question, but she wanted to express it properly, and she thought if she could just be left alone for a while she would be able to find the right words, so that she could make herself clearly understood—but they wouldn't leave her alone. They kept trying to rouse her, and yet when she spoke for any length of time they always silenced her by telling her it was God's will. She had accepted God's will all her life without argument, and she was not arguing now, but she knew that what had happened was not finished, and she was sure it was not God's will that she be left in this bewilderment. All she wanted was to say how she felt, but they mentioned God's will as though they were slamming a door between her and some territory that was forbidden to her. But only to her; everybody else knew all about it. She alone must lie quiet and silent under this semblance of ignorance that they wrapped about her like a shroud. They wanted her to be silent and not speak of this knowledge she had now, the knowledge that made her afraid. It was the same knowledge they all had, of course, but they did not want it spoken of. Everything about her seemed false, and Mrs. Bagot was tired of everything. She was tired of being told that she must do this for her own good and that she must do that for her own good, and it annoyed her when they said she was being brave—she was being what she had to be, she had no alternative. She felt very uncomfortable and out of place, and as though she had failed, but she did not know whether to push her failure away or comfort it, and in any case it seemed to have drifted out of reach.

She was not making sense. She could not get her thoughts sorted out. Something was drifting away—that was as far as she could go in her mind. No wonder she couldn't talk properly. What she wanted to say was really quite simple. Two things. First, there was the failure that had emptied and darkened her mind until nothing remained now but a black wash. Second, there was something that drifted and dwindled, always dwindling, until it was now no more than a small shape, very small, not to be identified except as something lost. Mrs. Bagot thought she was the only one who could still identify that shape, and she was afraid to take her eyes off it, because it became constantly smaller, showing as it diminished the new horizons it was reaching, although it drifted so gently it seemed not to move at all. Mrs. Bagot would never have dreamed her mind could stretch so far, or that her thoughts could follow so faithfully, or that she could watch so steadily, without tears or sleep.

The fierce demands that had been made on her body and on her attention were finished. She could have met all those demands, and more. She could have moved mountains. She had found that the more the child demanded of her, the more she had to give. Her strength came up in waves that had their source in a sea of calm and unconquerable devotion. The child's holy trust made her open her eyes, and she took stock of herself and found that everything was all right, and that she could meet what challenges arose and meet them well, and that she had nothing to apologize for—on the contrary, she had every reason to rejoice. Her days took on an orderliness that introduced her to a sense of ease and confidence she had never been told about. The house became a kingdom, significant, private, and safe. She smiled often, a smile of innocent importance.

Perhaps she had let herself get too proud. She had seen at once that the child was unique. She had been thankful, but perhaps not thankful enough. The first minute she had held him in her arms, immediately after he was born, she had seen his friendliness. He was fine. There was nothing in the world the matter with him. She had remarked to herself that his tiny face had a very humorous expression, as though he already knew exactly what was going on. And he was determined to live. He was full of fight. She had felt him fight toward life with all his strength, and then again, with all her strength. In a little while, he would have recognized her.

What she watched now made no demands on anyone. There was no impatience there, and no impatience in her, either. She lay on her side, and her hand beat gently on the pillow in obedience to words, an old tune, that had been sounding in her head for some time, and that she now began to listen to. It was an old song, very slow, a tenor voice from long ago and far away. She listened idly.

> *Oft in the stilly night,*
> *Ere slumber's chain has bound me,*
> *Fond memory brings the light*
> *Of other days around me . . .*

Over and over and over again, the same words, the same kind, simple words. Mrs. Bagot thought she must have heard that song a hundred times or more.

> *Oft in the stilly night,*
> *Ere slumber's chain has bound me,*
> *Fond memory brings the light*
> *Of other days around me;*
> *The smiles, the tears,*
> *Of boyhood's years,*
> *The words of love then spoken;*
> *The eyes that shone*
> *Now dimmed and gone,*
> *The cheerful hearts now broken.*

It was a very kind song. She had never noticed the words before, even though she knew them well. Loving words, loving eyes, loving hearts. The faraway voice she listened to was joined by others, as the first bird of dawn is joined by other birds, all telling the same story, telling it over and over again, because it is the only story they know.

There was the song, and then, there was the small shape that drifted uncomplainingly from distant horizon to still more distant horizon. Mrs. Bagot closed her eyes. She felt herself being beckoned to a place where she could hide, for the time being.

For the past day or so, she had turned from everyone, even from Martin. He no longer attempted to touch her. He had not even touched her hand since the evening he knelt down beside the bed and tried to put his arms around her. She struggled so fiercely against him that he had to let her go, and he stood up and stepped away from her. It really seemed she might injure herself, fighting against him, and that she would rather injure herself than lie quietly against him, even for a minute. He could not understand her. It was his loss as much as hers, but she behaved as though it had to do only with her. She pushed him away, and then when she was free of him she turned her face away from him and began crying in a way that pleaded for attention and consolation from someone, but not from him—that was plain. But before that, when she was pushing him away, he had seen her face, and the expression on it was of hatred. She might have been a wild animal, for all the control he had over her then, but if so she was a wild animal in a trap, because she was too weak to go very far. He pitied her, and the thought sped through his mind that if she could get up and run, or fly, he would let her go as far as she wished, and hope she would come back to him in her own time, when her anger and grief were spent. But he forgot that thought immediately in his panic at her distress, and he called down to the woman who had come in to help around the house, and asked her to come up at once. She had heard the noise and was on her way up anyway, and she was in the room almost as soon as he called—Mrs. Knox, a small, red-faced, gray-haired woman who enjoyed the illusion that life had nothing to teach her.

"Oh, I've been afraid of this all day," she said confidently, and she began to lift Mrs. Bagot up so that she could straighten the pillows and prop her up for her tea. But Mrs. Bagot struck out at the woman and began crying, "Oh, leave me alone, leave me alone. Why can't the two of you leave me alone." Then she wailed, "Oh, leave me alone," in a high strange voice, an artificial voice, and at that moment Mr. Bagot became convinced that she was acting, and that the best thing to do was walk off and leave her there, whether that was what she really wanted or not. Oh, but he loved her. He stared at her, and said to himself that it would have given him the greatest joy to see her lying there with the baby in her arms, but although that was true, the reverse was not true—to see her lying there as she was did not cause him terrible grief or anything like it. He felt ashamed and lonely and impatient, and he longed to say to her, "Delia, stop all this nonsense and let me talk to you." He wanted to appear masterful and kind and understanding, but she drowned him out with her wails, and he made up his mind she was acting, because if she was not acting, and if the grief she felt was real, then it was excessive grief, and perhaps incurable. She was getting stronger every day, the doctor had said so, and she had better learn to control herself or she would be a nervous wreck. And it wasn't a bit like her, to have no thought for him, or for what he might be suffering. It wasn't like her at all. She was always kind. He began to fear she would never be the same. He would have liked to kneel down beside the bed and talk to her in a very quiet voice, and make her understand that he knew what she was going through, and that he was going through much the same thing himself, and to ask her not to shut him away from her. But he felt afraid of her, and in any case Mrs. Knox was in the room. He was helpless. He was trying to think of something to say, not to walk out in silence, when Mrs. Knox came around the end of the bed and touched his arm familiarly, as though they were conspirators.

"The poor child is upset," she said. "We'll leave her by herself awhile, and then I'll bring her up something to eat. Now, you go along down. I have your own tea all ready."

Delia turned her head on the pillow and looked at him. "Martin," she said, "I am not angry with you."

He would have gone to her then, but Mrs. Knox spoke at once. "We know you're not angry, Mrs. Bagot," she said. "Now, you rest yourself, and I'll be back in a minute with your tray." She gave Martin a little push to start him out of the room, and since Delia was already turning her face away, he walked out and down the stairs.

There seemed to be no end to the damage—even the house looked bleak and the furniture looked poor and cheap. It was only a year since they moved into the house, and it had all seemed lovely then. Only a year. He was beginning to fear that Delia had turned against him. He had visions of awful scenes and strains in the future, a miserable life. He wished they could go back to the beginning and start all over again, but the place where they had stood together, where they had been happy, was all trampled over and so spoiled that it seemed impossible ever to make it smooth again. And how could they even begin to make it smooth with this one memory, which they should have shared, standing like an enemy between them and making enemies out of them. He would not let himself think of the baby. He might never be able to forget the shape of the poor little defeated bundle he had carried out of the bedroom in his arms, and that he had cried over down here in the hall, but he was not going to let his mind dwell on it, not for one minute. He wanted Delia as she used to be. He wanted the girl who would never have struck out at him, or spoken roughly to him. He was beginning to see there were things about her that he had never guessed at and that he did not want to know about. He thought, Better let her rest, and let this fit work itself out. Maybe tomorrow she'll be herself again. He had a fancy that when he next approached Delia it would be on tiptoe, going very quietly, hardly breathing, moving into her presence without a sound that might startle her, or surprise her, or even wake her up, so that he might find her again as she had been the first time he saw her, quiet, untroubled, hardly speaking, alone, altogether alone and all his.

Mrs. Bagot was telling the truth when she told Martin she was not angry with him. It irritated her that he thought all he had to do was put his arms around her and all her sorrow would go away, but she wasn't really angry with him. What it was—he held her so tightly that she was afraid she might lose sight of the baby, and the fear made her frantic. The baby must not drift out of sight, that was her only thought, and that is why she struck out at Martin and begged to be left alone. As he walked out of the room, she turned her face away so that he would not see the tears beginning to pour down her face again. Then she slept. When Martin came up to the room next time, she was asleep, and not, as he suspected, pretending to be asleep, but he was grateful for the pretense, if that is what it was, and he crept away, back downstairs to his book.

Mrs. Bagot slept for a long time. When she woke up, the room was dark and the house was silent. Outside was silent too; she could hear nothing. This was the front bedroom, where she and Martin slept together, and she lay in their big bed. The room was made irregular by its windows—a bow window, and then, in the flat section of wall that faced the door, French windows. The French windows were partly open, and the long white net curtains that covered them moved gently in a breeze Mrs. Bagot could not feel. She had washed all the curtains last week, and starched them, getting the room ready for the baby. In the dim light of the streetlamp, she could see the dark roof line of the row of houses across the street, and beyond the houses a very soft blackness, the sky. She was much calmer than she had been, and she no longer feared that she would lose sight of the small shape that had drifted, she noticed, much farther away while she slept. He was traveling a long way, but she would watch him. She was his mother, and it was all she could do for him now. She could do it. She was weak, and the world was very shaky, but the light of other days shone steadily and showed the truth. She was no longer bewildered, only dull, and the next time Martin came to stand hopefully beside her bed she smiled at him and spoke to him in her ordinary voice.

FRANK O'CONNOR

The American Wife

Elsie Colleary, who was on a visit to her cousins in Cork, was a mystery even to them. Her father, Jack Colleary's brother, had emigrated when he was a kid and done well for himself; he had made his money in the liquor business, and left it to go into wholesale produce when Elsie was growing up, because he didn't think it was the right background for a girl. He had given her the best of educations, and all he had got out of it was to have Elsie telling him that Irishmen were more manly, and that even Irish-Americans let their wives boss them too much. What she meant was that *he* let her mother boss him, and she had learned from other Irish people that this was not the custom at home. Maybe Mike Colleary, like a lot of other Americans, did give the impression of yielding too much to his wife, but that was because she thought she knew more about things than he did, and he was too softhearted to dissillusion her. No doubt the Americans, experienced in nostalgia, took Elsie's glorification of Irishmen good-humoredly, but it did not go down too well in Cork, where the men stood in perpetual contemplation of the dangers of marriage, like cranes standing on one leg at the edge of the windy water.

She stood out at the Collearys' quiet little parties, with her high waist and wide skirts, taking the men out to sit on the stairs while she argued with them about religion and politics. Women having occasion to go upstairs thought this very forward, but some of the men found it a pleasant relief. Besides, like all Americans, she was probably a millionaire, and the most unworldly of men can get a kick out of flirting with a real millionaire.

The man she finally fell in love with did not sit on the stairs with her at all, though, like her, he was interested in religion and politics. This was a chap called Tom Barry. Tom was thirty-five, tall and thin and good-looking, and he lived with his mother and two good-looking sisters in a tiny house near the Barrack, and he couldn't even go for a walk in the evening without the three of them lining up in the hallway to present him with his hat, his gloves, and his clean handkerchief. He had a small job in the courthouse, and was not without ambition; he had engaged in several small business enterprises with his friend Jerry Coakley, but all they had ever got out of these was some good stories. Jerry was forty, and *he* had an old mother who insisted on putting his socks on for him.

Elsie's cousins warned her against setting her cap at Tom, but this only seemed to make her worse. "I guess I'll have to seduce him," she replied airily, and her cousins, who had never known a well-bred Catholic girl to talk like that, were shocked. She shocked them even more before she was done. She called at his house when she knew he wasn't there and deluded his innocent mother and sisters into believing that she didn't have designs on him; she badgered Tom to death at the office, gave him presents, and even hired a car to take him for drives.

They weren't the only ones who were shocked. Tom was shocked himself when she asked him point-blank how much he earned. However, he put that down to unworldliness and told her.

"But that's not even a street-cleaner's wages at home," she said indignantly.

"I'm sure, Elsie," he said sadly. "But then, of course, money isn't everything."

"No, and Ireland isn't everything," she replied. It was peculiar, but from their first evening together she had never ceased talking about America to him—the summer heat, and the crickets chattering, and the leaves alive with fireflies. During her discussions on the stairs, she had apparently discovered a great many things wrong with Ireland, and Tom, with a sort of mournful pleasure, kept adding to them.

"Oh, I know, I know," he said regretfully.

"Then if you know, why don't you do something about it?"

"Ah, well, I suppose it's habit, Elsie," he said, as though he weren't quite sure. "I suppose I'm too old to learn new tricks."

But Elsie doubted if it was really habit, and it perplexed her that a man so clever and conscientious could at the same time be so lacking in initiative. She explained it finally to herself in terms of an attachment to his mother that was neither natural nor healthy. Elsie was a girl who loved explanations.

On their third outing she had proposed to him, and he was so astonished that he burst out laughing, and continued to laugh whenever he thought of it again. Elsie herself couldn't see anything to laugh at in it. Having been proposed to by men who were younger and better-looking and better off than he was, she felt she had been conferring an honor on him. But he was a curious man, for when she repeated the proposal, he said, with a cold fury that hurt her, "Sometimes I wish you'd think before you talk, Elsie. You know what I earn, and you know it isn't enough to keep a family on. Besides, in case you haven't noticed it, I have a mother and two sisters to support."

"You could earn enough to support them in America," she protested.

"And I told you already that I had no intention of going to America."

"I have some money of my own," she said. "It's not much, but it could mean I'd be no burden to you."

"Listen, Elsie," he said, "a man who can't support a wife and children has no business marrying at all. I have no business marrying anyway. I'm not a very cheerful man, and I have a rotten temper."

Elsie went home in tears, and told her astonished uncle that all Irishmen were pansies, and, as he had no notion what pansies were, he shook his head and admitted that it was a terrible country. Then she wrote to Tom and told him that what he needed was not a wife but a psychiatrist. The writing of this gave her great satisfaction, but next morning she realized that her mother would only say she had been silly. Her mother believed that men needed careful handling. The day after, she waited for Tom outside the courthouse, and when he came out she summoned him with two angry blasts on the horn. A rainy sunset was flooding the Western Road with yellow light that made her look old and grim.

"Well," she said bitterly, "I'd hoped I'd never see your miserable face again."

But that extraordinary man only smiled gently and rested his elbows on the window of the car.

"I'm delighted you came," he said. "I was all last night trying to write to you, but I'm not very good at it."

"Oh, so you got my letter?"

"I did, and I'm ashamed to have upset you so much. All I wanted to say was that if you're serious—I mean really serious—about this, I'd be honored."

At first she thought he was mocking her. Then she realized that he wasn't, and she was in such an evil humor that she was tempted to tell him she had changed her mind. Then common sense told her the man would be fool enough to believe her, and after that his pride wouldn't let him propose to her again. It was the price you had to pay for dealing with men who had such a high notion of their own dignity.

"I suppose it depends on whether you love me or not," she replied. "It's a little matter you forgot to mention."

He raised himself from the car window, and in the evening light she saw a look of positive pain on his lean, sad, gentle face. "Ah, I do, but " he was beginning when she cut him off and told him to get in the car. Whatever he was about to say, she didn't want to hear it.

They settled down in a modern bungalow outside the town, on the edge of the harbor. Elsie's mother, who flew over for the wedding, said dryly that she hoped Elsie would be able to make up to Tom for the loss of his mother's services. In fact, it wasn't long before the Barrys were saying she wasn't, and making remarks about her cooking and her lack of tidiness. But if Tom noticed there was anything wrong, which is improbable, he didn't mention it. Whatever his faults as a sweetheart, he made a good husband. It may have been the affection of a sensitive man for someone he saw as frightened, fluttering, and insecure. It could have been the longing of a frustrated one for someone that seemed to him remote, romantic, and mysterious. But whatever it was, Tom, who had always been God Almighty to his mother and sisters, was extraordinarily patient and understanding with Elsie, and she needed it, because she was often homesick and scared.

Jerry Coakley was a great comfort to her in these fits, for Jerry had a warmth of manner that Tom lacked. He was an insignificant-looking man with a ravaged dyspeptic face and a tubercular complexion, a thin, bitter mouth with bad teeth, and long lank hair; but he was so sympathetic and insinuating that at times he even gave you the impression that he was changing his shape to suit your mood. Elsie had the feeling that the sense of failure had eaten deeper into him than into Tom.

At once she started to arrange a match between him and Tom's elder sister, Annie, in spite of Tom's warnings that Jerry would never marry till his mother died. When she realized that Tom was right, she said it was probably as well, because Annie wouldn't put his socks on him. Later she admitted that this was unfair, and that it would probably be a great relief to poor Jerry to be allowed to put on his socks himself. Between Tom and him there was one of those passionate relationships that spring up in small towns where society narrows itself down to a handful of erratic and explosive friendships. There were always people who weren't talking to other people, and friends had all to be dragged into the disagreement, no matter how trifling it might be, and often it happened that the principals had already become fast friends again when *their* friends were still ignoring one another in the street. But Jerry and Tom refused to disagree. Jerry would drop in for a bottle of stout, and Tom and he would denounce the country, while Elsie wondered why they could never find anything more interesting to talk about than stupid priests and crooked politicians.

Elsie's causes were of a different kind. The charwoman, Mrs. Dorgan, had six children and a husband who didn't earn enough to keep them. Elsie concealed from Tom how much she really paid Mrs. Dorgan, but she couldn't conceal that Mrs. Dorgan wore her clothes, or that she took the Dorgan family to the seaside in the summer. When Jerry suggested to Tom that the Dorgans might be doing too well out of Elsie, Tom replied, "Even if they were, Jerry, I wouldn't interfere. If 'tis people's nature to be generous, you must let them be generous."

For Tom's causes she had less patience. "Oh, why don't you people do something about it, instead of talking?" she cried.

"What could you do, Elsie?" asked Jerry.

"At least you could show them up," said Elsie.

"Why, Elsie?" he asked with his mournful smile. "Were you thinking of starting a paper?"

"Then, if you can't do anything about it, shut up!" she said. "You and Tom seem to get some queer masochistic pleasure out of these people."

"Begor, Elsie, you might have something there," Jerry said, nodding ruefully.

"Oh, we adore them," Tom said mockingly.

"You do," she said. "I've seen you. You sit here night after night denouncing them, and then when one of them gets sick you're round to the house to see if there's anything you can do for him, and when he dies you start a collection for his wife and family. You make me sick." Then she stamped out to the kitchen.

Jerry hunched his shoulders and exploded in splutters and giggles. He reached out a big paw for a bottle of stout, with the air of someone snaring a rabbit.

"I declare to God, Tom, she has us taped," he said.

"She has you taped anyway," said Tom.

"How's that?"

"She thinks you need an American wife as well."

"Well, now, she mightn't be too far out in that, either," said Jerry with a crooked grin. "I often thought it would take something like that."

"She thinks you have *problems*," said Tom with a snort. Elsie's favorite word gave him the creeps.

"She wouldn't be referring to the mother, by any chance?"

For a whole year Elsie had fits of depression because she thought she wasn't going to have a baby, and she saw several doctors, whose advice she repeated in mixed company, to the great embarrassment of everybody except Jerry. After that, for the best part of another year, she had fits of depression because she was going to have a baby, and she informed everybody about that as well, including the occasion of its conception and the probable date of its arrival, and again they were all embarrassed only Jerry. Having reached the age of eighteen before learning that there was any real difference between the sexes, Jerry found all her talk fascinating, and also he realized that Elsie saw nothing immodest in it. It was just that she had an experimental interest in her body and mind. When she gave him bourbon he studied its taste, but when he gave her Irish she studied its effect —it was as simple as that. Jerry, too, liked explanations, but he liked them for their own sake, and not with the intention of doing anything with them. At the same time, Elsie was scared by what she thought was a lack of curiosity on the part of the

Cork doctors, and when her mother learned this she began to press Elsie to have the baby in America, where she would feel secure.

"You don't think I should go back, Tom?" she asked guiltily. "Daddy says he'll pay my fare."

It came as a shock to Tom, though the idea had crossed his mind that something of the kind might happen. "If that's the way you feel about it, I suppose you'd better, Elsie," he replied.

"But you wouldn't come with me."

"How can I come with you? You know I can't just walk out of the office for a couple of months."

"But you could get a job at home."

"And I told you a dozen times I don't want a job in America," he said angrily. Then, seeing the way it upset her, he changed his tone. "Look, if you stay here, feeling the way you do, you'll work yourself into a real illness. Anyway, sometime you'll have to go back on a visit, and this is as good an occasion as any."

"But how can I, without you?" she asked. "You'd only neglect yourself."

"I would not neglect myself."

"Would you stay at your mother's?"

"I would not stay at my mother's. This is my house, and I'm going to stop here."

Tom worried less about the effect Elsie's leaving would have on him than about what his family would say, particularly Annie, who never lost the chance of a crack at Elsie. "You let that girl walk on you, Tom Barry," she said. "One of these days she'll walk too hard." Then, of course, Tom walked on *her*, in the way that only a devoted brother can, but that was no relief to the feeling that something had come between Elsie and him and that he could do nothing about it. When he was driving Elsie to the liner, he knew that she felt the same, for she didn't break down until they came to a long gray bridge over an inlet of water, guarded by a lonely gray stone tower. She had once pointed it out to him as the first thing she had seen that represented Ireland to her, and now he had the feeling that this was how she saw him—a battered old tower by a river mouth that was no longer of any importance to anyone but the sea gulls.

She was away longer than she or anyone else had expected. First there was the wedding of an old school friend; then her mother's birthday; then the baby got ill. It was clear that she was enjoying herself immensely, but she wrote long and frequent letters, sent snapshots of herself and the baby, and—most important of all—had named the baby for Jerry Coakley. Clearly Elsie hadn't forgotten them. The Dorgan kids appeared on the road in clothes that had obviously been made in America, and whenever Tom met them he stopped to speak to them and give them the pennies he thought Elsie would have given them.

Occasionally Tom went to his mother's for supper, but otherwise he looked after himself. Nothing could persuade him that he was not a natural housekeeper, or that whatever his sisters could do he could not do just as well himself. Sometimes Jerry came and the two men took off their coats and tried to prepare a meal out of one of Elsie's cookbooks. "Steady, squad!" Tom would murmur as he wiped his hands before taking another peep at the book. "You never know when this might come in handy." But whether it was the result of Tom's supervision or Jerry's helplessness, the meal usually ended in a big burnup, or a tasteless mess from which some essential ingredient seemed to be missing, and they laughed over it as they consoled themselves with bread and cheese and stout. "Elsie is right," Jerry would say, shaking his head regretfully. "We have problems, boy! We have problems!"

Elsie returned at last with trunks full of new clothes, a box of up-to-date kitchen stuff, and a new gaiety and energy. Every ten minutes Tom would make an excuse to tiptoe upstairs and take another look at his son. Then the Barrys arrived, and Elsie gave immediate offense by quoting Gesell and Spock. But Mrs. Barry didn't seem to mind as much as her daughters. By some extraordinary process of association, she had discovered a great similarity between Elsie and herself in the fact that she had married from the south side of the city into the north and had never got used to it. This delighted Elsie, who went about proclaiming that her mother-in-law and herself were both displaced persons.

The next year was a very happy one, and less trying on Elsie, because she had another woman to talk to, even if most of the time she didn't understand what her mother-in-law was telling her, and had the suspicion that her mother-in-law didn't understand her either. But then she got pregnant for the second time, and became restless and dissatisfied once more, though now it wasn't only with hospitals and doctors but with schools and schoolteachers as well. Tom and Jerry had impressed on her that the children were being turned into idiots, learning through the medium of a language they didn't understand—indeed, according to Tom, it was a language that nobody understood. What chance would the children have?

"Ah, I suppose the same chance as the rest of us, Elsie," said Jerry in his sly, mournful way.

"But you and Tom don't want chances, Jerry," she replied earnestly. "Neither of you has any ambition."

"Ah, you should look on the bright side of things. Maybe with God's help they won't have any ambition either."

But this time it had gone beyond a joke. For days on end, Tom was in a rage with her, and when he was angry he seemed to withdraw into himself like a snail into a shell.

Unable to get at him, Elsie grew hysterical. "It's all your damned obstinacy," she sobbed. "You don't do anything in this rotten hole, but you're too conceited to get out of it. Your family treat you as if you were God, and then you behave to me as if you were. God! God! God!" she screamed, and each time she punched him viciously with her fist, till suddenly the humor of their situation struck him and he went off into laughter.

After that, he could only make his peace with her and make excuses for her leaving him again, but he knew that the excuses wouldn't impress his sisters. One evening when he went to see them, Annie caught him, as she usually did, when he was going out the front door, and he stood looking sidewise down the avenue.

"Are you letting Elsie go off to America again, Tom?" she asked.

"I don't know," Tom said, pulling his long nose with an air of affected indifference. "I can't very well stop her, can I?"

"Damn soon she'd be stopped if she hadn't the money," said Annie. "And you're going to let her take young Jerry?"

"Ah, how could I look after Jerry? Talk sense, can't you!"

"And I suppose we couldn't look after him either? We're not sufficiently well-read."

"Ah, the child should be with his own mother, Annie," Tom said impatiently.

"And where should his mother be? Ah, Tom Barry," she added bitterly, "I told you what that one was, and she's not done with you yet. Are you sure she's going to bring him back?"

Then Tom exploded on her in his cold, savage way. "If you want to know, I am not," he said, and strode down the avenue with his head slightly bowed.

Something about the cut of him as he passed under a street lamp almost broke Annie's heart. "The curse of God on that bitch!" she said when she returned to her mother in the kitchen.

"Is it Elsie?" her mother cried angrily. "How dare you talk of her like that!"

"He's letting her go to America again," said Annie.

"He's a good boy, and he's right to consider her feelings," said her mother anxiously. "I often thought myself I'd go back to the south side and not be ending my days in this misfortunate hole."

The months after Elsie's second departure were bitter ones for Tom. A house from which a woman is gone is bad enough, but one from which a child is gone is a deadhouse. Tom would wake in the middle of the night thinking he heard Jerry crying, and be half out of bed before he realized that Jerry was thousands of miles away. He did not continue his experiments with cooking and housekeeping. He ate at his mother's, spent most of his time at the Coakleys, and drank far too much. Like all inward-looking men he had a heavy hand on the bottle. Meanwhile Elsie wavered and procrastinated worse than before, setting dates, cancelling her passage, sometimes changing her mind within twenty-four hours. In his despondency Tom resigned himself to the idea that she wouldn't return at all, or at least persuaded himself that he had.

"Oh, she'll come back all right," Jerry said with a worried air. "The question is, will she stay back. . . . You don't mind me talking about it?" he asked.

"Indeed no. Why would I?"

"You know, Tom, I'd say ye had family enough to last ye another few years."

Tom didn't look up for a few moments, and when he did he smiled faintly. "You think it's that?"

"I'm not saying she knows it," Jerry added hastily. "There's nothing calculating about her, and she's crazy about you."

"I thought it was something that went with having the baby," Tom said thoughtfully. "Some sort of homing instinct."

"I wouldn't say so," said Jerry. "Not altogether. I think she feels that eventually she'll get you through the kids."

"She won't," Tom said bitterly.

"I know, sure, I know. But Elsie can't get used to the— the irremediable." The last word was so unlike Jerry that Tom felt he must have looked it up in a dictionary, and the absurdity of this made him feel very close to his old crony. "Tell me, Tom," Jerry added gently, "wouldn't you do it? I know it wouldn't be easy, but wouldn't you try it, even for a while, for Elsie's sake? 'Twould mean a hell of a lot to her."

"I'm too old, Jerry," Tom said so deliberately that Jerry knew it had been in his mind as well.

"Oh, I know, I know," Jerry repeated. "Even ten years ago I might have done it myself. It's like jail. The time comes when you're happier in than out. And that's not the worst of it," he added bitterly. "The worst is when you pretend you like it."

It was a strange evening that neither of them ever forgot, sitting in that little house to which Elsie's absence seemed a rebuke, and listening to the wind from the harbor that touched the foot of the garden. They knew they belonged to a country whose youth was always escaping from it, out beyond that harbor, and that was middle-aged in all its attitudes and institutions. Of those that remained, a little handful lived with defeat and learned fortitude and humor and sweetness, and these were the things that Elsie, with her generous idealism, loved in them. But she couldn't pay the price. She wanted them where she belonged herself, among the victors.

A few weeks later, Elsie was back; the house was full of life again, and that evening seemed only a bad dream. It was almost impossible to keep Jerry Og, as they called the elder child, away from Tom. He was still only a baby, and a spoiled one at that, but when Tom took him to the village Jerry Og thrust out his chest and took strides that were too big for him, like any small boy with a father he adored. Each day, he lay in wait for the postman and then took the post away to sort it for himself. He sorted it by the pictures on the stamps, and Elsie noted gleefully that he reserved all the pretty pictures for his father.

Nobody had remembered Jerry's good advice, even Jerry himself, and eighteen months later Elsie was pregnant again. Again their lives took the same pattern of unrest. But this time Elsie was even more distressed than Tom.

"I'm a curse to you," she said. "There's something wrong with me. I can't be natural."

"Oh, you're natural enough," Tom replied bitterly. "You married the wrong man, that's all."

"I didn't, I didn't!" she protested despairingly. "You can say anything else but that. If I believed that, I'd have nothing left, because I never cared for anyone but you. And in spite of what you think, I'm coming back," she went on, in tears. "I'm coming back if it kills me. God, I hate this country; I hate every God damn thing about it; I hate what it's done to you and Jerry. But I'm not going to let you go."

"You have no choice," Tom said patiently. "Jerry Og will have to go to school, and you can't be bringing him hither and over, even if you could afford it."

"Then, if that's what you feel, why don't you keep him?" she cried. "You know perfectly well you could stop me taking him with me if you wanted to. You wouldn't even have to bring me into court. I'll give him to you now. Isn't that proof enough that I'm coming back?"

"No, Elsie, it is not," Tom replied, measuring every word. "And I'm not going to bring you into court, either. I'm not going to take hostages to make sure my wife comes back to me."

And though Elsie continued to delude herself with the belief that she would return, she knew Tom was right. It would all appear different when she got home. The first return to Ireland had been hard, the second had seemed impossible. Yet, even in the black hours when she really considered the situation, she felt she could never resign herself to something that had been determined before she was born, and she deceived herself with the hope that Tom would change his mind and follow her. He must follow her. Even if he was prepared to abandon her, he would never abandon Jerry Og.

And this, as Big Jerry could have told her, was where she made her biggest mistake, because if Tom had done it at all it would have been for her. But Big Jerry had decided that the whole thing had gone beyond his power to help. He recognized the irremediable, all right, sometimes perhaps even before it became irremediable. But that, as he would have said himself, is where the ferryboat had left him.

Thanks to Elsie, the eldest of the Dorgans now has a job in Boston and in the course of years the rest of them will probably go there as well. Tom continues to live in his little bungalow beside the harbor. Annie is keeping house for him, which suits her fine, because Big Jerry's old mother continued to put his socks on for him a few years too long, and now Annie has only her brother to worship. To all appearances they are happy enough, as happiness goes in Cork. Jerry still calls, and the two men discuss the terrible state of the country. But in Tom's bedroom there are pictures of Elsie and the children, the third of whom he knows only through photographs, and apart from that, nothing has changed since Elsie left it five years ago. It is a strange room, for one glance is enough to show that the man who sleeps there is still in love, and that everything that matters to him in the world is reflected there. And one day, if he comes by the dollars, he will probably go out and visit them all, but it is here he will return and here, no doubt, he will die. As Jerry says in his wise way, sometimes it all seems like a fairy tale.

CARL SANDBURG

Sea Chest

There was a woman loved a man
   as the man loved the sea.
Her thoughts of him were the same
   as his thoughts of the sea.
They made an old sea chest
   for their belongings together.

O HENRY

The Gift
of the Magi

One dollar and eighty-seven cents. That was all. And sixty cents of it was in pennies. Pennies saved one and two at a time by bulldozing the grocer and the vegetable man and the butcher until one's cheeks burned with silent imputation of parsimony that such close dealing implied. Three times Della counted it. One dollar and eighty-seven cents. And the next day would be Christmas.

There was clearly nothing to do but flop down on the shabby little couch and howl. So Della did it. Which instigates the moral reflection that life is made up of sobs, sniffles, and smiles, with sniffles predominating.

While the mistress of the home is gradually subsiding from the first stage to the second, take a look at the home. A furnished flat at $8 per week. It did not exactly beggar description, but it certainly had that word on the lookout for the mendicancy squad.

In the vestibule below was a letter box into which no letter would go, and an electric button from which no mortal finger could coax a ring. Also appertaining thereunto was a card bearing the name "Mr. James Dillingham Young."

FROM THE FOUR MILLION BY O. HENRY. REPRINTED BY PERMISSION OF DOUBLEDAY & CO., INC.

The "Dillingham" had been flung to the breeze during a former period of prosperity when its possessor was being paid $30 a week. Now, when the income was shrunk to $20, the letters of "Dillingham" looked blurred, as though they were thinking seriously of contracting to a modest and unassuming D. But whenever Mr. James Dillingham Young came home and reached his flat above, he was called "Jim" and greatly hugged by Mrs. James Dillingham Young, already introduced to you as Della. Which is all very good.

Della finished her cry and attended to her cheeks with the powder rag. She stood by the window and looked out dully at a gray cat walking a gray fence in a gray back yard. Tomorrow would be Christmas Day, and she had only $1.87 with which to buy Jim a present. She had been saving every penny she could for months, with this result. Twenty dollars a week doesn't go far. Expenses had been greater than she had calculated. They always are. Only $1.87 to buy a present for Jim. Her Jim. Many a happy hour she had spent planning something nice for him. Something fine and rare and sterling—something just a little bit near to being worthy of the honor of being owned by Jim.

There was a pier-glass between the windows of the room. Perhaps you have seen a pier-glass in an $8 flat. A very thin and very agile person may, by observing his reflection in a rapid sequence of longtitudinal strips, obtain a fairly accurate conception of his looks. Della, being slender, had mastered the art.

Suddenly she whirled from the window and stood before the glass. Her eyes were shining brilliantly, but her face had lost its color within twenty seconds. Rapidly she pulled down her hair and let it fall to its full length.

Now, there were two possessions of the James Dillingham Youngs in which they both took a mighty pride. One was Jim's gold watch that had been his father's and his grandfather's. The other was Della's hair. Had the Queen of Sheba lived in the flat across the airshaft, Della would have let her hair hang out the window some day to dry just to depreciate her majesty's jewels

and gifts. Had King Solomon been the janitor, with all his treasures piled up in the basement, Jim would have pulled out his
watch every time he passed, just to see him pluck at his beard
from envy.

So now Della's beautiful hair fell about her, rippling and
shining like a cascade of brown waters. It reached below her
knee and made itself almost a garment for her. And then she did
it up again nervously and quickly. Once she faltered for a minute
and stood still while a tear or two splashed on the worn red
carpet.

On went her old brown jacket; on went her old brown hat.
With a whirl of skirts and with the brilliant sparkle still in her
eyes she fluttered out the door and down the stairs to the street.

Where she stopped the sign read: "Mme. Sofronie. Hair
Goods of All Kinds." One flight up Della ran, and collected herself, panting. Madame, large, too white, chilly, hardly looked
the "Sofronie."

"Will you buy my hair?" asked Della.

"I buy hair," said Madame. "Take yer hat off and let's have
a sight at the looks of it."

Down rippled the brown cascade.

"Twenty dollars," said madame, lifting the mass with a practiced hand.

"Give it to me quick," said Della.

Oh, and the next two hours tripped by on rosy wings. Forget
the hashed metaphor. She was ransacking the stores for Jim's
present.

She found it at last. It surely had been made for Jim and no
one else. There was no other like it in any of the stores, and she
had turned all of them inside out. It was a platinum fob chain,
simple and chaste in design, properly proclaiming its value by
substance alone and not by meretricious ornamentation—as all
good things should do. It was even worthy of The Watch. As
soon as she saw it she knew that it must be Jim's. It was like him.
Quietness and value—the description applied to both. Twenty-

one dollars they took from her for it, and she hurried home with the 87 cents. With that chain on his watch Jim might be properly anxious about the time in any company. Grand as the watch was, he sometimes looked at it on the sly on account of the old leather strap that he used in place of a chain.

When Della reached home her intoxication gave way a little to prudence and reason. She got out her curling irons and lighted the gas and went to work repairing the ravages made by generosity added to love. Which is always a tremendous task, dear friends—a mammoth task.

Within forty minutes her head was covered with tiny, closelying curls that made her look wonderfully like a truant schoolboy. She looked at her reflection in the mirror long, carefully, and critically.

"If Jim doesn't kill me," she said to herself, "before he takes a second look at me, he'll say I look like a Coney Island chorus girl. But what could I do—oh! what could I do with a dollar and eighty-seven cents?"

At seven o'clock the coffee was made and the frying pan was on the back of the stove hot and ready to cook the chops.

Jim was never late. Della doubled the fob chain in her hand and sat on the corner of the table near the door that he always entered. Then she heard his step on the stair, way down on the first flight, and she turned white for just a moment. She had a habit of saying little silent prayers about the simplest everyday things, and now she whispered: "Please, God, make him think I am still pretty."

The door opened and Jim stepped in and closed it. He looked thin and very serious. Poor fellow, he was only twenty-two— and to be burdened with a family! He needed a new overcoat and he was without gloves.

Jim stopped inside the door, as immovable as a setter at the scent of quail. His eyes were fixed upon Della, and there was an expression in them that she could not read, and it terrified her. It was not anger, nor surprise, nor disapproval, nor horror, nor any of the sentiments that she had been prepared for. He simply stared at her fixedly with that peculiar expression on his face.

Della wriggled off the table and went for him.

"Jim, darling," she cried, "don't look at me that way. I had my hair cut off and sold it because I couldn't have lived through Christmas without giving you a present. It'll grow out again—you won't mind, will you? I just had to do it. My hair grows awfully fast. Say 'Merry Christmas!' Jim, and let's be happy. You don't know what a nice—what a beautiful, nice gift I've got for you."

"You've cut off your hair?" asked Jim, laboriously, as if he had not arrived at that patent fact yet even after the hardest mental labor.

"Cut it off and sold it," said Della. "Don't you like me just as well, anyhow? I'm me without my hair, ain't I?"

Jim looked about the room curiously.

"You say your hair is gone?" he said, with an air almost of idiocy.

"You needn't look for it," said Della. "It's sold, I tell you—sold and gone, too. It's Christmas Eve, boy. Be good to me, for it went for you. Maybe the hairs of my head were numbered," she went on with a sudden seriousness, "but nobody could ever count my love for you. Shall I put the chops on, Jim?"

Out of his trance Jim seemed quickly to wake. He enfolded his Della. For ten seconds let us regard with discreet scrutiny some inconsequential object in the other direction. Eight dollars a week or a million a year—what is the difference? A mathematician or a wit would give you the wrong answer. The Magi brought valuable gifts, but that was not among them. This dark assertion will be illuminated later on.

Jim drew a package from his overcoat pocket and threw it upon the table.

"Don't make any mistake, Della," he said, "about me. I don't think there's anything in the way of a haircut or a shave or a shampoo that could make me like my girl any less. But if you'll unwrap that package you may see why you had me going for a while at first."

White fingers and nimble tore at the string and paper. And then an ecstatic scream of joy; and then, alas! a quick feminine change to hysterical tears and wails, necessitating the immediate employment of all the comforting powers of the lord of the flat.

For there lay The Combs—the set of combs, side and back, that Della had worshiped for long in a Broadway window. Beautiful combs, pure tortoise shell, with jeweled rims—just the shade to wear in the beautiful vanished hair. They were expensive combs, she knew, and her heart had simply craved and yearned over them without the least hope of possession. And now they were hers, but the tresses that should have adorned the coveted adornments were gone.

But she hugged them to her bosom, and at length she was able to look up with dim eyes and a smile and say: "My hair grows so fast, Jim!"

And then Della leaped up like a little singed cat and cried, "Oh, oh!"

Jim had not yet seen his beautiful present. She held it out to him eagerly upon her open palm. The dull precious metal seemed to flash with a reflection of her bright and ardent spirit.

"Isn't it a dandy, Jim? I hunted all over town to find it. You'll have to look at the time a hundred times a day now. Give me your watch. I want to see how it looks on it."

Instead of obeying, Jim tumbled down on the couch and put his hands under the back of his head and smiled.

"Della," said he, "let's put our Christmas presents away and keep 'em a while. They're too nice to use just at present. I sold the watch to get the money to buy your combs. And now suppose you put the chops on."

The Magi, as you know, were wise men—wonderfully wise men—who brought gifts to the Babe in the manger. They invented the art of giving Christmas presents. Being wise, their gifts were no doubt wise ones, possibly bearing the privilege of exchange in case of duplication. And here I have lamely related to you the uneventful chronicle of two foolish children in a flat who most unwisely sacrificed for each other the greatest treasures of their house. But in a last word to the wise of these days let it be said that of all who give gifts these two were the wisest. Of all who give and receive gifts, such as they are wisest. Everywhere they are wisest. They are the Magi.

SEAN O'FAOLAIN

The Fur Coat

When Maguire became Parliamentary Secretary to the Minister
for Roads and Railways his wife wound her arms around his
neck, lifted herself on her toes, gazed into his eyes and said,
adoringly:

"Now, Paddy, I must have a fur coat."

"Of course, of course, me dear," Maguire cried, holding her
out from him admiringly; for she was a handsome little woman
still, in spite of the graying hair and the first hint of a stoop.
"Get two fur coats! Switzer's will give us any amount of tick
from now on."

Molly sat back into her chair with her fingers clasped between her knees and said, chidingly:

"You think I'm extravagant!"

"Indeed, then, I do not. We've had some thin times together
and it's about time we had a bit of comfort in our old age. I'd
like to see my wife in a fur coat. I'd love to see my wife take a
shine out of some of those straps in Grafton Street—painted jades
that never lifted a finger for God or man, not to as much as
mention the word *Ireland*. By all means get a fur coat. Go down
to Switzer's tomorrow morning," he cried with all the innocence
of a warm-hearted, inexperienced man, "and order the best fur
coat that money can buy."

Molly Maguire looked at him with affection and irritation. The years had polished her hard—politics, revolution, husband in and out of prison, children reared with the help of relatives and Prisoners' Dependents' Funds. You could see the years on her fingertips, too pink, too coarse, and in her diamond-bright eyes.

"Paddy, you big fool, do you know what you'd pay for a mink coat? Not to mention a sable? And not as much as to whisper the word broadtail?"

"Say a hundred quid," said Paddy, manfully. "What's a hundred quid? I'll be handling millions of public money from now on. I have to think big."

She replied in her warm Limerick singsong; sedately and proudly as befitted a woman who had often, in her father's country store, handled thousands of pound notes.

"Do you know, Paddy Maguire, what a really bang-up fur coat could cost you? It could cost you a thousand guineas, and more."

"One thousand guineas? For a coat? Sure, that's a whole year's salary."

"It is."

Paddy drew into himself. "And," he said, in a cautious voice, "is that the kind of coat you had in mind?"

She laughed, satisfied at having taken him off his perch.

"Yerrah, not at all. I thought I might pick up a nice little coat for, maybe, thirty or forty or, at the outside, fifty quid. Would that be too much?"

"Go down to Switzer's in the morning and bring it home on your back."

But, even there, she thought she detected a touch of the bravo, as if he was still feeling himself a great fellow. She let it pass. She said she might have a look around. There was no hurry. She did not bring up the matter again for quite fifteen minutes.

"Paddy! About that fur coat. I sincerely hope you don't think I'm being *vulgar*?"

"How could you be vulgar?"

"Oh, sort of *nouveau riche*. I don't want a fur coat for show-off." She leaned forward eagerly. "Do you know the reason why I want a fur coat?"

"To keep you warm. What else?"

"Oh, well, that too, I suppose, yes," she agreed shortly. "But you must realize that from this on we'll be getting asked out to parties and receptions and so forth. And—well—I haven't a rag to wear!"

"I see," Paddy agreed; but she knew that he did not see.

"Look," she explained, "what I want is something I can wear any old time. I don't want a fur coat for grandeur." (This very scornfully.) "I want to be able to throw it on and go off and be as well dressed as anybody. You see, you can wear any old thing under a fur coat."

"That sounds a good idea." He considered the matter as judiciously as if he were considering a memorandum for a projected bypass. She leaned back, contented, with the air of a woman who has successfully laid her conscience to rest.

Then he spoiled it all by asking, "But, tell me, what do all the women do who haven't fur coats?"

"They dress."

"Dress? Don't ye all dress?"

"Paddy, don't be silly. They think of nothing else but dress. I have no time for dressing. I'm a busy housewife and, anyway, dressing costs a lot of money." (Here she caught a flicker in his eye which obviously meant that forty quid isn't to be sniffed at either.) "I mean they have costumes that cost twenty-five pounds. Half a dozen of 'em. They spend a lot of time and thought over it. They live for it. If you were married to one of 'em you'd soon know what it means to dress. The beauty of a fur coat is that you can just throw it on and you're as good as the best of them."

"Well, that's fine! Get the ould coat."

He was evidently no longer enthusiastic. A fur coat, he had learned, is not a grand thing—it is just a useful thing. He drew his brief case towards him. There was that pier down in Kerry to be looked at. "Mind you," he added, "it'd be nice and warm, too. Keep you from getting a cold."

"Oh, grand, yes, naturally, cozy, yes, all that, yes, yes!"

And she crashed out and banged the door after her and put the children to bed as if she were throwing sacks of turf into a cellar. When she came back he was poring over maps and specifications. She began to patch one of the boy's pajamas. After a while she held it up and looked at it in despair. She let it sink into her lap and looked at the pile of mending beside her.

"I suppose when I'm dead and gone they'll invent plastic pajamas that you can wash with a dishcloth and mend with a lump of glue."

She looked into the heart of the turf fire. A dozen pajamas . . . underwear for the whole house . . .

"Paddy!"

"Huh?"

"The last thing that I want anybody to start thinking is that I, by any possible chance, could be getting grand notions."

She watched him hopefully. He was lost in his plans.

"I can assure you, Paddy, that I loathe—I simply loathe all this modern show-off."

"That's right."

"Those wives that think they haven't climbed the social ladder until they've got a fur coat!"

He grunted at the map of the pier.

"Because I don't care what you or anybody else says, Paddy, there *is* something vulgar about a fur coat. There's no shape to them. Especially musquash. What I was thinking of was black Indian lamb. Of course, the real thing would be ocelot. But they're much too dear. The real ones. And I wouldn't be seen dead in an imitation ocelot."

He glanced sideways from the table. "You seem to know a lot about fur." He leaned back and smiled benevolently. "I never knew you were hankering all this time after a fur coat."

"Who said I'm hankering! I am *not*. What do you mean? Don't be silly. I just want something decent to wear when we go out to a show, or to wear over a dance frock, that's all. What do you mean—hankering?"

"Well, what's wrong with that thing you have with the fur on the sleeves? The shiny thing with the what-do-you-call-'ems —sequins, is it?"

"*That!* Do you mean *that?* For heaven's sake, don't be talking about what you don't know anything about. I've had *that* for fourteen years. It's like something me grandmother wore at her own funeral."

He laughed. "You used to like it."

"Of course, I liked it when I got it. Honestly, Paddy Maguire, there are times when . . ."

"Sorry, sorry, sorry. I was only trying to be helpful. How much is an ocelot?"

"Eighty-five or ninety—at the least."

"Well, why not?"

"Paddy, tell me honestly. Honestly, now! Do you seriously think that I could put eighty-five pounds on my back?"

With his pencil Maguire frugally drew a line on the map, reducing the pier by five yards, and wondered would the county surveyor let him get away with it.

"Well, the question is: will you be satisfied with the Indian lamb? What color did you say it is? Black? That's a very queer lamb."

Irritably he rubbed out the line. The wretched thing would be too shallow at low water if he cut five yards off it.

"It's dyed. You could get it brown, too," she cried. "You could get all sorts of lamb. Broadtail is the fur of unborn Persian lambs."

That woke him up: the good farmer stock in him was shocked.

"Unborn lambs!" he cried. "Do you mean to say that they . . ."

"Yes, isn't it awful? Honest to Heaven, Paddy, anyone that'd wear broadtail ought to be put in prison. Paddy, I've made up

my mind. I just couldn't buy a fur coat. I just won't buy it.
That's the end of it."

She picked up the pajamas again and looked at them with
moist eyes. He turned to devote his full attention to her problem.

"Molly, darling, I'm afraid I don't understand what you're
after. I mean, do you or do you not want a fur coat? I mean,
supposing you didn't buy a fur coat, what else could you do?"

"Just exactly what do you mean?"—very coldly.

"I mean, it isn't apparently necessary that you should buy a
fur coat. I mean, not if you don't really want to. There must be
some other way of dressing besides fur coats? If you have a
scunner against fur coats, why not buy something else just as
good? There's hundreds of millions of other women in the world
and they all haven't fur coats."

"I've told you before that they dress! And I've no time to
dress. I've explained all that to you."

Maguire got up. He put his back to the fire, his hands behind
him, a judicial look on him. He addressed the room.

"All the other women in the world can't all have time to dress.
There must be some way out of it. For example, next month
there'll be a garden party up at the President's house. How many
of all these women will be wearing fur coats?" He addressed
the armchair. "Has Mrs. de Valera time to dress?" He turned
and leaned over the turf basket. "Has Mrs. General Mulcahy
time to dress? There's ways and means of doing everything."
(He shot a quick glance at the map of the pier; you could always
knock a couple of feet off the width of it.) "After all, you've
told me yourself that you could purchase a black costume for
twenty-five guineas. Is that or is that not a fact? Very well then,"
triumphantly, "why not buy a black costume for twenty-five
guineas?"

"Because, you big fathead, I'd have to have shoes and a blouse
and hat and gloves and a fur and a purse and everything to match
it, and I'd spend far more in the heel of the hunt, and I haven't

time for that sort of thing and I'd have to have two or three costumes—Heaven above, I can't appear day after day in the same old rig, can I?"

"Good! Good! That's settled. Now, the question is: shall we or shall we not purchase a fur coat? Now! What is to be said for a fur coat?" He marked off the points on his fingers. "Number one: it is warm. Number two: it will keep you from getting cold. Number three . . ."

Molly jumped up, let a scream out of her, and hurled the basket of mending at him.

"Stop it! I told you I don't want a fur coat! And you don't want me to get a fur coat! You're too mean, that's what it is! And, like all the Irish, you have the peasant streak in you. You're all alike, every bloody wan of ye. Keep your rotten fur coat. I never wanted it . . ."

And she ran from the room sobbing with fury and disappointment.

"Mean?" gasped Maguire to himself. "To think that anybody could say that I . . . Mean!"

She burst open the door to sob:

"I'll go to the garden party in a mackintosh. And I hope that'll satisfy you!" and ran out again.

He sat miserably at his table, cold with anger. He murmured the hateful word over and over, and wondered could there be any truth in it. He added ten yards to the pier. He reduced the ten to five, and then, seeing what he had done, swept the whole thing off the table.

It took them three days to make it up. She had hit him below the belt, and they both knew it. On the fourth morning she found a check for a hundred and fifty pounds on her dressing table. For a moment her heart leaped. The next moment it died in her. She went down and put her arms about his neck and laid the check, torn in four, into his hand.

"I'm sorry, Paddy," she begged, crying like a kid. "You're not mean. You never were. It's me that's mean."

"You! Mean?" he said, fondly holding her in his arms.

"No, I'm not mean. It's not that. I just haven't the heart, Paddy. It was knocked out of me donkeys' years ago." He looked at her sadly. "You know what I'm trying to say?"

He nodded. But she saw that he didn't. She was not sure that she knew herself. He took a deep, resolving breath, held her out from him by the shoulders, and looked her straight in the eyes. "Molly, tell me the truth. You want this coat?"

"I do. O God, I do!"

"Then go out and buy it."

"I couldn't, Paddy. I just couldn't."

He looked at her for a long time. Then he asked:

"Why?"

She looked straight at him and, shaking her head sadly, she said in a little sobbing voice:

"I don't know."

SEYMOUR EPSTEIN

Wheat Closed Higher, Cotton Was Mixed

Bernie Halper met and married Sue several years after the war ended. They both were taking part in an amateur production of *The Sea Gull*. Bernie directed. Sue played the role of Masha. A newspaper theater critic was present at the performance, and he shed a few lines of grace over the efforts of the group. He wrote that some professionals heavy-laden with success might spend a profitable hour watching the enthusiasm and intelligence of these young people.

That same evening the whole cast—extras, helpers, all—met at someone's apartment and picked over those few words like augurs over the entrails of a chicken. Visions of triumph mingled with the cigarette smoke, and each one made out the shape of his own destiny.

"I still say the important word is 'intelligence,' " Bernie declared at one o'clock in the morning. "There are any number of dopes with the gift of talent, but an actor without brains is like a plant without water. He just won't grow."

From REDBOOK, June 1961.

Since all present were still too young to admit of any short-coming, this remark was found to be acceptable as a parting shot. About fifteen people filed out of a room that would take two days to ventilate. In the street they deployed singly and in pairs toward the various subways that would take them home. It was no accident that Bernie fell in with Sue.

Throughout rehearsals he had managed to avoid so much as a single glance of partiality. This despite her gray eyes and cute nose and hair as dark and ample as a moonless sea. There was an amplitude in her figure as well, which filled every hollow of Bernie's desire. Nor was that desire made up of loneliness and inexperience. Bernie had known women, being himself hand-some in the way of physical virility and generous features. He wasn't tall but he was large: big head, heavy shoulders, large mouth, prominent nose. His neck could have used another inch, and he had a way of hunching forward when he walked. A foot-ball coach would have singled him out in any group of freshmen.

Bernie and Sue walked toward the Seventh Avenue subway, where the New Lots train would take Sue to her home in Brook-lyn. Even Manhattan can be quiet along its side streets at one in the morning, and their footsteps sounded brash and intrusive. A young man to whom words came easily, Bernie found himself stricken with silence. It was Sue who spoke.

"I'd like to ask you a question," she said. "Would you tell me the truth?"

Bernie smiled. "If I know the truth," he replied.

"Do you think I have intelligence?"

This was as he had expected. The appeal to his honesty missed its target, deflected by self-interest.

"Only people who have intelligence question it," he answered, feeling that he did not so much lie as bedeck his love with silks and spangles.

For Bernie Halper was in love, right there on Forty-eighth Street between Fifth and Sixth avenues at one in the morning. He walked on as if nothing had happened, but he felt as if he had been dealt a blow that passed through his flesh, broke no bones, and landed smack on the core of his being. He could have doubled over with the pain of his joy.

"I wish you would tell me the truth," Sue repeated.

"You are intelligent," Bernie stated flatly. "And lovely," he added.

"Sometimes I wonder if I can act at all," she said, exacting gentle usury.

Bernie lifted his face to the neon-obscured sky. In his mind was an image of Sue as she had stepped out of the wings in her long dress and tiara of braided hair. She had held her hands as he had shown her (precisely, a blueprint, no variation of her own) and spoken her lines in the same way. If Truth was Beauty, then Sue was Truth. And can Truth be anything but intelligent? That she could not act was a matter of some regret and questionable significance. A deception for her sake was already coloring his love with poignance.

"You can act," Bernie said, ready to sign checks for any amount. "You can act beautifully. Why do you ask? I know. It's like being in love. You can't hear the words often enough. Are you in love, Sue?"

She turned and looked at him with her remarkable gray eyes. "Now, do you mean?"

"Ever."

"Yes."

"Are you in love with someone now?"

"No."

"Good. Will you see me tomorrow? Will you go with me to a movie? A play? Dinner? Anything?"

"All right," she said.

Two months later Bernie asked Sue to marry him. Sue said yes, but made it clear that she intended to go on with her acting career.

"What do you take me for?" Bernie cried. "I know a little something about ambition myself. Why should I deny it to you? . . . Listen, darling, will you do me a favor? I ask it only because

I'll shrivel up and die if I don't hear you say it soon. Say you love me. I must have said it to you no less than six million times."

"Of course I love you," Sue said, taking his face between her hands. "Bernie . . ."

"Please don't say anything else," he pleaded.

"Tell me the truth. . . ."

Bernie swore that she had a rare, rich and beautiful talent and that the world would know it someday.

They married in August and almost perished from the heat in their wonderful room-and-a-half on East Twentieth. They took long walks in the city, since they could afford little else, and Bernie made every view and quaintness his personal gift to Sue. He gave her Greenwich Village, Chinatown, Riverside Drive, and all the magnificent bridges of New York.

About the Queensboro Bridge he said: "I was driving over it once before the war. It was just about twilight. Maybe a little later. Anyway, I was coming from the Queens side into the city, and I saw Manhattan lighted up like the Arabian Nights. I felt like climbing to the top of the bridge and taking a flying swan dive right into the city. I thought: What else do you want? If you can't make it here, you can't make it anywhere."

"Make what?" Sue asked.

"Anything! Golden apples! My private fairy tale! Turn thrice, Bernie Halper, Lord Mayor of Third Avenue!"

"Why not Fifth?"

"Fifth it is!"

"How much money *do* we have, Lord Mayor?" Sue asked.

Bernie took out a handkerchief and wiped his face. "There's a couple of hundred in the bank and about eight hundred in bonds. We're on Easy Street. Don't worry. I'm a provider."

It was Bernie who did the worrying. He had been promised a showcase production around the end of September, but there was no money in that. The immediate future was resplendent with moneyless doings. Sue was already cast in the Synge play Bernie planned to do. That too would contribute a big fat zero to their income. In addition, Sue was continuing her drama classes at the Academy. She miserably suggested that she quit and take a job.

Bernie burst into laughter at the look on her face. "Honey-bunch, slash my wrists and see what you can get at the blood bank!" he said mockingly.

"I didn't say it that way at all," Sue protested.

"Please remember that expression," Bernie said. "It was great!"

But the question of money yipped at his heels like a Pekingese, too insignificant to be menacing yet embarrassing in its persistence. He had held a variety of jobs after finishing school on the GI Bill. He had worked in a department store as a salesman. His father had thrown some house-painting jobs his way. For a few months he crouched next to the driver and pointed out the splendors of New York in a plastic-domed bus. And just before taking on the production in which he had met Sue, Bernie had discovered a dormant ability. He became a worker in leather.

It happened that a friend of his with a real ability for the craft had set up shop in Greenwich Village as a custom maker of leather handbags and sandals. Very arty and bizarre stuff, but requiring innate skill if a lot of expensive leather was not to go to waste. The friend did quite well, in the marginal way of such businesses. Bernie dropped in often at the shop and began toying with the knife and awl. It became immediately apparent to both Bernie and his friend that he had the touch. He was able to pick up a few dollars helping out on occasional afternoons.

When Bernie cashed in the second hundred-dollar bond he paid a visit to his friend in the Village. The friend said yes, sure, he could use some help.

The Playboy of the Western World scourged Bernie. He gripped his skull between his hands as though he wanted to crush it. He asked himself in hoarse supplications why he had to pick such a play. To take innocent children from the Bronx, Brooklyn, New Jersey, God knows where, and make lilting Irishers out of them! Madness! He had counseled himself a thousand times never to make the sinful error of going on with a thing merely because he had begun, and here he was treading quicksand up to his neck. All right, the lead part was good. That boy would be an actor. But everyone else, including Sue . . . It was a goulash.

He had his first bad fight with Sue.

"Ear," he said to her, pulling on the lobe of his own. "You listen and then you reproduce the accent, the inflection. An actor who doesn't have an ear is a tone-deaf singer."

"I hate you!" Sue screamed.

The production rolled downhill like a vehicle without brakes. When certain death stared him in the face Bernie's nervous system reacted with a charge of adrenaline. He took the leading man aside and asked him if he could play it straight, no accent. The answer was yes. Then Bernie assembled the cast and informed them that they could stop torturing themselves. No brogues. He challenged them all to capture the spirit of the lines without the music. It would fail, he assured them, but it would fail interestingly rather than ludicrously. That was the best he could offer them at that late date.

The effect was somewhat like that on a baseball player who has swung three or four bats so that the one he wields at the plate will seem light. Just playing the roles without having to worry about the treachery of their tongues broke the tension and gave them an art and ease above their normal level.

The performance annoyed some, puzzled many and persuaded an all-important few. There is an attractive legend that great discoveries have been made through the inadvertence of somebody's maid leaving something where it shouldn't have been. Bernie's "experiment," as it was called, fell into such a category of fruitful accident. The same reviewer who had found *The Sea Gull* an enthusiastic and intelligent production found *Playboy* "a worthwhile experiment with a play that normally has to wait upon a miraculous pooling of accents and talents. It is to Mr. Halper's credit that he persevered in the face of what he must have known would seem high treason to lovers of the

Irish theater. Certainly we missed the melodies of Synge, but we did enjoy a good play, well acted."

In their apartment afterward, Bernie improvised a wild Irish dance while whistling a jig through his teeth. Sue held on to his hands like the tail of a kite on a windy day. Then Bernie went down to the German delicatessen and bought two pounds of roast beef, a rye bread with caraway seeds, four bottles of beer and a container of Russian dressing. They made sandwiches, just the two of them, and ate and drank until their ears rang.

As a result of that one good review and several complimentary mentions, the production wound up having an unprecedented, if profitless, run of three months. More important, Bernie received an invitation from a producer to "read" a play. The producer wanted Bernie to submit his judgment on an original play, and if he found it good, to offer some suggestions about casting and direction. There were no promises and no contract—just a chance, if Bernie Halper wished to take it. Bernie Halper wished, in all modesty and trembling, to take the chance.

There followed days of perfect wholeness, into which hope and activity flowed in ideal proportion. Sue was acting, receiving a nightly potion of applause, which her thirsting heart drank greedily. She would come back to the apartment a stimulated drunk, a courtesan.

Bernie was spending his days at home. He read the play the producer had given him. It was not, to his mind, a good play, but he also knew that a producer doesn't go around asking people their opinions of what he considers a bad play. And it was not a bad play; it was just not a good one. With proper direction it could be made into something.

Bernie paced endless miles from the sink to the windows to the bathroom—an isosceles triangle at the apex of which he finally had his revelation. One character played as a self-perceiving opportunist instead of a Chekhovian failure not only made that character's lines wink with humor but added a wonderful ingredient of exasperation to all the other parts. It only remained to get his ideas on paper and see the producer.

There was no hurry about this. The producer had said he would like to see something in about a month, and Bernie had had the play in his possession for only a week. He checked his impulse to run with both hands full of bright ideas. There might have been some gain in doing this, but he succumbed to a more subtle pleasure.

It seemed now to Bernie that he had never doubted his eventual success. His personal contract with fate permitted much latitude, and at a guess Bernie would have put the date of delivery well beyond his twenty-ninth birthday. His twenty-ninth birthday was only four months away, and fate appeared to be frantically busy with gift wrapping and silver bows. Bernie wanted to pause. He wanted to savor. He wanted time to walk around like a long-barren woman confirmed in her first pregnancy, patronizing the world out of the overflow of her secret wealth.

Sue left their place at ten in the morning. She had her classes at the Academy, which were over by five. She then came home for an early dinner with Bernie before leaving for the theater. This left him the afternoons completely free.

He spent those afternoons roaming around the city. Even the thought that there was less than three hundred dollars between the Halpers and starvation couldn't put him off his tour of euphoria. The days were cloudy and cold, and this, for some reason, was in perfect keeping with his mood of ordainment. He strolled around the Village and looked into stores where he and Sue had mentally tagged items against their day of affluence. He walked into little coffee shops at off hours, delighting in the atmosphere of detachment generated by empty stools and apathetic counter girls. The city was busy, busy—but Bernie Halper would open a book, sit sideways and cross his legs (since there was no one on either side of him), and take a criminally long time over his Dutch apple pie and coffee.

His wanderings took him as far north as the Cloisters and as far south as the Battery. In all his life he had never enjoyed the city as much as he did in those few weeks. It spoke to him of creation and joy, of his name on billboards, of rights he could claim because he was a gifted young man beloved of the gods. Now was the time when he could have clambered up the Queensboro Bridge and taken his magnificent swan dive into all that awaited him.

At four o'clock, wherever he was, he would start back home. He would stop at a market on Third Avenue and buy things for their dinner.

"I won't have you cooking," Sue said.

"How are you going to stop me?" Bernie asked.

"But you *shouldn't!*" she protested. "You have your own work. How are you doing on the play?"

He had given her no inkling of the beautiful silk purse he had fashioned out of a sow's ear. He didn't know exactly when he would reveal it to her, but it would probably be about the time he had exhausted his little affair with Bernie Halper.

"It's a stinker," he told her, "but I've got ideas. . . . I don't know why it is, but my finest inspirations come to me over the stove. My boiling point is about the same as water's."

After Sue left, Bernie would clean up the dishes. He really didn't mind kitchen chores. He performed them with a background of music provided by the tinny little radio Sue had brought with her from Brooklyn. At that hour there was only the soppiest kind of music on the air—neither good jazz nor good swing nor good classical—tearoom tunes, the kind of stuff that could start a forest fire out of a spark of melancholy. But Bernie enjoyed it. It edged his thoughts with a pleasing blankness, like the margins of a printed page. It also created a time stasis for what followed.

Bernie always managed to finish the last of the dishes just as the seven o'clock news broadcast was concluding. He had regulated his tempo to synchronize. At the end of the news broadcast there was a summary of the market activity for the day. Bernie wasn't interested in stocks. He wouldn't have been interested if he'd had thousands of dollars lying around begging for safe investment. But during these days of solitary and delicious communion with his life—present and future—he had discovered a phrase that was a perfect distillation of all he felt. Perfect because it meant nothing and evoked everything· "   Wheat closed higher and cotton was mixed. . . ."

Wheat didn't always close higher, nor was cotton eternally mixed—whatever the devil either meant. There were variations to the formula, but for the sake of keeping his symbol pure Bernie translated every market report into that precise phrase. And when it fell upon his ears Bernie Halper contracted his whole being into one transcendent discharge of love and hope. The million artifacts in the city that had assumed the shape of his dreams, his love for Sue, the long lifetime of good and happy work that lay before him—all these streamed into Bernie from every direction. These and the one ineffable thing no man can describe when he is young, stammers about in his middle years and replaces with sleep when he has grown old. Perhaps it is a secret suspicion of immortality—a narcissism so profound that it finds its reflection in every facet of life, including death.

Bernie didn't get to direct that original play. In fact, he never even had the satisfaction of having his ideas discussed. The producer simply vanished—or he might as well have. He left for California. This was the information Bernie received when he called the number the producer had given him.

"Any idea when he'll be back?" Bernie asked.

"Dunno," was the answer. "Couple of months. Maybe more."

"Is this his home?" Bernie asked.

"No. This is the Consolidated Syndicate."

"The *what?*"

"Con—It's a buying office."

Bernie ultimately met people who knew the producer. He talked to them. They told him that the man was known for his erratic behavior. Yes, he had produced several plays on Broadway, but he was essentially a businessman. His muse was money, and he followed his muse wherever it yelled the loudest. Forget it, they told him.

Bernie naturally didn't forget it. He didn't mind his own loss of time and effort or the man's defection so much as he did the feeling of foolishness he was left with. The warm flow of felicity suddenly froze, and everything was caught in a posture of mockery.

"The city is full of nuts," Sue said by way of consolation.

But she failed to console. She said all the things a man might expect to hear from his wife under the circumstances, but she said them as one who understands rather than feels. The disappointment was not as much hers as his, and this crack of distinction marred the surface of his love.

"Don't take on so," Bernie said to her. "You'll get over it."

"What do you mean by that?" she asked.

"Nothing."

"Well, it's not the end of the world," Sue said, aware of her failure of feeling. "You said yourself it would be idiotic to pin any hopes on a thing like that."

"So I did. So it was. Amen."

"I don't know what you expect me to do."

"Shed one honest tear," Bernie snapped. "Just one of the many you would have shed if something of this sort had happened to you!"

Then Sue did cry, but her tears were not for the right thing.

Bernie went job hunting. He had no negotiable skill outside the theater, and the salaries offered him were ridiculous. He took a job selling a food-freezer plan to housewives and closed three deals the first day. That evening he figured out what the housewife was getting for her money and he didn't show up the next day. He went to see his friend in the Village.

"Look," said his friend, "I can use you, but I can't have you hopping in for a couple of hours a week. Can you give me three or four eight-hour days?"

"Sure," said Bernie.

Things settled down to what is normal for young people who hope to earn their bread in the arts. The bread was earned elsewhere and the arts glittered like stars. They may have been several million light-years away, but in the dark, clear night of longing it seemed as though you had only to reach out your hand to pluck one.

Sue continued with her drama classes during the day and found occasional work as an usher in a Broadway theater in the evening. Bernie became more proficient in leathercraft and his friend allowed him to design some bags of his own, for which he received a percentage when they were sold. His and Sue's combined incomes, however, added up to the kind of financial uncertainty acceptable only to those whose eyes are fixed firmly on the heavens.

If they couldn't have heaven (the particular heaven they sought), they could at least gather together with other apprentice angels and imitate the noises of Paradise. Their friends were people like themselves: young, predatorily ambitious, and chronically separated from their rightful status by a hairbreadth of prejudice. They gathered at one another's cubicles in the city and drank wine or beer while flagellating this senile actress or that cretinous actor. If someone of their acquaintance made good in a Broadway show, they were loud in their acclamation—so loud as to stifle the cries of pain rasping in their throats.

And after these prayer meetings Bernie and Sue would return to their apartment so confirmed in their belief, so absolute in their hunger, that it seemed as if fate could not much longer withstand the pressure. It would succumb merely to get the Halpers off its neck.

On one such night Bernie and Sue lay unspeaking in their dark room, their thoughts privately prating in the silence.

Then Sue whispered, "Bernie . . ."

"Yeah?"

"I didn't know if you were asleep."

"Not even close. What did you want?"

"I'm not a good actress," she said.

"You are."

"I'm not. I know I'm not. I've always known it. What am I going to do? I thought maybe I'd get over it, but it gets worse all the time. There's nothing else I want. . . . Bernie, do you want very much to succeed as a director?"

"I can taste it."

"What would you do for it?"

"I don't get you."

"I mean," said Sue, "supposing you could make a pact with God. You could have success but at a sacrifice—like five years of your life, or someone who means very much to you. . . . You know, something important. Would you do it?"

"I wouldn't sacrifice you, if that's what you mean," Bernie said. "Would you me?"

"No."

"Meaning yes."

"I said no."

"I know you did," said Bernie, "but you were thinking something else. I'll tell you what you were thinking. You were thinking that sleeping with the right guy would be such a small thing compared to what you might get that you wonder how I could possibly make a fuss about it."

Her own unguardedness and Bernie's terrible accuracy left Sue bereft of words.

"Bernie . . ." she said after a moment.

Bernie moved his arm and touched her, not in a caress but adjuringly, as one might put his hand on a child to forestall its panic penitence. "There's a good likelihood neither one of us will amount to a damn in the theater," he said in a voice dry and lifeless enough to be prophetic. "Why ruin everything?"

When Sue became pregnant she was in rehearsals for her first Broadway production. It was a musical.

"You did it on purpose!" she raged and sobbed at Bernie. "You couldn't stand to see me get ahead!"

Bernie caught the fists she tried to use against him between his big hands and held them captive. "Think a minute!" he said beseechingly. "For God's sake, Sue, think a minute! It's no one's fault. And look, no one has to know. For months! There's no chance of your endangering yourself. It's just a walk-on part. . . ."

A walk-on part, and a miracle of percentages. A thousand-to-one shot. The director at that point had simply been looking at faces, and Sue's was one of the faces he chose. There were exactly three speaking lines—forty-two words—and these were to be spoken in chorus with six other girls.

"You can certainly be in rehearsals until the show opens," Bernie said soothingly. "And even if you have to quit afterward, you'll still have the show to your credit."

"And what happens after that?"

"Didn't you expect you'd ever have children?" Bernie asked her.

She didn't answer. There was nothing to say. The question wasn't fair or honest—neither of them had thought of the possibility. There was no more room in their lives for a child than there was for a grand piano in their apartment.

Sue didn't allow herself to dwell on the future. Bernie did. He went to see his father.

The elder Halper scratched the bristles on his cheeks with nails as tough as bears' claws. Three decades of house painting had changed the composition of his flesh. It had the dry, grainy look of sun-baked wood.

"How much'll you need?" Mr. Halper asked.

"I figure I can set up shop for a thousand," Bernie said.

His father nodded. "A thousand I got," he said.

"This is a loan," Bernie said. "I want it made out in regular form. A note."

Mr. Halper nodded again without smiling. "Tomorrow I'll see a lawyer," he said.

With the thousand dollars Bernie went searching for a vacant store in the Village, as far away from his friend's shop as possible. When he found one he signed a year's lease and then set about purchasing the materials of his trade. He knew where to look. He had found out while working for his friend.

The show in which Sue appeared closed after one week. The reviews were awful and the backers pulled out. Sue cried half the night and lay silently awake the other half while Bernie slept. She woke Bernie at six in the morning to tell him they would have to go to the doctor.

Sue stayed in the hospital for several days after her miscarriage. Bernie went every day with a fresh bunch of flowers. He tried to console her for everything—for the show that closed, for the child she didn't want, for the child she didn't have. She listened to him, her remarkable gray eyes ringed with a tired bewilderment.

"Sue, I've started in business for myself," he finally told her. "A leather shop. I borrowed some money from my father."

"Why did you do that?"

"We were going to have a child!"

"What are you going to do with it now?"

"Keep it," said Bernie. "We've got to have something to fall back on."

*   *   *

The jobs Sue found were transient, as though those who employed her understood that she would be a transient too. She was a receptionist, a salesgirl, a poll taker and of course, intermittently, an usher.

There were amateur acting groups all over the city, and Sue was always among them. Sometimes she had a part. Sometimes she sat on a folding chair in a church basement or social hall and listened to other voices resound loudly in the emptiness.

Bernie's workday began at noon. He kept the shop open until ten in the evening on weekdays and eleven on Saturday. At times he wondered if he had given a single thought to the hours this business would entail.

Half the thousand was gone the first month in business, and Bernie saw that he wouldn't make it with the output of his own hands. So he rearranged the store, putting his workshop in the rear and taking in other merchandise he could turn over more quickly. He now sold ceramics and silver jewelry in addition to his leatherwork. It was just another store in the Village, but Bernie was saved from the worst implications by thinking of it as temporary.

At times rebellion seethed in his heart, and he would put out the lights and close the door of the shop. He would walk aimlessly around the streets for an hour, biting seeds of bitterness, telling himself it was impossible, absolutely impossible, to go back and face another desultory customer who fingered a dozen items and walked out with empty hands and a vague smile. But he would finally go back, because not to go back would commit him to something of which he had grown afraid.

"This is ridiculous," he said to Sue. "I must have some time to myself. I see no one. I'm a slave to that damn store."

"Get rid of it," Sue replied.

He looked at her. Her style as a woman had come to full flower. She had put on some flesh, just enough to bring to perfection her gray-eyed voluptuousness. . . . My Russian princess, Bernie thought to himself, limp with helplessness and dread.

"I'll close the store at seven two nights a week," he said. "The hell with it. Let's see some people."

So they began to invite people to their apartment again. Since they had more money now, they served liquor and elaborate spreads of food. The people who came were something like themselves, but not exactly. They were a little younger, a great deal more certain of their future. But the excitement generated by these evenings was almost the same.

Bernie would watch Sue at these parties. He saw with a sick heart the encroachment of mannerisms he knew too well. The extravagant gesture, the elocutionary speech, the whole synthetic bag of tricks of the would-be actress who hadn't made it and never would. He watched these things as a man might observe the symptoms of a fatal disease, and he felt a searing pity for his pretty, afflicted darling.

When one such evening had come to an end, and they had cleaned up the mess and mounted the fan on a window sill to exhaust the fumes, Bernie turned to see Sue standing in the center of the room, her beautiful arms lifted as she slowly removed the pins from her hair. Her eyes met his, and in that instant before she spoke, Bernie made out his life.

He saw this room and all the rooms they would eventually occupy. He saw the store, every item in it, and the small segment of sky vouchsafed from the window. He could hear the eternal seven o'clock news broadcast telling of trouble and the fact that wheat closed higher and cotton was mixed. But the words evoked nothing, because he had pinched off the nerve that fed illusion.

"Bernie . . ." Sue said.

"Yes."

"Tell me the truth. . . ."

Then Bernie went to her, kissed her, and carefully chose the words he would have to go on saying.

ANTON CHEKHOV

The Chemist's Wife

The little town of B———, consisting of two or three crooked streets, was sound asleep. There was a complete stillness in the motionless air. Nothing could be heard but far away, outside the town no doubt, the barking of a dog in a thin, hoarse tenor. It was close upon daybreak.

Everything had long been asleep. The only person not asleep was the young wife of Tchernomordik, a qualified dispenser who kept a chemist's shop at B———. She had gone to bed and got up again three times, but could not sleep, she did not know why. She sat at the open window in her nightdress and looked into the street. She felt bored, depressed, vexed . . . so vexed that she felt quite inclined to cry—again she did not know why. There seemed to be a lump in her chest that kept rising into her throat. . . . A few paces behind her Tchernomordik lay curled up close to the wall, snoring sweetly. A greedy flea was stabbing the bridge of his nose, but he did not feel it, and was positively smiling, for he was dreaming that everyone in the town had a cough, and was buying from him the King of Denmark's cough-drops. He could not have been wakened now by pinpricks or by cannon or by caresses.

The chemist's shop was almost at the extreme end of the town, so that the chemist's wife could see far into the fields. She could see the eastern horizon growing pale by degrees, then turning crimson as though from a great fire. A big broad-faced moon peeped out unexpectedly from behind bushes in the distance. It was red (as a rule when the moon emerges from behind bushes it appears to be blushing).

Suddenly in the stillness of the night there came the sounds of footsteps and a jingle of spurs. She could hear voices.

"That must be the officers going home to the camp from the Police Captain's," thought the chemist's wife.

Soon afterwards two figures wearing officers' white tunics came into sight: one big and tall, the other thinner and shorter. . . . They slouched along by the fence, dragging one leg after the other and talking loudly together. As they passed the chemist's shop, they walked more slowly than ever, and glanced up at the windows.

"It smells like a chemist's," said the thin one. "And so it is! Ah, I remember. . . . I came here last week to buy some castor-oil. There's a chemist here with a sour face and the jawbone of an ass! Such a jawbone, my dear fellow! It must have been a jawbone like that that Samson killed the Philistines with."

"M'yes," said the big one in a bass voice. "The pharmacist is asleep. And his wife is asleep too. She is a pretty woman, Obtyosov."

"I saw her. I liked her very much. . . . Tell me, doctor, can she possibly love that jawbone of an ass? Can she?"

"No, most likely she does not love him," sighed the doctor, speaking as though he were sorry for the chemist. "The little woman is asleep behind the window, Obtyosov, what? Tossing with the heat, her little mouth half open . . . and one little foot hanging out of bed. I bet that fool the chemist doesn't realize what a lucky fellow he is. . . . No doubt he sees no difference between a woman and a bottle of carbolic!"

"I say, doctor," said the officer, stopping. "Let us go into the shop and buy something. Perhaps we shall see her."

"What an idea—in the night!"

"What of it? They are obliged to serve one even at night. My dear fellow, let us go in!"

"If you like. . . ."

The chemist's wife, hiding behind the curtain, heard a muffled ring. Looking round at her husband, who was smiling and snoring sweetly as before, she threw on her dress, slid her bare feet into her slippers, and ran to the shop.

On the other side of the glass door she could see two shadows. The chemist's wife turned up the lamp and hurried to the door to open it, and now she felt neither vexed nor bored nor inclined to cry, though her heart was thumping. The big doctor and the slender Obtyosov walked in. Now she could get a view of them. The doctor was corpulent and swarthy; he wore a beard and was slow in his movements. At the slightest motion his tunic seemed as though it would crack, and perspiration came on to his face. The officer was rosy, clean-shaven, feminine-looking, and as supple as an English whip.

"What may I give you?" asked the chemist's wife, holding her dress across her bosom.

"Give us . . . er—er . . . four pennyworth of peppermint lozenges!"

Without haste the chemist's wife took down a jar from a shelf and began weighing out lozenges. The customers stared fixedly at her back; the doctor screwed up his eyes like a well-fed cat, while the lieutenant was very grave.

"It's the first time I've seen a lady serving in a chemist's shop," observed the doctor.

"There's nothing out of the way in it," replied the chemist's wife, looking out of the corner of her eye at the rosy-cheeked officer. "My husband has no assistant, and I always help him."

"To be sure. . . . You have a charming little shop! What a number of different . . . jars! And you are not afraid of moving about among the poisons? Brrr!"

The chemist's wife sealed up the parcel and handed it to the doctor. Obtyosov gave her the money. Half a minute of silence followed. . . . The men exchanged glances, took a step towards the door, then looked at one another again.

"Will you give me two pennyworth of soda?" said the doctor.

Again the chemist's wife slowly and languidly raised her hand to the shelf.

"Haven't you in the shop anything . . . such as . . ." muttered Obtyosov, moving his fingers, "something, so to say, allegorical . . . revivifying . . . seltzer-water, for instance? Have you any seltzer--water?"

"Yes," answered the chemist's wife.

"Bravo! You're a fairy, not a woman! Get us three bottles!"

The chemist's wife hurriedly sealed up the soda and vanished through the door into the darkness.

"A peach!" said the doctor, with a wink. "You wouldn't find a pineapple like that in the island of Madeira! Eh? What do you say? Do you hear the snoring, though? That's his worship the chemist enjoying sweet repose."

A minute later the chemist's wife came back and set five bottles on the counter. She had just been in the cellar, and so was flushed and rather excited.

"Sh-sh! . . . quietly!" said Obtyosov when, after uncocking the bottles, she dropped the corkscrew. "Don't make such a noise; you'll wake your husband."

"Well, what if I do wake him?"

"He is sleeping so sweetly . . . he must be dreaming of you. . . . To your health!"

"Besides," boomed the doctor, hiccupping after the seltzer-water, "husbands are such a dull business that it would be very nice of them to be always asleep. How good a drop of red wine would be in this water!"

"What an idea!" laughed the chemist's wife.

"That would be splendid. What a pity they don't sell spirits in chemist's shops! Though you ought to sell wine as a medicine. Have you any *vinum gallicum rubrum?*"

"Yes."

"Well, then, give us some! Bring it here, damn it!"

"How much do you want?"

"*Quantum satis.* . . . Give us an ounce each in the water, and afterwards we'll see. . . . Obtyosov, what do you say? First with water and afterwards *per se.* . . ."

The doctor and Obtyosov sat down to the counter, took off their caps, and began drinking the wine.

"The wine, one must admit, is wretched stuff! *Vinum nastissimum!* Though in the presence of . . . er . . . it tastes like nectar. You are enchanting, madam! In imagination I kiss your hand."

"I would give a great deal to do so not in imagination," said Obtyosov. "On my honour, I'd give my life."

"That's enough," said Madame Tchernomordik, flushing and assuming a serious expression.

"What a flirt you are, though!" the doctor laughed softly, looking slyly at her from under his brows. "Your eyes seem to be firing shot: piff-paff! I congratulate you: you've conquered! We are vanquished!"

The chemist's wife looked at their ruddy faces, listened to their chatter, and soon she, too, grew quite lively. Oh, she felt so gay! She entered into the conversation, she laughed, flirted, and even, after repeated requests from the customers, drank two ounces of the wine.

"You officers ought to come in oftener from the camp," she said; "it's awful how dreary it is here. I'm simply dying of it."

"I should think so!" said the doctor indignantly. "Such a peach, a miracle of nature, thrown away in the wilds! How well Griboyedov said, 'Into the wilds, to Saratov'! It's time for us to be off, though. Delighted to have made your acquaintance . . . very. How much do we owe you?"

The chemist's wife raised her eyes to the ceiling and her lips moved for some time.

"Twelve roubles forty-eight kopecks," she said.

Obtyosov took out of his pocket a fat pocketbook, and after fumbling for some time among the notes, paid.

"Your husband's sleeping sweetly . . . he must be dreaming,"
he muttered, pressing her hand at parting.

"I don't like to hear silly remarks. . . ."

"What silly remarks? On the contrary, it's not silly at all . . .
even Shakespeare said: 'Happy is he who in his youth is young.' "

"Let go of my hand."

At last after much talk and after kissing the lady's hand at
parting, the customers went out of the shop irresolutely, as
though they were wondering whether they had not forgotten
something.

She ran quickly into the bedroom and sat down in the same
place. She saw the doctor and the officer, on coming out of the
shop, walk lazily away a distance of twenty paces; then they
stopped and began whispering together. What about? Her heart
throbbed, there was a pulsing in her temples, and why she did
not know. . . . Her heart beat violently as though those two
whispering outside were deciding her fate.

Five minutes later the doctor parted from Obtyosov and
walked on, while Obtyosov came back. He walked past the shop
once and a second time. . . . He would stop near the door and
then take a few steps again. At last the bell tinkled discreetly.

"What? Who is there?" the chemist's wife heard her husband's voice suddenly. "There's a ring at the bell, and you don't
hear it," he said severely. "Is that the way to do things?"

He got up, put on his dressing-gown, and staggering, half
asleep, flopped in his slippers to the shop.

"What . . . is it?" he asked Obtyosov.

"Give me . . . give me four pennyworth of peppermint
lozenges."

Sniffing continually, yawning, dropping asleep as he moved,
and knocking his knees against the counter, the chemist went to
the shelf and reached down the jar.

Two minutes later the chemist's wife saw Obtyosov go out
of the shop, and, after he had gone some steps, she saw him
throw the packet of peppermints on the dusty road. The doctor

came from behind a corner to meet him. . . . They met and, gesticulating, vanished in the morning mist.

"How unhappy I am!" said the chemist's wife, looking angrily at her husband, who was undressing quickly to get into bed again. "Oh, how unhappy I am!" she repeated, suddenly melting into bitter tears. "And nobody knows, nobody knows. . . ."

"I forgot fourpence on the counter," muttered the chemist, pulling the quilt over him. "Put it away in the till, please. . . ."

And at once he fell asleep again.

JOHN UPDIKE

Wife-wooing

Oh my love. Yes. Here we sit, on warm broad floorboards, before a fire, the children between us, in a crescent, eating. The
girl and I share one half-pint of French-fried potatoes; you and
the boy share another; and in the center, sharing nothing, making
simple reflections within himself like a jewel, the baby, mounted
in an Easybaby, sucks at his bottle with frowning mastery, his
selfish, contemplative eyes stealing glitter from the center of the
flames. And you. You. You allow your skirt, the same black skirt
in which this morning you with woman's soft bravery mounted
a bicycle and sallied forth to play hymns in difficult keys on the
Sunday school's old piano—you allow this black skirt to slide off
your raised knees down your thighs, slide *up* your thighs in your
body's absolute geography, so the parallel whiteness of their
undersides is exposed to the fire's warmth and to my sight. Oh.
There is a line of Joyce. I try to recover it from the legendary,
imperfectly explored grottoes of *Ulysses:* a garter snapped, to
please Blazes Boylan, in a deep Dublin den. What? Smackwarm.
That was the crucial word. Smacked smackwarm on her smack-
able warm woman's thigh. Something like that. A splendid man,
to feel that. Smackwarm woman's. Splendid also to feel the curious and potent, inexplicable and irrefutably magical life language leads within itself. What soul took thought and knew that

adding "wo" to man would make a woman? The difference exactly. The wide w, the receptive o. Womb. In our crescent the children for all their size seem to come out of you toward me, wet fingers and eyes, tinted bronze. Three children, five persons, seven years. Seven years since I wed wide warm woman, whitethighed. Wooed and wed. Wife. A knife of a word that for all its final bite did not end the wooing. To my wonderment.

We eat meat, meat I wrested warm from the raw hands of the hamburger girl in the diner a mile away, a ferocious place, slick with savagery, wild with chrome; young predators snarling dirty jokes menaced me, old men reached for me with coffee-warmed paws; I wielded my wallet, and won my way back. The fat brown bag of buns was warm beside me in the cold car; the smaller bag holding the two tiny cartons of French-fries emitted an even more urgent heat. Back through the black winter air to the fire, the intimate cave, where halloos and hurrahs greeted me, the deer, mouth agape and its cotton throat gushing, stretched dead across my shoulders. And now you, beside the white O of the plate upon which the children discarded with squeals of disgust the rings of translucent onion that came squeezed in the hamburgers—you push your toes an inch closer to the blaze, and the ashy white of the inside of your deep thigh is lazily laid bare, and the eternally elastic garter snaps smackwarm against my hidden heart.

Who would have thought, wide wife, back there in the white tremble of the ceremony (in the corner of my eye I held, despite the distracting hail of ominous vows, the vibration of the cluster of stephanotis clutched against your waist), that seven years would bring us no distance, through all those warm beds, to the same trembling point, of beginning? The cells change every seven years, and down in the atom, apparently, there is a strange discontinuity; as if God wills the universe anew every instant. (Ah God, dear God, tall friend of my childhood, I will never forget you, though they say dreadful things. They say rose windows in cathedrals are vaginal symbols.) Your legs, exposed as fully as by a bathing suit, yearn deeper into the amber wash of heat. Well: begin. A green jet of flame spits out sideways from a pocket of resin in a log, crying, and the orange shadows on the ceiling sway with fresh life. Begin.

"Remember, on our honeymoon, how the top of the kerosene heater made a great big rose window on the ceiling?"

"Vnn." Your chin goes to your knees, your shins draw in, all is retracted. Not much to remember, perhaps, for you; blood badly spilled, clumsiness of all sorts. "It was cold for June."

"Mommy, what was cold? What did you say?" the girl asks, enunciating angrily, determined not to let language slip on her tongue and tumble her so that we laugh.

"A house where Daddy and I stayed one time."

"I don't like dat," the boy says, and throws a half bun painted with chartreuse mustard onto the floor.

You pick it up and with beautiful sombre musing ask, "Isn't that funny? Did any of the others have mustard on them?"

"I *hate* dat," the boy insists; he is two. Language is to him thick vague handles swirling by; he grabs what he can.

"Here. He can have mine. Give me his." I pass my hamburger over, you take it, he takes it from you, there is nowhere a ripple of gratitude. There is no more praise of my heroism in fetching Sunday supper, saving you labor. Cunning, you sense, and sense that I sense your knowledge, that I had hoped to hoard your energy toward a more ecstatic spending. We sense everything between us, every ripple, existent and nonexistent; it is tiring. Courting a wife takes tenfold the strength of winning an ignorant girl. The fire shifts, shattering fragments of newspaper that carry in lighter gray the ghost of the ink of their message. You huddle your legs and bring the skirt back over them. With a sizzling noise like the sighs of the exhausted logs, the baby sucks the last from his bottle, drops it to the floor with its distasteful hoax of vacant suds, and begins to cry. His egotist's mouth opens; the delicate membrane of his satisfaction tears. You pick him up and stand. You love the baby more than me.

Who would have thought, blood once spilled, that no barrier

would be broken, that you would be each time healed into a
virgin again? Tall, fair, obscure, remote, and courteous.

We put the children to bed, one by one, in reverse order of
birth. I am limitlessly patient, paternal, good. Yet you know.
We watch the paper bags and cartons ignite on the breathing
pillow of embers, read, watch television, eat crackers, it does not
matter. Eleven comes. For a tingling moment you stand on the
bedroom rug in your underpants, untangling your nightie; oh,
fat white sweet fat fatness. In bed you read. About Richard
Nixon. He fascinates you; you hate him. You know how he defeated Jerry Voorhis, martyred Mrs. Douglas, how he played
poker in the Navy despite being a Quaker, every fiendish trick,
every low adaptation. Oh my Lord. Let's let the poor man go to
bed. We're none of us perfect. "Hey let's turn out the light."

"Wait. He's just about to get Hiss convicted. It's very
strange. It says he acted honorably."

"I'm sure he did." I reach for the switch.

"No. Wait. Just till I finish this chapter. I'm sure there'll be
something at the end."

"Honey, Hiss was guilty. We're all guilty. Conceived in con-
cupiscence, we die unrepentant." Once my ornate words wooed
you.

I lie against your filmy convex back. You read sideways, a
sleepy trick. I see the page through the fringe of your hair, sharp
and white as a wedge of crystal. Suddenly it slips. The book has
slipped from your hand. You are asleep. Oh cunning trick, cunning. In the darkness I consider. Cunning. The headlights of cars
accidentally slide fanning slits of light around our walls and
ceiling. The great rose window was projected upward through
the petal-shaped perforations in the top of the black kerosene
stove, which we stood in the center of the floor. As the flame on
the circular wick flickered, the wide soft star of interlocked
penumbrae moved and waved as if it were printed on a silk cloth
being gently tugged or slowly blown. Its color soft blurred
blood. We pay dear in blood for our peaceful homes.

In the morning, to my relief, you are ugly. Monday's wan breakfast light bleaches you blotchily, drains the goodness from your thickness, makes the bathrode a limp stained tube flapping disconsolately, exposing sallow decolletage. The skin between your breasts a sad yellow. I feast with the coffee on your drabness. Every wrinkle and sickly tint a relief and a revenge. The children yammer. The toaster sticks. Seven years have worn this woman.

The man, he arrows off to work, jousting for right-of-way, veering on the thin hard edge of the legal speed limit. Out of domestic muddle, softness, pallor, flaccidity: into the city. Stone is his province. The winning of coin. The maneuvering of abstractions. Making heartless things run. Oh the inanimate, adamant joys of job!

I return with my head enmeshed in a machine. A technicality it would take weeks to explain to you snags my brain; I fiddle with phrases and numbers all the blind evening. You serve me supper as a waitress—as less than a waitress, for I have known you. The children touch me timidly, as they would a steep girder bolted into a framework whose height they don't understand. They drift into sleep securely. We survive their passing in calm parallelity. My thoughts rework in chronic right angles the same snagging circuits on the same professional grid. You rustle the book about Nixon; vanish upstairs into the plumbing; the bathtub pipes cry. In my head I seem to have found the stuck switch at last: I push at it; it jams; I push; it is jammed. I grow dizzy, churning with cigarettes. I circle the room aimlessly.

So I am taken by surprise at a turning when at the meaningful hour of ten you come with a kiss of toothpaste to me moist and girlish and quick; the momentous moral of this story being, An expected gift is not worth giving.

EXCERPT FROM

The Song
of Songs

How beautiful you are, how pleasing, my love, my delight!
Your very figure is like a palm tree, your breasts are like clusters.
I said: I will climb the palm tree, I will take hold of its branches.
Now let your breasts be like clusters of the vine and the fra-
grance of your breath like apples, and your mouth like an excellent wine that flows smoothly for my lover, spreading over the
lips and the teeth. I belong to my lover and for me he yearns.
Come, my lover, let us go forth to the fields and spend the night
among the villages. Let us go early to the vineyards, and see if
the vines are in bloom, if the buds have opened, if the pomegran-
ates have blossomed; there will I give you my love.

JOHN UPDIKE

Ace in the Hole

The moment his car touched the boulevard heading home, Ace
flicked on the radio. He needed the radio, especially today. In
the seconds before the tubes warmed up, he said aloud, doing it
just to hear a human voice, "Jesus. She'll pop her lid." His voice,
though familiar, irked him; it sounded thin and scratchy, as if
the bones in his head were picking up static. In a deeper register
Ace added, "She'll murder me." Then the radio came on, warm
and strong, so he stopped worrying. The Five Kings were doing
"Blueberry Hill"; to hear them made Ace feel so sure inside that
from the pack pinched between the car roof and the sun shield
he plucked a cigarette, hung it on his lower lip, snapped a match
across the rusty place on the dash, held the flame in the instinc-
tive spot near the tip of his nose, dragged, and blew out the
match, all in time to the music. He rolled down the window and
snapped the match so it spun end over end into the gutter. "Two
points," he said, and cocked the cigarette toward the roof of the
car, sucked powerfully, and exhaled two plumes through his
nostrils. He was beginning to feel like himself, Ace Anderson,
for the first time that whole day, a bad day. He beat time on the
accelerator. The car jerked crazily. "On Blueberry Hill," he
sang, "my heart stood still. The wind in the wil-low tree"—he
braked for a red light—"played love's suh-*weet* melodee—"

"Go, Dad, bust your lungs!" a kid's voice blared. The kid was riding in a '52 Pontiac that had pulled up beside Ace at the light. The profile of the driver, another kid, was dark over his shoulder.

Ace looked over at him and smiled slowly, just letting one side of his mouth lift a little. "Ram it," he said, good-naturedly. It was only a couple of years since he had been their age.

But the kid, who looked Greek, lifted his thick upper lip and spat out the window. The spit gleamed on the asphalt like a half-dollar.

"Now isn't that pretty?" Ace said, keeping one eye on the light. "You miserable wop. You are *mis*erable." While the kid was trying to think of some smart comeback, the light changed. Ace dug out so hard he smelled burned rubber. In his rear-view mirror he saw the Pontiac lurch forward a few yards, then stop dead, right in the middle of the intersection.

The idea of them stalling their fat tin Pontiac kept him in a good humor all the way home. He decided to stop at his mother's place and pick up the baby, instead of waiting for Evey to do it. His mother must have seen him drive up. She came out on the porch holding a plastic spoon and smelling of cake.

"You're out early," she told him.

"Friedman fired me," Ace told her.

"Good for you," his mother said. "I always said he never treated you right." She brought a cigarette out of her apron pocket and tucked it deep into one corner of her mouth, the way she did when something pleased her.

Ace lighted it for her. "Friedman was O.K. personally," he said. "He just wanted too much for his money. I didn't mind working Saturdays, but until eleven, twelve Friday nights was too much. Everybody has a right to some leisure."

"Well, I don't dare think what Evey will say, but I, for one, thank dear God you had the brains to get out of it. I always said that job had no future to it—no future of any kind, Freddy."

"I guess," Ace admitted. "But I wanted to keep at it, for the family's sake."

"Now, I know I shouldn't be saying this, but any time Evey —this is just between us—any time Evey thinks she can do better, there's room for you *and* Bonnie right in your father's house." She pinched her lips together. He could almost hear the old lady think, There, I've said it.

"Look, Mom, Evey tries awfully hard, and anyway you know she can't work that way. Not that *that*—I mean, she's a realist, too . . ." He let the rest of the thought fade as he watched a kid across the street dribbling a basketball around a telephone pole that had a backboard and net nailed on it.

"Evey's a wonderful girl of her own kind. But I've always said, and your father agrees, Roman Catholics ought to marry among themselves. Now I know I've said it before, but when they get out in the greater world—"

"*No*, Mom."

She frowned, smoothed herself, and said, "Your name was in the paper today."

Ace chose to let that go by. He kept watching the kid with the basketball. It was funny how, though the whole point was to get the ball up into the air, kids grabbed it by the sides and squeezed. Kids just didn't think.

"Did you hear?" his mother asked.

"Sure, but so what?" Ace said. His mother's lower lip was coming at him, so he changed the subject. "I guess I'll take Bonnie."

His mother went into the house and brought back his daughter, wrapped in a blue blanket. The baby looked dopey. "She fussed all day," his mother complained. "I said to your father, 'Bonnie is a dear little girl, but without a doubt she's her mother's daughter.' You were the best-natured boy."

"Well I *had* everything," Ace said with impatience. His mother blinked like an owl. He nicely dropped his cigarette into a brown flowerpot on the edge of the porch and took his daughter into his arms. She was getting heavier, solid. When he reached the end of the cement walk, his mother was still on the porch, waving to him. He was so close he could see the fat around her elbow jiggle, and he only lived a half block up the street, yet here she was, waving to him as if he was going to Japan.

At the door of his car, it seemed stupid to him to drive the measly half block home. "Never ride where you can walk," Coach Behn used to tell his boys. Ace left the ignition keys in his pocket and ran along the pavement with Bonnie laughing and bouncing at his chest. He slammed the door of his land-lady's house open and shut, pounded up the two flights of stairs, and was panting so hard when he reached the door of his apart-ment that it took him a couple of seconds to fit the key into the lock.

The run must have tuned Bonnie up. As soon as he lowered her into the crib, she began to shout and wave her arms. He didn't want to play with her. He tossed some blocks and a rattle into the crib and walked into the bathroom, where he turned on the hot water and began to comb his hair. Holding the comb under the faucet before every stroke, he combed his hair for-ward. It was so long, one strand curled under his nose and touched his lips. He whipped the whole mass back with a single pull. He tucked in the tufts around his ears, and ran the comb straight back on both sides of his head. With his fingers he felt for the little ridge at the back where the two sides met. It was there, as it should have been. Finally, he mussed the hair in front enough for one little lock to droop over his forehead, like Alan Ladd. It made the temple seem lower than it was. Every day, his hairline looked higher. He had observed all around him how blond men went bald first. He remembered reading somewhere, though, that baldness shows virility.

On his way to the kitchen he flipped the left-hand knob of the television. Bonnie was always quieter with the set on. Ace didn't see how she could understand much of it, but it seemed to mean something to her. He found a can of beer in the refrig-erator behind some brownish lettuce and those hot dogs Evey never got around to cooking. She'd be home any time. The clock said 5:12. She'd pop her lid.

Ace didn't see what he could do but try and reason with her. "Evey," he'd say, "you ought to thank God I got out of it. It had no future to it at all." He hoped she wouldn't get too mad, because when she was mad he wondered if he should have married her, and doubting that made him feel crowded. It was bad enough, his mother always crowding him. He punched the two triangles in the top of the beer can, the little triangle first, and then the big one, the one he drank from. He hoped Evey wouldn't say anything that couldn't be forgotten. What women didn't seem to realize was that there were things you knew but shouldn't say.

He felt sorry he had called the kid in the car a wop.

Ace balanced the beer on a corner where two rails of the crib met and looked under the chairs for the morning paper. He had trouble finding his name, because it was at the bottom of a column on an inside sports page, in a small article about the county basketball statistics:

> "Dusty" Tremwick, Grosvenor Park's sure-fingered center, copped the individual scoring honors with a season's grand (and we do mean grand) total of 376 points. This is within eighteen points of the all-time record of 394 racked up in the 1949–1950 season by Olinger High's Fred Anderson.

Ace angrily sailed the paper into an armchair. Now it was Fred Anderson; it used to be Ace. He hated being called Fred, especially in print, but then the sportswriters were all office boys anyway, Behn used to say.

"Do not just ask for shoe polish," a man on television said, "but ask for *Emu Shoe Gloss,* the *only* polish that absolutely *guarantees* to make your shoes look shinier than new." Ace turned the sound off, so that the man moved his mouth like a fish blowing bubbles. Right away, Bonnie howled, so Ace turned it up loud enough to drown her out and went into the kitchen, without knowing what he wanted there. He wasn't hungry; his stomach was tight. It used to be like that when he walked to the gymnasium alone in the dark before a game and could see the people from town, kids and parents, crowding in at the lighted doors. But once he was inside, the locker room would be bright and hot, and the other guys would be there, laughing and towel-slapping, and the tight feeling would leave. Now there were whole days when it didn't leave.

A key scratched at the door lock. Ace decided to stay in the kitchen. Let *her* find *him*. Her heels clicked on the floor for a step or two; then the television set went off. Bonnie began to cry. "Shut up, honey," Evey said. There was a silence.

"I'm home," Ace called.

"No kidding. I thought Bonnie got the beer by herself."

Ace laughed. She was in a sarcastic mood, thinking she was Lauren Bacall. That was all right, just so she kept funny. Still smiling, Ace eased into the living room and got hit with, "What are *you* smirking about? Another question: What's the idea running up the street with Bonnie like she was a football?"

"You saw that?"

"Your mother told me."

"You saw her?"

"Of course I saw her. I dropped by to pick up Bonnie. What the hell do you think?—I read her tiny mind?"

"Take it easy," Ace said, wondering if Mom had told her about Friedman.

"Take it easy? Don't coach *me*. Another question: Why's the car out in front of her place? You give the car to her?"

"Look, I parked it there to pick up Bonnie, and I thought I'd leave it there."

"Why?"

"What do you mean, why? I just did. I just thought I'd walk. It's not that far, you know."

"No, I don't know. If you'd be on your feet all day a block would look like one hell of a long way."

"Okay. I'm sorry."

She hung up her coat and stepped out of her shoes and walked around the room picking up things. She stuck the newspaper in the wastebasket.

Ace said, "My name was in the paper today."

"They spell it right?" She shoved the paper deep into the basket with her foot. There was no doubt; she knew about Friedman.

"They called me Fred."

"Isn't that your name? What *is* your name anyway? Hero J. Great?"

There wasn't any answer, so Ace didn't try any. He sat down on the sofa, lighted a cigarette, and waited.

Evey picked up Bonnie. "Poor thing stinks. What does your mother do, scrub out the toilet with her?"

"Can't you take it easy? I know you're tired."

"You should. I'm always tired."

Evey and Bonnie went into the bathroom; when they came out, Bonnie was clean and Evey was calm. Evey sat down in an easy chair beside Ace and rested her stocking feet on his knees. "Hit me," she said, twiddling her fingers for the cigarette.

The baby crawled up to her chair and tried to stand, to see what he gave her. Leaning over close to Bonnie's nose, Evey grinned, smoke leaking through her teeth, and said, "Only for grownups, honey."

"Eve," Ace began, "there was no future in that job. Working all Saturday, and then Friday nights on top of it."

"I know. Your mother told *me* all that, too. All I want from you is what happened."

She was going to take it like a sport, then. He tried to remember how it *did* happen. "It wasn't my fault," he said. "Friedman told me to back this '51 Chevvy into the line that faces Church Street. He just bought it from an old guy this morning who said it only had thirteen thousand on it. So in I jump and start her up. There was a knock in the engine like a machine gun. I almost told Friedman he'd bought a squirrel, but you know I cut that smart stuff out ever since Palotta laid me off."

"You told me that story. What happens in this one?"

"Look, Eve. I *am* telling ya. Do you want me to go out to a movie or something?"

"Suit yourself."

"So I jump in the Chevvy and snap it back in line, and there was a kind of scrape and thump. I get out and look and Friedman's running over, his arms going like *this*"—Ace whirled his own arms and laughed—"and here was the whole back fender of a '49 Merc mashed in. Just looked like somebody took a planer and shaved off the bulge, you know, there at the back." He tried to show her with his hands. "The Chevvy, though, didn't have a dent. It even gained some paint. But *Friedman*, to *hear* him—Boy, they can rave when their pocketbook's hit. He said"—Ace laughed again—"never mind."

Evey said, "You're proud of yourself."

"No, listen. I'm not happy about it. But there wasn't a thing I could *do*. It wasn't my driving at all. I looked over on the other side, and there was just two or three inches between the Chevvy and a Buick. *Nobody* could have gotten into that hole. Even if it had hair on it." He thought this was pretty good.

She didn't. "You could have looked."

"There just wasn't the *space*. Friedman said stick it in; I stuck it in."

"But you could have looked and moved the other cars to make more room."

"I guess that would have been the smart thing."

"I guess, too. Now what?"

"What do you mean?"

"I mean now what? Are you going to give up? Go back to the Army? Your mother? Be a basketball pro? What?"

"You know I'm not tall enough. Anybody under six-six they don't want."

"Is that so? Six-six? Well, please listen to this, Mr. Six-Foot-Five-and-a-Half: I'm fed up. I'm ready as Christ to let you run." She stabbed her cigarette into an ashtray on the arm of the chair so hard the ashtray jumped to the floor. Evey flushed and shut up.

What Ace hated most in their arguments was these silences after Evey had said something so ugly she wanted to take it back. "Better ask the priest first," he murmured.

She sat right up. "If there's one thing I don't want to hear about from you it's priests. You let the priests to me. You don't know a damn thing about it. Not a damn thing."

"Hey, look at Bonnie," he said, trying to make his tone easy.

Evey didn't hear him. "If you think," she went on, "if for one rotten moment you think, Mr. Fred, that the be-all and end-all of my life is you and your hot-shot stunts—"

"Look, Mother," Ace pleaded, pointing at Bonnie. The baby had picked up the ashtray and put it on her head for a hat.

Evey glanced down angrily. "Cute," she said. "Cute as her daddy."

The ashtray slid from Bonnie's head and she groped after it.

"Yeah, but watch," Ace said. "Watch her hands. They're sure."

"You're nuts," Evey said.

"No, honest. Bonnie's great. She's a natural. Get the rattle for her. Never mind, I'll get it." In two steps, Ace was at Bonnie's crib, picking the rattle out of the mess of blocks and plastic rings and beanbags. He extended the rattle toward his daughter, shaking it delicately. Made wary by this burst of attention, Bonnie reached with both hands; like two separate animals they approached from opposite sides and touched the smooth rattle simultaneously. A smile worked up on her face. Ace tugged weakly. She held on, and then tugged back. "She's a natural," Ace said, "and it won't do her any good because she's a girl. Baby, we got to have a boy."

"I'm not your baby," Evey said, closing her eyes.

Saying "Baby" over and over again, Ace backed up to the radio and, without turning around, manipulated the volume knob. In the moment before the tubes warmed up, Evey had time to say, "Wise up, Freddy. What shall we do?"

The radio came in on something slow: dinner music. Ace

picked Bonnie up and set her in the crib. "Shall we dance?" he asked his wife, bowing.

"I want to talk."

"Baby. It's the cocktail hour."

"This is getting us no place," she said, rising from her chair, though.

"Fred Junior. I can see him now," he said, seeing nothing.

"We will have no Juniors."

In her crib, Bonnie whimpered at the sight of her mother being seized. Ace fitted his hand into the natural place on Evey's back and she shuffled stiffly into his lead. When, with a sudden injection of saxophones, the tempo quickened, he spun her out carefully, keeping the beat with his shoulders. Her hair brushed his lips as she minced in, then swung away, to the end of his arm; he could feel her toes dig into the carpet. He flipped his own hair back from his eyes. The music ate through his skin and mixed with the nerves and small veins; he seemed to be great again, and all the other kids were around them, in a ring, clapping time.

RUTH SUCKOW

Golden Wedding

You ought to change your clothes, pa."

"What you in such a hurry to get my clothes changed for?"

"Well, you want to be ready when George comes in, don't you?"

"Aw, he won't get in today. How can he get the car through all this snow?"

"He will, too. Didn't they invite us out there?"

"Yeah, but they didn't know it was goin' tuh snow like this."

"You go now and put your other clothes on."

He grumbled, but finally obeyed—which was just like him.

Yes, but why did he always have to act this way? He had been doing it ever since they were married. He went through just so much grumbling first before he would do anything that he knew he must. It was the same thing over again every time they went anywhere; and all her prodding hadn't done any good that she could see.

"Won't get in today." That was just like him, too. If he knew that she was counting on anything, he had to hold out and belittle it, raise objections. He never wanted to admit that anything was going to turn out right. He always had good arguments to oppose to her faith, which he declared didn't take any account of the facts. But she still held to this blind faith of hers, and he to his objections. Sometimes things worked out her way; sometimes his. She pulling ahead, he pulling back. But the pulling had amounted to this much in fifty years—that he usually gave in in the end; and that she was a little worried in spite of her hopeful assertions that things were going to justify her belief.

So that now she did have to admit to herself that it was snowing hard. She was sure that George would come . . . but her eyes screwed up anxiously as she looked out over the plants at air thick with misty flakes. It looked as if it wasn't going to stop all day. The covered plants and peony-bushes just outside were big clumps of whiteness. Fine dark twigs stuck out from the snow humped over the bending raspberry-bushes. When she peered down the street, she could barely see the willow-trees at the farther end, bluish and dim. Few passers-by came down this little side street where the old Willeys lived. The glimmery softness of the white road showed only two crooked tracks from a morning milk-wagon that were already nearly filled, and as white as all the rest of the world.

Just the same, she believed that George was going to get in somehow.

Mr. Willey came back into the room.

She looked up sharply, and cried in despair: "Oh, pa, why did you have to go put on that old necktie?"

"What old necktie?"

"Oh, you know what I mean! That old thing that I should think you'd be ashamed to wear around the place any more, let alone where we're going today. Go and put on your nice one—the one Jenny sent you for Christmas."

"Whatta I wanta put that on fur! To ride out in the snow?"

"Snow!" she scoffed. "How's the snow going to hurt it? Can't you cover it up? Now you go and put that on. Try and look decent for once, today. You don't know who may be there to see us."

"Yes, you keep talkin' about that. Who do you think's goin' to be there?"

"Well, pa, you know the dinner's for us."

"Oh, I guess they ain't such a whole grist of folks comin' out in all this snow jest to eat dinner with *us*."

"You go and put that other tie on."

He went. But her small frail hands, bluish and veined, shook a little at the crocheting with which she was trying to fill in the time. Her eyes moistened, and her mouth tightened into a childish grimace of weeping. Why did pa have to be so mean—and just today? They knew each other with such terrible intimacy that each had an uncanny perception of just what tiny things could hurt the other. Pretending this dinner wasn't going to amount to anything; depreciating her proud glory as a bride of fifty years; bringing up the sense of all the intimate, dingy happenings to tarnish the splendor of this occasion. Putting on that old tie today was a blow at her importance as his wife, at their marriage. He was always insisting upon their age and insignificance . . . and the silent, ghost-white street, the meagerness of their little yard with the few bushes, the bleak lines of the storm entry, those half-filled wheel tracks—all bore him out. Two old people, out of things, living in a little house off the main road. Denying the significance of their one achievement of continuity.

It made her bitter, too. What did it amount that they had been married fifty years? Pa was so mean. Sentimental thoughts with which she had begun the day—unconsciously framing themselves in her mind in the grandiloquent terms of the town paper—were stringently checked by the terrible familiarity of his attitude. Just then, she didn't see why she *had* been such a fool as to have lived with him fifty years—why anyone should celebrate it.

Oh, well—but then, that was pa. After all, she knew how much the grumbling amounted to. Why did she let herself be so riled by it every time? Her best dress of dark-gray silk, shimmering so nicely in the light from the window, raised the occasion, would not let her feel harsh. She knew that all those objections were partly a defense against the ill fortune of which they had had enough—he was not going to admit that things might turn out well, so that he wouldn't be disappointed again. He had had to make an assertion with that old tie to conceal a sneaking hope that this dinner might be a big affair, with people met to celebrate. Their long years together stretched out before her inner vision. . . . He'd been a pretty good husband after all, had worked hard, hadn't spent his money for drink or run after other women. She supposed you couldn't have everything.

She cried excitedly: "Pa! Here comes George! Now you hurry up and get yourself ready."

But she was the one, after all, who had to scurry to the dresser for a last hairpin to stick into her neat little knob of hair, to re-fasten her brooch in her lace collar, search for another handkerchief. He was ready, tie and all, and she was still in the bedroom when George, their son-in-law, came stamping in, scuffing the thick soft snow off his big overshoes.

"Ain't you ready, folks?"

"Ma! Hurry up! Well, what in thunder's she doing? Thought she was ready an hour ago."

II

"I didn't know as you'd get here, George."

"Yep—oh, there's lots of ways of gettin' in."

"The old bobs still come in pretty handy, I'll tell ye," Mr. Willey said.

"Wrapped up good, grandma?"

"Oh, yes, I know how to bundle." Her voice came muffled through the fascinator that she had wound around her head over a knitted hood. She stepped along blindly behind George, down the covered walk, squinting against the misty flakes, trying to keep hold of the coarse brown hair of George's fur coat . . . feet making soft cavernous dents in the thick snow. . . . "Why, there's Reverend and Mrs. Baxter in the bob, ain't it?"

"Yeah, they're going along with us. Can yuh get in, grandma?"

George lifted her over the side of the bob, and with a little scramble she managed to get in. The Methodist minister and his wife were tucked snugly into a corner. Mr. Baxter shouted jovial greetings. Mrs. Baxter smiled and nodded, only glints of eyes showing between squinted eyelids, two little hard red cheeks and a ruddy blob of nose let out of the big scarf tied over her head.

"Get in. Lots of room."

Four ministerial feet in heavy, shining rubbers were hitched awkwardly over the thick robe covering the floor of the bob, through little holes of which stuck bent yellow straws. The old people squatted down stiffly, and Mr. Baxter drew the fur robe over them.

"Well, how's the wedding party?"

"Oh . . . I guess they're all right," Mrs. Willey said with shy pleasure.

"Looks more like a silver wedding than a golden wedding today."

"Yes, ain't the snow bad!"

"All fixed back there?" George called.

"All fixed! Let 'er go!"

"*Gid*-dap!"

The two big horses gave a plunge forward, the bob rocked, tilted up on the edge of the road. . . . They passed the snowy willows and got out on the main road, where there were already silvery-smooth bob tracks above the gravel, no ruts to make the women give little shrieks and put out their hands blindly. The horses settled into an even trot.

"Isn't this nice, though?" Mrs. Baxter exulted.

All felt the exhilaration. The strangeness of the snow made the day a festival.

They stopped trying to shout things at one another, getting the wet small flakes in their mouths. They snuggled down on the straw under the fur robe. The bob went softly through the new, pure whiteness. Snow kept falling, gentle as mist—tiny flakes, and big tufted splotches. The road ahead and the road behind were lost—there was only a place of dim white silence, and they moving in it.

"Are we there?"

"Why, I guess we are!"

"I didn't hardly know where we're getting."

The bob trundled over the wooden planks across the ditch and into the drive between the willow-trees that were blue-brown through the snow . . . misty, dreamlike, strange. The place had a festive air, too, because of the magic difference the snow made—the big barn roof white against the shrouded sky; the old wagon standing out there softly covered, rounded, all its stark angles gone.

"Well, I guess I didn't spill anybody out," George said.

They plodded to the house. George had let them out near the back door. They went up the steps, with a great stamping and scuffing—Clara in the doorway urging them in, they protesting that they must "sweep themselves off."

"Aw, it's just the kitchen—won't hurt this floor—come on in."

They went in, brushing and shaking. At once they were enveloped in warmth from the big range, with scents of chicken browning, biscuits, coffee, that their nostrils breathed in with a sharp deliciousness . . . snow melting on their wraps, shaking off in a fine chill spray, making pools on the linoleum. They had a glimpse of Darlene, the youngest girl, at the stove, her face flushed a deep hot rose under the brown hair. Many dishes about. . . .

"Oh, don't stay in here!" Clara was urging. "No, your things won't hurt anything. Ain't the first time there's been snow in this house today."

Mrs. Baxter and Mrs. Willey found themselves pushed into the chilly downstairs bedroom, where they unwrapped scarfs and fascinators, and where Mrs. Baxter—with apology and an alert glance at the door—yanked up her skirt and revealed black woolen tights which she tugged off her portly legs.

"Didn't know but what the snow might get in," she panted.

"So I thought I'd come prepared. I guess I won't shock you ladies getting these off—hope none of the men'll look in here—might see a sight—"

"They ain't around," Clara said comfortingly. "That's just all right—just the thing to wear."

Clara stood until the wraps were off. She was heated, so that her grayish-brown hair looked dry and sheeny above her flushed face. She wore a bungalow apron. And yet she looked festive, too. Extra clean, her mother thought, with her fat arms bare to the elbow, her perspiring neck.

"Well, if you've got everything you want—"

"Oh, yes! Don't pay any attention to us, Clara. I'll come out and help you just as soon as I get my things off."

"No, now, ma. You go in the parlor and visit with Mrs. Baxter. I don't want either of you in the kitchen. Minnie'll help me."

"Oh, is Minnie and John here?"

"Yes, they're here. Minnie's here and the rest are coming."

"Well, I guess we'll have to obey," Mrs. Willey said with a pleased flattered laugh.

They went into the parlor and seated themselves nicely.

Mrs. Willey bent down to pick off a tiny straw clinging to her gray silk dress. Then she folded her hands and rocked.

She had half expected all along to find people here. And she saw no one but Clara and Darlene, and her daughter-in-law Minnie, who peeped in a moment. But the minister's family being here made it all right to have worn the gray silk—justified her in having ordered the necktie. Mrs. Baxter had on a dark-blue taffeta that rustled as she rocked.

All the same, the old lady could sense an air of preparation. The odors in the kitchen, that quick, half-realized glimpse of dishes . . . Even the bedroom had been specially clean; a glossy white scarf on the dresser, and the tatting-edged pillow shams. Clara had her best things out. The dining-room door was closed. Yes, and in the parlor too the chairs were set so neatly. The perfect order of the mission table suggested something beyond the everyday. As they rocked, Mrs. Willey was alert for every sound. There was a shrill excited tone in the noise and laughter in the kitchen, abruptly stilled, and then breaking out again; a tramping, a going back and forth that suggested more people in the house than were apparent; children's voices in some upstairs room.

The realization of the occasion brought back heightened memories. As she looked about the parlor, with its new Victrola and davenport and miscellaneous chairs, Mrs. Willey was on the point of saying to Mrs. Baxter: "This don't look much the way the place did when Mister and I first came here!" But she could not communicate that poignant memory of the old rooms, that was somewhere deep in her mind . . . small, bare, the few walnut furnishings, the feeling of raw openness all around. . . . She rocked. Her eyes had a distant look.

She was excited by the scents from the kitchen, the subdued bustle there.

Shouts came from outside. Mrs. Willey turned quickly to the window—the shouts an answer to her expectation.

A great bob load was coming up to the house, rocking as it turned into the drive—people shouting, waving. Mrs. Willey's hands felt trembling, her heart beat sharply, as she rose. The two old people stood blinking, she gratified, he sheepish, as a confused lot of people came tramping in, and crying:

"Where's the bridal couple? Look at the blushing groom! Well, well, well—many happy returns of the day!"

III

The dining-room door opened—

"Go in, ma."

"Yes, the bridal couple must lead the way."

The old people protested, as a matter of duty, but inwardly pleased to be pushed in ahead of the others, to sit at the head of the long table. Old Mr. Willey looked sheepish—all this splendor for an old couple like them. But Mrs. Willey was exalted. She saw the room in a heightened dazzle of bright confusion—glitter of tumblers, plates and silver, shine of white and yellow. Laughing, calling, appreciative murmurs . . . and then all of them standing there, suddenly and uncomfortably grave, Mrs. Willey still tremulous with excitement, while the minister gave the blessing, appropriately solemn and loud-toned . . . only one high, unconscious piping from the children's table in the corner."

The company seated themselves. The laughter, the murmurs broke out again.

"My, isn't this lovely!"

"Well, grandma, what do you think of it?"

"Well, I . . . I don't hardly know *what* to say," the old lady quavered.

The others laughed delightedly.

But as she sat at the head of the table, waited upon, getting served first, gradually things began to emerge out of that first shining confusion. She had known that this would happen, marvelous as it was. She recognized her daughter-in law Minnie's best table-cloth, pieced out at the farther end (where George sat) with one of Clara's—that table-cloth with a crocheted border, that had been laid away in a chiffonier drawer to be peeped at by admiring women, that had been used only at the weddings of Minnie's daughters. The granddaughters must have brought their best wedding silver in carefully packed baskets. Clara and George had never accumulated any silver. But even more thrilling than this was the festive look of the room, with its decorations—the yellow crepe paper drawn from the center-piece and tied in bows at the four corners, the yellow tissue paper flowers (Gertrude was the one who had made those) at every place . . . and all the decorations converging significantly toward the center of the table where a huge cake frosted in yellow, frilled about with paper and flowers, stood under a hanging, ruffly, yellow wedding bell.

She looked about the long, crowded table. They were all there—all the people whose lives were bound up with hers and pa's. Clara and George, Minnie and John, grandsons and grandsons-in-law, "connections" from Prospect and the country around; even Nels Olson, a prosperous merchant in town now, but years ago the Willeys' hired man. The children at the square table were gleeful, and in their best.

And it was for them—for her and pa. She felt that exalted swelling in her breast, and tears stayed just behind the surface glisten of her eyes. Let pa say again that they were old and left behind, that no one thought of them, their day was over! No, this occasion was as glorious as she had been imagining it, in spite of his pessimistic objections. After all these work-filled years— fifty years—that had seemed at times to be petering out into a small meager loneliness, to sit here, honored, receiving again the delicious food and wine of personal recognition. All her people met to do her honor, to show that her life work had counted. . . . There was just one little twinge of disappointment. Robert had not come from Seattle. She had thought against all reason that when she opened the door, she would miraculously find Robert. She was glad she had mentioned it to no one. Pa's scoffing would have been justified.

It showed the grandeur of the occasion that Clara was "sitting down to table" beside George; although she gave hasty uneasy glances toward the kitchen. She had changed her apron, at the last minute, for her best dark green taffeta, above which her fat neck and face were flushed hotly. The granddaughters were waiting on the table, squeezing in between the chairs and the wall with their great platters of fowl, and bowls of gravy, and shining coffee-pot. The meal was like an old-time harvest dinner in abundance—beside the chicken, two big platters of goose that Minnie had cooked at home and brought over warm, and covered, to be heated in Clara's oven; potatoes, baked beans, escalloped corn and peas, three kinds of bread and biscuits, relishes and jellies and pickles. But there were, beside, the special dishes that marked the importance of wedding and reunion dinners in Prospect and the country around—perfection salad, made the day before by the married granddaughters, great biscuit pans full of it;

mayonnaise; and the women guests at the table had already discerned that the huge, yellow-frosted cake was Golden Companion, for which Lottie Disbrow had the community recipe.

The first absorption in food was giving way to a chatter. The children at the small table were yielding pieces of chicken that they had snatched, consenting to wait for "something *awful* good" promised by mothers in a deep whisper. Faces shone and glistened with warmth and food . . . and past the windowpanes drifted the last aimless flakes of the big snowfall.

There were satisfied, admiring comments on the food. . . . "Ain't these biscuits just fine! You make these, Clara?" "Yes. I was afraid they wasn't going to come out good." "Oh, they're lovely!" . . . "More chicken? Well, sir, I've had a good deal already. Do you let folks have their third piece?" A worried "Oh, now, Henry, you want to be careful. You've had enough." "Aw, go on and take it, Reverend. You need that drumstick."

John said expansively: "Don't pay any attention to the womenfolks! This is the time when a fellow can eat all he pleases. Can't have a golden-wedding dinner every day."

"Yes, but then you'll expect your wives to run around for you maybe half the night because you eat too much again," Minnie put in smartly.

All the wives murmured: "I guess so!" And laughed significantly.

But the men said: "Time enough to worry about that afterwards. Anyway, I can't see but you're eatin' plenty yourself."

Talk, clatter of dishes, shrill voices of children, babies waking and wailing in the bedroom. Mrs. Baxter said: "It seems a shame to eat, and spoil this lovely table." But it was spoiled now—littered—the hand-painted jelly dishes messy, the salad bowls nearly empty, some of the crepe paper torn and pushed askew. The dinner was ending. The girls brought heaping dishes of home-made ice cream with chocolate sauce.

"Oh, my! Look at this! I don't know where the room for it's coming from, but I'll have to find some."

Mr. Willey muttered: "What's this stuff on here?"

Mrs. Willey nudged him. "Pa! That's choc'late."

"Huh! Well, I dunno—"

"You rather have yours without, grandpa?"

"No, no!" Mrs. Willey protested, shocked. "He'll eat it this way. It looks lovely." She gave him a look.

The women perceived—felt in the air—what was about to come. But some of the men took up their spoons, began to eat, were reprimanded by their wives, and looked about, belligerent and then subdued. Mrs. Willey knew what it meant. Her small, faded mouth quivered. Clara was getting ready, half apologetic, to make the people listen. Gertrude stood behind her grandmother's chair, smiling.

"Sh! Sh!"

Clara got up with difficulty, squeezed between the table and her chair. Her voice had the toneless quavering of one unaccustomed and half ashamed to speak before others.

"Friends . . . and—a . . . As long as this is our mother's and father's golden-wedding day, maybe now we better ask mother to cut the wedding cake."

Mr. Baxter relieved the silent moment that followed by a loud, cheerful "That's right—let the bride do it." There were repetitions of "bride"; and they all laughed and murmured. Gertrude handed her grandmother the large knife; and the old lady, her hands trembling slightly, cut through the Golden Companion. The first wedge came out, moist, rich and yellow. They applauded. There were shouts of laugher when Mr. Baxter found the old maid's thimble in his piece. Lottie Disbrow had marked the location of the ring, and Gertrude gave that piece to her grandmother.

"I'm gonna be rich—look, mamma, I'm gonna be rich!" one of the children cried, holding up the coin.

The wedding cake was passed about the table. The groom's cake—a dark, spicy fruit cake—was brought in already cut. Plates of angel food were passed about—"Better eat this, girls," the women told the unmarried girls, "and save your wedding cake to sleep on!" Now all the table relaxed into a warm, easy, chattering exhilaration. Even old Mr. Willey had dropped his defenses, carried along by the spirit of the hour.

How did everyone feel it now? But those still talking relapsed into startled silence. Throat-clearings. The men looked down, rigid, embarrassed. The children turned with round, bright, fascinated eyes. Mrs. Willey's heart pounded. Clara's eyes began to water.

The Reverend Mr. Baxter rose, tapped on his glass with his knife.

"Sh—sh!" to the children.

Silence.

Mr. Baxter began to speak. Although he spoke in the slow, portentous voice that he used for the texts of his sermons, only significant phrases stood out, echoed and diminished in the minds of the listeners . . . "met together today . . . do honor to these two people . . . long journey together . . . achievement . . . God's blessing on this couple . . ." Words irradiated by the winter sunshine that came through the windows now, sparkling off the snow, and striking iridescence from the silver and glass, the glossy table-cloth, the warm shining heads of the listening children. The old couple at the head of the table took on a deep significance into which a lifetime of meaning was compressed, brought to a sudden realization. . . . "And now I have been asked by all these good people to present this token of the occasion. And may it always bring to your minds, Mr. and Mrs. Willey, the memory of the affection of your children and neighbors, and their appreciation of your having reached this day."

He took the package that Gertrude handed him. Old Mr. Willey had to receive it—unwrap it—show to everyone the silver loving-cup. There were applause, hand-clappings, nose-blowings. A telegram from Robert was read. The sun shone warmly on the silver cup with its gilt lining, flashed off the two handles. The old lady could only murmur that she "thanked her dear children and neighbors." But the old man was flushed, carried beyond himself. He saw everything heightened . . . and his vision, like his wife's, stretched back and back to scenes so long ago that he

scarcely knew how to communicate his sense of them. But he
had to say something if she didn't.

He remembered when he first came out to Ioway, he said.
The bob ride had brought back old times. Things that the children had thought old stuff, the tales that old men tell sitting on
benches in front of the hotel—they listened to now with a sense of
drama and event, of time passing. When he talked about the
wedding day fifty years ago, the children heard him with delighted appreciation.

"In them days, we didn't go to all this fuss we do now for
weddings. When folks wanted to git married, they just hitched
up and drove into town, and that ended it. Well, sir, I was thinking what kind of a day that was. Not snowy—one of them real
muddy days—and I tell ye, there *was* mud in those times! You
fellers talk about roads, but you don't know what roads can be.
Well, sir, we'd fixed on that day—and I was willing to put it off
—but *she*'d got her mind set on it and of course it had to be.
["Asa!" Applause from the men, protests from the women.] We
took my brother Luke's team, and him and me and her and
Luke's girl—girl he had then, name of Tressy Bowers, she went
out to Dakoty later—we started, with the horses all slicked up
and their manes combed out, to drive into Prospect. Well, good
enough goin' for a ways—and then jest out here beyond where
Ted Bloomquist's place is now, we run into one of them mud-
holes about three foot deep. Mud splashes up—girls screeches—
and them two horses gits stuck so they can't pull out. Well, then
the womenfolks had a time! They don't want us to git out in the
mud because it'll spoil our wedding clothes, and they ain't nothing else for us to do but set there until somebody comes along.
Well, a fellow did, and he helped us, and we got out.

"But then me and Luke's about as muddy as the team, and
the women thought it was awful to go into town to the
preacher's that way. So before we reached town—right down
there by the crick, in what's Hibbert's pasture now—they made
us fellers git out; and the girls they took sticks and whatever
they could find handy, and tore a big chunk out o' their under-

skirts—women wore plenty o' clothes them days—and they made us fellers stand up and hev the mud scraped off our pants—and then when we's cleaned up a little, we went along to the preacher's and got married."

"And it's lasted quite a while!"

"Yes, sir. He done a good job of it."

Mrs. Willey was flustered, protesting—"You know it wasn't near as bad as that! What do you want to go and tell such things for?"—blushing when the underskirts were mentioned. In the warm, relieved, easy glow that followed, the loving-cup was passed about the table and admired. The names of all the givers were engraved upon it; and beneath the names of Asa Willey and Angie Pilgrim Willey, the two dates:

1874 - 1924

Finally it was time to leave the table. The granddaughters would not let the older women into the kitchen. Carrie Gustafson had been called to help out with the dishwashing. The others went into the parlor, all the women urging one another to take the best rockers; looking out of the windows and commenting that the day had "turned out nice" after all. They were moving still in that warm, easy exhilaration that came from food and coffee and that high moment at the table. "Tired, grandma?" "Oh, no, I ain't tired." The sun glistened on the snow. Mrs. Willey sat in an ease in which it seemed that she could never know what fatigue was—strangely free, her spirit exulting, doing what it pleased with her body. The great dinner was over, but the day was not ended yet. There were things to come. And then there would be the afterglow lingering for a long, long time.

"Guess we'll have a little music, folks," George said.

They listened, sentimentally gratified, when a mellifluous baritone with an overdone accent sang *Silver Threads among the Gold*. But the murmuring and chatter, the pleas and shouts of children, sounded above the music—George's few "good" records, conscientiously played: *Il Trovatore*, *A Perfect Day*, *The Last Rose of Summer*. George began to yield to the children's

pleas for "This one, grandpa," "Play this one, Uncle George"—
Morning in the Barnyard and the "Uncle Josh" monologue. The
room was filled with a high noise of chatter, laughter, resolute
music, sounds from the kitchen . . . and outside, the sun sparkling
off the great, untouched spread of snow across the yard and
fields.

Shouts from the road, and then a running to the windows.
Charlie, one of George's boys, came tramping into the house,
ruddy-faced, in his sheepskin coat . . . from somewhere a jingle
of sleigh-bells. The girls followed him from the kitchen, dish
towels in their hands.

"Well, grandma and grandpa, do you want a sleigh-ride?
Team's out here ready."

The others urged, laughing, excited, pushing toward the
dining-room windows from which—through a blinding sparkle
—they could see the sleigh. The young men were out there,
patting the horses. They had got the Tomlinsons' old two-seated
sleigh, that had been packed away in a musty, cluttered barn
corner for years. It was furbished, decked with sleigh-bells the
boys had found somewhere; John's big horses stamping, shaking
and turning their heads to see where the jingling came from,
letting out clouds of silvery vapor.

"It ain't cold—just grand! Better go, grandma."

"Take your wedding journey!"

The bedroom was full of women laughing, encouraging,
helping to bundle her into heavy wraps—shouting to George to
get his fur coat for grandpa. There was discussion as to who
should have the place beside Charlie. "You go, Clara," "Oh, no—
some of the rest of you." "Mr. and Mrs. Baxter—" "Oh, no, no!
Let some of these little people." "Me, mamma! I want a sleigh-
ride!" "No, you children can have lots of fun here." "I think
Clara'd ought to go. She's the only one ain't had a ride today."
Clara would not go without Minnie. The two plump women
were packed into the front seat, with Charlie squeezed between
them. The old Willeys had the place of honor in the back of the
sleigh.

All the company flung on wraps, shawls, whatever they could pick up, and hurried out to the back steps to watch the sleighing party leave. The women hugged their arms in their shawls, squinted against the sharp flash of sun from the drive and glistening shed roofs.

"Look-a there! Ain't that great?"

They pointed to the placard that the boys had fastened with a white streamer to the back of the sleigh—

JUST MARRIED

"Get back—get those kids back. These horses are rarin' to go."

The clustered company waved, shouted, as the sleigh started with a jerk and frosty jingle of bells; watched it out of sight around the turn; then went back to the house, away from the white emptiness in which the new sleigh-tracks had left steely marks.

Bobs had been along this road since it had stopped snowing, making the going easier. The jingling bells, the sky a dazzle of blue after the snowfall. . . . The world they were passing through was as shining, remote, as those ethereal, silvery hills and thickets drawn on frosty window-panes. The sunlight glittered on the horses' smooth-curving backs. The sleigh runners left narrow, hard, flashing tracks. The low rounded hills were crusted deep with sparkling white. Corn stalks, humped with snow, shone stiff and pale gold. They had to close their eyes against that blinding radiance.

They drove into Prospect—not down that little street where the old people lived, but "right through the main part of town." People halted at the sound of bells, laughed at the placard, waved and called out greetings. The sleighing party, warmed still by the happy intoxication of the wedding dinner, responded hilariously.

"What's this—an elopement?" Judge Brubaker shouted.

"We've got to stop for you to have your pictures taken," Clara turned to say.

"Oh, no!" Mrs. Willey protested.

But she liked it—even grandpa liked it.

They climbed the sloping wooden stairs to the gallery, covered with thick soft snow. The photograph would be in the Des Moines paper. "Prospect Couple Celebrate Golden Wedding." It would have their names—tell about the loving-cup, and Robert's telegram. The long room of the gallery, filled with snowy light, had the same dazzle as the street today.

The old man was lifted above his gloom and forebodings. He raised his wife's hand clasped in his, and shouted back at people. A crowd of little boys swarmed out into the road, making for the sleigh with ludicrous determination. "Hop on, boys!" he called jovially. They clung until a jerk at the corner threw them off the runners, and they still trailed the sleigh for a block or two.

IV

"Well, was the ride nice, grandma?"

"Oh, it was fine!"

"Get cold?"

"Not a bit cold. . . . I guess I am a little chilly now, though."

And as she trudged up through the heavy snow to the farmhouse again, she realized that the afternoon was late, the best of the sunshine over. When she went into the house, too, there was a different feeling. The big bob-load of people had left during the sleigh-ride. Now there were only the family themselves—the granddaughters sitting wearily in the parlor after their long siege in the kitchen. "Oh, children, be still awhile. You make such a racket." Carrie Gustafson was plodding about in the kitchen doing the last of the cleaning up.

Standing in the bedroom, taking off her many wraps, Mrs. Willey realized that the chill of the winter day had sunk into her. Her eyes were reddened, her small faded lips were blue. Her thin frail hands felt stiff and chilled.

"I guess you did get kind o' cold, grandma."

"Oh, not so very. It was awful nice."

They sat about in the parlor, where the grandchildren were playing with undiminished liveliness, even wilder than at noon. The older people were tired. The men talked, and the women, in two camps. Then some of the women went out to the kitchen to "set out a few things for supper."

"Now, don't go to a lot of trouble. We don't really need a thing after all we've et."

"Oh, the men'll want something. We'll just put on what's left."

But when they went to the table, the cold goose and chicken, the warmed-over potatoes, the different bits of salad, tasted good after all. There was a revived cheer, an intimacy in gathering around the remnants of the great meal after the outsiders had left. The glossy table-cloth had spots of jelly. The yellow bell still hung there; but the flowers and crepe paper and wedding cake were gone. Plates of angel food and fruit cake, a little crumbled, were put on. The coffee tasted better than anything else.

Under the old woman's smile lay tremulous fatigue. She could scarcely sit at the table. As soon as the meal was over, George hitched up the bob to take the old people and some of the grandchildren home.

"Well, sir, it's been quite a day!"

Now they had seen too much to notice the whiteness of the fields that they passed, the willows dim and motionless. The straw was warm under the robe on the floor of the bob. The *plop-plop-plop* of the big horses' hoofs was magically soothing . . . and the slight jolt and sway of the bob, going over rough places in the road, turning corners. . . .

They were all surprised when the bob stopped.

"Are we here?"

"Sure. Where'd you think we was?"

"Why, I didn't hardly know."

"Wait a minute, grandma, I'll lift you out."

George lifted her over the side of the bob. When he put her down, her legs felt stiff and queer, and she could scarcely make her feet move. She looked with a kind of wonder at the house standing bleak, silent, no shine from the windows, no smoke from the chimney. She entered it with the feeling of a traveler from splendid scenes who still carries a trace of their radiance with him to shed upon the familiar home. The little entry was cold.

"Wait a minute," George said. "I'll get your fire going for you."

"Oh, you needn't to bother, George."

"Sure. Only take a minute."

The sound of his heavy boots, the crackle of wood and rattle of coal, made a cheerful bustle. "There! I guess she'll warm up now." Then he was gone. Shouts of good-by from the bob—it trundled off down the snowy street, around a corner.

It seemed as if the day could not be over. But they were in the house together. There was nothing for them to do, after all, but to go to bed.

V

Their bedroom was chilly.

It took the old woman longer to put away all her cherished best things—her silk dress and lace collar and brooch. He was in bed long before she was, and impatient. She wanted to linger. The silk dress kept the feeling of occasion. There was still a sense of exaltation—a jumbled memory of the dinner, the shining table, the jangle of bells and the sparkling snow, the greetings along the street.

But the old pieces of furniture, set with a meager exactness in the chilly room, exerted the long-known influence of the every day. After all, it was this that they must come back to. The day had been fine, but the day was over and would not come again. Now, when they were alone, they had so little to say. Their room was too close, too familiar. Their knowledge of each other was too intimate for their speech to go outside its daily boundaries— they were afraid of that. They fell so quickly into the old ways with each other. She struggled against admitting this. "The cake was nice, wa'nt it?"

"Hm?"

"The cake. It was nice."

"Um. Yeah. Ain't you nearly ready?"

"It was nice of the children to plan it for us that way, a surprise like that."

. . . But it was no use. He would never talk about things. He was pulling her down to the old level again. She folded away the lace collar, put the brooch in the small jeweler's box with her watch chain and an old ring. She would have liked to go over the whole day, picking out and holding up the intimate and significant details—but he wanted the light out, wanted to get to sleep. She was softened toward him, thinking of that moment on the snowy street when he had lifted their two hands. She was not ready to let the day go. Why couldn't pa ever talk things over with her? He'd talk more to anybody than to her.

She felt the still, frosty wonder of the night, as she stood a moment at the small window. And because she could not share this—felt so helpless—a little old, thin bitterness seeped through her proud exaltation, tincturing it with the familiar quality of every day. . . .

He turned over restlessly. "Well, ma! Ain't ye ever comin' to bed?"

"Well, can't you give me time to put away my things?"

"Hmp . . . 'time'!" And other mutterings, half intelligible.

But when she put out the light and climbed into the creaking bed beside him, he was at ease. He soon went to sleep. She lay beside him, awake for a long time.

The irritation died away into calm, and she lay holding in the solitude of her own mind deeply felt, wordless things . . . as she had done in countless other nights; holding quiet both the beauty and the bitterness, encompassing them in the tranquillity of her comprehension . . . not so ill content, after all, that he should drop off childlike to sleep, and leave her and those incommunicable thoughts alone.

WASHINGTON IRVING

The Wife

The treasures of the deep are not so precious
As are the conceal'd comforts of a man
Locked up in woman's love. I scent the air
Of blessings, when I come but near the house.
What a delicious breath marriage sends forth ...
The violet bed's not sweeter.

MIDDLETON

I have often had the occasion to remark the fortitude with which women sustain the most overwhelming reverses of fortune. Those disasters which break down the spirit of a man, and prostrate him in the dust, seem to call forth all energies of the softer sex, and give such intrepidity and elevation to their character, that at times it approaches to sublimity. Nothing can be more touching than to behold a soft and tender female, who had been all weakness and dependence, and alive to every trivial roughness, while treading the prosperous paths of life, suddenly rising in mental force to be the comforter and support of her husband under misfortune, and abiding, with unshrinking firmness, the bitterest blasts of adversity.

As the vine, which has long twined its graceful foliage about the oak, and been lifted by it into sunshine, will, when the hardy plant is rifted by the thunderbolt, cling round it with its caressing tendrils and bind up its shattered boughs, so is it beautifully ordered by Providence, that woman, who is the mere dependent and ornament of man in his happier hours, should be his stay and solace when smitten with sudden calamity; winding herself into the rugged recesses of his nature, tenderly supporting the drooping head, and binding up the broken heart.

I was once congratulating a friend, who had around him a blooming family, knit together in the strongest affection. "I can wish you no better lot," said he with enthusiasm, "than to have a wife and children. If you are prosperous, there they are to share your prosperity; if otherwise, there they are to comfort you." And indeed, I have observed that a married man falling into misfortune is more apt to retrieve his situation in the world than a single one; partly because he is more stimulated to exertion by the necessities of the helpless and beloved beings who depend upon him for subsistence; but chiefly because his spirits are soothed and relieved by domestic endearments, and his self-respect kept alive by finding that, though all abroad is darkness and humiliation, yet there is still a little world of love at home, of which he is the monarch. Whereas a single man is apt to run to waste and self-neglect; to fancy himself lonely and abandoned, and his heart to fall to ruin like some deserted mansion, for want of an inhabitant.

These observations call to mind a little domestic story, of which I was once a witness. My intimate friend, Leslie, had married a beautiful and accomplished girl, who had been brought up in the midst of fashionable life. She had, it is true, no fortune, but that of my friend was ample; and he delighted in the anticipation of indulging her in every elegant pursuit, and administering to those delicate tastes and fancies that spread a kind of witchery about the sex.—"Her life," said he, "shall be like a fairy tale."

The very difference in their characters produced a harmonious combination: he was of a romantic and somewhat serious cast; she was all life and gladness. I have often noticed the mute rapture with which he would gaze upon her in company, of which her sprightly powers made her the delight; and how, in the midst of applause, her eyes would still turn to him, as if there alone she sought favor and acceptance. When leaning on his arm, her slender form contrasted finely with his tall manly person. The fond confiding air with which she looked up at him seemed to call forth a flush of triumphant pride and cherishing tenderness, as if he doted on his lovely burden for its very helplessness. Never did a couple set forward on the flowery path of early and well-suited marriage with a fairer prospect of felicity.

It was the misfortune of my friend, however, to have embarked his property in large speculations; and he had not been married many months when, by a succession of sudden disasters, it was swept from him, and he found himself reduced almost to penury. For a time he kept his situation to himself, and went about with a haggard countenance and a breaking heart. His life was but a protracted agony; and what rendered it more insupportable was the necessity of keeping up a smile in the presence of his wife; for he could not bring himself to overwhelm her with the news. She saw, however, with the quick eye of affection, that all was not well with him. She marked his altered looks and stifled sighs, and was not to be deceived by his sickly and vapid attempts at cheerfulness. She tasked all her sprightly powers and tender blandishments to win him back to happiness; but she only drove the arrow deeper into his soul. The more he saw cause to love her, the more torturing was the thought that he was soon to make her wretched. A little while, thought he, and the smile will vanish from that cheek—the song will die away from those lips—the lustre of those eyes will be quenched with sorrow; and the happy heart, which now beats lightly in that bosom, will be weighed down like mine by the cares and miseries of the world.

At length he came to me one day, and related his whole situation in a tone of the deepest despair. When I heard him through I inquired, "Does your wife know all this?"—At the question he burst into an agony of tears. "For God's sake!" cried he, "if you have any pity on me, don't mention my wife; it is the thought of her that drives me almost to madness!"

"And why not?" said I. "She must know it sooner or later: you cannot keep it long from her, and the intelligence may break upon her in a more startling manner, than if imparted by yourself; for the accents of those we love soften the harshest tidings. Besides, you are depriving yourself of the comforts of her sympathy; and not merely that, but also endangering the only bond that can keep hearts together—an unreserved community of thought and feeling. She will soon perceive that something is secretly preying upon your mind; and true love will not brook reserve; it feels under-valued and outraged, when even the sorrows of those it loves are concealed from it."

"Oh, but my friend! to think what a blow I am to give to all her future prospects—how I am to strike her very soul to the earth by telling her that her husband is a beggar; that she is to forego all the elegancies of life—all the pleasures of society—to shrink with me into indigence and obscurity! To tell her that I have dragged her down from the sphere in which she might have continued to move in constant brightness—the light of every eye—the admiration of every heart!—How can she bear poverty? she has been brought up in all the refinements of opulence. How can she bear neglect? she has been the idol of society. Oh! it will break her heart—it will break her heart!—"

I saw his grief was eloquent, and I let it have its flow; for sorrow relieves itself by words. When his paroxysm had subsided, and he had relapsed into moody silence, I resumed the subject gently, and urged him to break his situation at once to his wife. He shook his head mournfully, but positively.

"But how are you going to keep it from her? It is necessary she should know it, that you may take the steps proper to the alteration of your circumstances. You must change your style of living—nay," observing a pang to pass across his countenance, "don't let that afflict you. I am sure you have never placed your happiness in outward show—you have yet friends, warm friends, who will not think the worse of you for being less splendidly lodged; and surely it does not require a palace to be happy with Mary—"

"I could be happy with her," cried he, convulsively, "in a hovel!—I could go down with her into poverty and the dust!—I could—I could—God bless her!—God bless her!" cried he, bursting into a transport of grief and tenderness.

"And believe me, my friend," I said, stepping up and grasping him warmly by the hand, "believe me she can be the same with you. Ay, more: it will be a source of pride and triumph to her—it will call forth all the latent energies and fervent sympathies of her nature; for she will rejoice to prove that she loves you for yourself. There is in every true woman's heart a spark of heavenly fire, which lies dormant in the broad daylight of prosperity; but which kindles up and beams and blazes in the dark hour of adversity. No man knows what the wife of his bosom is—no man knows what a ministering angel she is—unless he has gone with her through the fiery trials of this world."

There was something in the earnestness of my manner, and the figurative style of my language, that caught the excited imagination of Leslie. I knew the auditor I had to deal with; and following up the impression I had made, I finished by persuading him to go home and unburden his sad heart to his wife.

I must confess, notwithstanding all I had said, I felt some little solicitude for the result. Who can calculate on the fortitude of one whose life has been a round of pleasures? Her gay spirits might revolt at the dark downward path of low humility suddenly pointed out before her, and might cling to the sunny regions in which they had hitherto revelled. Besides, ruin in fashionable life is accompanied by so many galling mortifications, to which in other ranks it is a stranger.—In short, I could not meet Leslie the next morning without trepidation. He had made the disclosure.

"And how did she bear it?"

"Like an angel! It seemed rather to be a relief to her mind, for she threw her arms round my neck, and asked if this was all that had lately made me unhappy.—But, poor girl," added he, "she cannot realize the change we must undergo. She has no idea of poverty but in the abstract; she has only read of it in poetry, where it is allied to love. She feels as yet no privation; she suffers no loss of accustomed conveniences nor elegancies. When we come practically to experience its sordid cares, its paltry wants, its petty humilitations—then will be the real trial."

"But," said I, "now that you have got over the severest task, that of breaking it to her, the sooner you let the world into the secret the better. The disclosure may be mortifying; but then it is a single misery and soon over: whereas you otherwise suffer it in anticipation, every hour of the day. It is not poverty so much as pretence, that harasses a ruined man—the struggle between a proud mind and an empty purse—the keeping up a hollow show that must soon come to an end. Have the courage to appear poor and you disarm poverty of its sharpest sting." On this point I found Leslie perfectly prepared. He had no false pride himself, and as to his wife, she was only anxious to conform to their altered fortunes.

Some days afterwards he called upon me in the evening. He had disposed of his dwelling house and taken a small cottage in the country, a few miles from town. He had been busied all day in sending out furniture. The new establishment required few articles, and those of the simplest kind. All the splendid furniture of his late residence had been sold, excepting his wife's harp. That, he said, was too closely associated with the idea of herself; it belonged to the little story of their loves; for some of the sweetest moments of their courtship were those when he had leaned over that instrument and listened to the melting tones of her voice. I could not but smile at this instance of romantic gallantry in a doting husband.

He was now going out to the cottage, where his wife had been all day superintending its arrangements. My feelings had become strongly interested in the progress of this family story, and, as it was a fine evening, I offered to accompany him.

He was wearied with the fatigues of the day, and as he walked out, fell into a fit of gloomy musing.

"Poor Mary!" at length broke, with a heavy sigh, from his lips.

"And what of her?" asked I: "has anything happened to her?"

"What," said he, darting an impatient glance, "is it nothing to be reduced to this paltry situation—to be caged in a miserable cottage—to be obliged to toil almost in the menial concerns of her wretched habitation?"

"Has she then repined at the change?"

"Repined! she has been nothing but sweetness and good humor. Indeed, she seems in better spirits than I have ever known her; she has been to me all love, and tenderness, and comfort!"

"Admirable girl!" exclaimed I. "You call yourself poor, my friend; you never were so rich—you never knew the boundless treasures of excellence you possess in that woman."

"Oh! but, my friend, if this first meeting at the cottage were over, I think I could then be comfortable. But this is her first day of real experience; she has been introduced into a humble dwelling—she has been employed all day in arranging its miserable equipments—she has, for the first time, known the fatigues of domestic employment—she has, for the first time, looked round her on a home destitute of everything elegant,—almost of everything convenient; and may now be sitting down, exhausted and spiritless, brooding over a prospect of future poverty."

There was a degree of probability in this picture that I could not gainsay, so we walked on in silence.

After turning from the main road up a narrow lane, so thickly shaded with forest trees as to give it a complete air of seclusion, we came in sight of the cottage. It was humble enough in its appearance, for the most pastoral poet; and yet it had a pleasing rural look. A wild vine had overrun one end in a profusion of foliage; a few trees threw their branches gracefully over it; and I observed several pots of flowers tastefully disposed about the door and on the grassplot in front. A small wicket gate opened upon a footpath that wound through some shrubbery to the door. Just as we approached, we heard the sound of music—Leslie grasped my arm; we paused and listened. It was Mary's voice singing, in a style of the most touching simplicity, a little air of which her husband was peculiarly fond.

I felt Leslie's hand tremble on my arm. He stepped forward to hear more distinctly. His step made a noise on the gravel walk. A bright beautiful face glanced out at the window and vanished—a light footstep was heard—and Mary came tripping forth to meet us: she was in a pretty rural dress of white; a few wild flowers were twisted in her fine hair; a fresh bloom was on her cheek; her whole countenance beamed with smiles—I had never seen her look so lovely.

"My dear George," cried she, "I am so glad you are come! I have been watching and watching for you; and running down the lane, and looking out for you. I've set out a table under a beautiful tree behind the cottage; and I've been gathering some of the most delicious strawberries for I know you are fond of them—and we have such excellent cream—and everything is so sweet and still here—Oh!" said she, putting her arm within his, and looking up brightly in his face, "Oh, we shall be so happy!"

Poor Leslie was overcome. He caught her to his bosom—he folded his arms round her—he kissed her again and again—he could not speak, but the tears gushed into his eyes; and he has often assured me, that though the world has since gone prosperously with him, and his life has, indeed, been a happy one, yet never has he experienced a moment of more exquisite felicity.

CARSON McCULLERS

A Domestic Dilemma

On Thursday Martin Meadows left the office early enough
to make the first express bus home. It was the hour when the
evening lilac glow was fading in the slushy streets, but by the
time the bus had left the Mid-town terminal the bright city
night had come. On Thursdays the maid had a half-day off and
Martin liked to get home as soon as possible, since for the past
year his wife had not been—well. This Thursday he was very
tired and, hoping that no regular commuter would single him
out for conversation, he fastened his attention to the newspaper
until the bus had crossed the George Washington Bridge. Once
on 9-W Highway Martin always felt that the trip was halfway
done, he breathed deeply, even in cold weather when only rib-
bons of draught cut through the smoky air of the bus, confident
that he was breathing country air. It used to be that at this point
he would relax and begin to think with pleasure of his home.
But in this last year nearness brought only a sense of tension and
he did not anticipate the journey's end. This evening Martin
kept his face close to the window and watched the barren fields
and lonely lights of passing townships. There was a moon, pale
on the dark earth and areas of late, porous snow; to Martin the

---

countryside seemed vast and somehow desolate that evening. He took his hat from the rack and put his folded newspaper in the pocket of his overcoat a few minutes before time to pull the cord.

The cottage was a block from the bus stop, near the river but not directly on the shore; from the living-room window you could look across the street and opposite yard and see the Hudson. The cottage was modern, almost too white and new on the narrow plot of yard. In summer the grass was soft and bright and Martin carefully tended a flower border and a rose trellis. But during the cold, fallow months the yard was bleak and the cottage seemed naked. Lights were on that evening in all the rooms in the little house and Martin hurried up the front walk. Before the steps he stopped to move a wagon out of the way.

The children were in the living room, so intent on play that the opening of the front door was at first unnoticed. Martin stood looking at his safe, lovely children. They had opened the bottom drawer of the secretary and taken out the Christmas decorations. Andy had managed to plug in the Christmas tree lights and the green and red bulbs glowed with out-of-season festivity on the rug of the living room. At the moment he was trying to trail the bright cord over Marianne's rocking horse. Marianne sat on the floor pulling off an angel's wings. The children wailed a startling welcome. Martin swung the fat little baby girl up to his shoulder and Andy threw himself against his father's legs.

'Daddy, Daddy, Daddy!'

Martin set down the little girl carefully and swung Andy a few times like a pendulum. Then he picked up the Christmas tree cord.

'What's all this stuff doing out? Help me put it back in the drawer. You're not to fool with the light socket. Remember I told you that before. I mean it, Andy.'

The six-year-old child nodded and shut the secretary drawer.

Martin stroked his fair soft hair and his hand lingered tenderly on the nape of the child's frail neck.

'Had supper yet, Bumpkin?'

'It hurt. The toast was hot.'

The baby girl stumbled on the rug and, after the first surprise of the fall, began to cry; Martin picked her up and carried her in his arms back to the kitchen.

'See, Daddy,' said Andy. 'The toast—— '

Emily had laid the childrens' supper on the uncovered porcelain table. There were two plates with the remains of cream-of-wheat and eggs and silver mugs that had held milk. There was also a platter of cinamon toast, untouched except for one tooth-marked bite. Martin sniffed the bitten piece and nibbled gingerly. Then he put the toast into the garbage pail.

'Hoo—phui—What on earth!'

Emily had mistaken the tin of cayenne for the cinnamon.

'I like to have burnt up,' Andy said. 'Drank water and ran outdoors and opened my mouth. Marianne didn't eat none.'

'Any,' corrected Martin. He stood helpless, looking around the walls of the kitchen. 'Well, that's that, I guess,' he said finally. 'Where is your mother now?'

'She's up in you alls' room.'

Martin left the children in the kitchen and went up to his wife. Outside the door he waited for a moment to still his anger. He did not knock and once inside the room he closed the door behind him.

Emily sat in the rocking chair by the window of the pleasant room. She had been drinking something from a tumbler and as he entered she put the glass hurriedly on the floor behind the chair. In her attitude there was confusion and guilt which she tried to hide by a show of spurious vivacity.

'O, Marty! You home already? The time slipped up on me. I was just going down——' She lurched to him and her kiss was strong with sherry. When he stood unresponsive she stepped back a pace and giggled nervously.

'What's the matter with you? Standing there like a barber pole. Is anything wrong with you?'

'Wrong with *me?*'' Martin bent over the rocking chair and picked up the tumbler from the floor. 'If you could only realize how sick I am—how bad it is for all of us.'

Emily spoke in a false, airy voice that had become too familiar to him. Often at such times she affected a slight English accent, copying perhaps some actress she admired. 'I haven't the vaguest idea what you mean. Unless you are referring to the glass I used for a spot of sherry. I had a finger of sherry— maybe two. But what is the crime in that, pray tell me? I'm quite all right. Quite all right.'

'So anyone can see.'

As she went into the bathroom Emily walked with careful gravity. She turned on the cold water and dashed some on her face with her cupped hands, then patted herself dry with the corner of a bath towel. Her face was delicately featured and young, unblemished.

'I was just going down to make dinner.' She tottered and balanced herself by holding to the door frame.

'I'll take care of dinner. You stay up here. I'll bring it up.'

'I'll do nothing of the sort. Why, whoever heard of such a thing?'

'Please,' Martin said.

'Leave me alone. I'm quite all right. I was just on the way down———'

'Mind what I say.'

'Mind your grandmother.'

She lurched toward the door, but Martin caught her by the arm. 'I don't want the children to see you in this condition. Be reasonable.'

'Condition!' Emily jerked her arm. Her voice rose angrily. 'Why, because I drink a couple of sherries in the afternoon you're trying to make me out a drunkard. Condition! Why, I don't even touch whiskey. As well you know. *I* don't swill liquor at bars. And that's more than you can say. I don't even have a cocktail at dinnertime. I only sometimes have a glass of sherry. What, I ask you, is the disgrace of that? Condition!'

Martin sought words to calm his wife. 'We'll have a quiet supper by ourselves up here. That's a good girl.' Emily sat on the side of the bed and he opened the door for a quick departure.

'I'll be back in a jiffy.'

As he busied himself with the dinner downstairs he was lost in the familiar question as to how this problem had come upon his home. He himself had always enjoyed a good drink. When they were still living in Alabama they had served long drinks or cocktails as a matter of course. For years they had drunk one or two—possible three drinks before dinner, and at bedtime a long nightcap. Evenings before holidays they might get a buzz on, might even become a little tight. But alcohol had never seemed a problem to him, only a bothersome expense that with the increase in the family they could scarcely afford. It was only after his company had transferred him to New York that Martin was aware that certainly his wife was drinking too much. She was tippling, he noticed, during the day.

The problem acknowledged, he tried to analyze the source. The change from Alabama to New York had somehow disturbed her; accustomed to the idle warmth of a small Southern town, the matrix of the family and cousinship and childhood friends, she had failed to accommodate herself to the stricter, lonelier mores of the North. The duties of motherhood and housekeeping were onerous to her. Homesick for Paris City, she had made no friends in the suburban town. She read only magazines and murder books. Her interior life was insufficient without the artifice of alcohol.

The revelations of incontinence insidiously undermined his previous conceptions of his wife. There were times of unexplainable malevolence, times when the alcoholic fuse caused an explosion of unseemly anger. He encountered a latent coarseness in Emily, inconsistent with her natural simplicity. She lied about drinking and deceived him with unsuspected stratagems.

Then there was an accident. Coming home from work one evening about a year ago, he was greeted with screams from the children's room. He found Emily holding the baby, wet and naked from her bath. The baby had been dropped, her frail, frail skull striking the table edge, so that a thread of blood was soaking into the gossamer hair. Emily was sobbing and intoxicated. As Martin cradled the hurt child, so infinitely precious at that moment, he had an affrighted vision of the future.

The next day Marianne was all right. Emily vowed that never again would she touch liquor, and for a few weeks she was sober, cold and downcast. Then gradually she began—not whiskey or gin—but quantities of beer, or sherry, or outlandish liqueurs; once he had come across a hatbox of empty crème de menthe bottles. Martin found a dependable maid who managed the household completely. Virgie was also from Alabama and Martin had never dared tell Emily the wage scale customary in New York. Emily's drinking was entirely secret now, done before he reached the house. Usually the effects were almost imperceptible—a looseness of movement or the heavy-lidded eyes. The times of irresponsibilities, such as the cayenne-pepper toast, were rare, and Martin could dismiss his worries when Virgie was at the house. But, nevertheless, anxiety was always latent, a threat of indefined disaster that underlaid his days.

'Marianne!' Martin called, for even the recollection of that time brought the need for reassurance. The baby girl, no longer hurt, but no less precious to her father, came into the kitchen with her brother. Martin went on with the preparations for the meal. He opened a can of soup and put two chops in the frying pan. Then he sat down by the table and took his Marianne on his knees for a pony ride. Andy watched them, his fingers wobbling the tooth that had been loose all that week.

'Andy-the-candyman!' Martin said. 'Is that old critter still in your mouth? Come closer, let Daddy have a look.'

'I got a string to pull it with.' The child brought from his pocket a tangled thread. 'Virgie said to tie it to the tooth and tie the other end to the doorknob and shut the door real suddenly.'

Martin took out a clean handkerchief and felt the loose tooth carefully. 'That tooth is coming out of my Andy's mouth tonight. Otherwise I'm awfully afraid we'll have a tooth tree in the family.'

'What?'

'A tooth tree,' Martin said. 'You'll bite into something and swallow that tooth. And the tooth will take root in poor Andy's stomach and grow into a tooth tree with sharp little teeth instead of leaves.'

'Shoo, Daddy,' Andy said. But he held the tooth firmly between his grimy little thumb and forefinger. 'There ain't any tree like that. I never seen one.'

'There *isn't* any tree like that and I never *saw* one.'

Martin tensed suddenly. Emily was coming down the stairs. He listened to her fumbling footsteps, his arm embracing the little boy with dread. When Emily came into the room he saw from her movements and her sullen face that she had again been at the sherry bottle. She began to yank open drawers and set the table.

'Condition!' she said in a furry voice. 'You talk to me like that. Don't think I'll forget. I remember every dirty lie you say to me. Don't you think for a minute that I forget.'

'Emily!' he begged. 'The children———'

'The children—yes! Don't think I don't see through your dirty plots and schemes. Down here trying to turn my own children against me. Don't think I don't see and understand.'

'Emily! I beg you—please go upstairs.'

'So you can turn my children—my very own children———' Two large tears coursed rapidly down her cheeks. 'Trying to turn my little boy, my Andy, against his own mother.'

With drunken impulsiveness Emily knelt on the floor before the startled child. Her hands on his shoulders balanced her. 'Listen, my Andy—you wouldn't listen to any lies your father tells you? You wouldn't believe what he says? Listen, Andy, what was your father telling you before I came downstairs?' Uncertain, the child sought his father's face. 'Tell me. Mama wants to know.'

'About the tooth tree.'

'What?'

The child repeated the words and she echoed them with un-believing terror. 'The tooth tree!' She swayed and renewed her grasp on the child's shoulder. 'I don't know what you're talking about. But listen, Andy, Mama is all right, isn't she?' The tears were spilling down her face and Andy drew back from her, for he was afraid. Grasping the table edge, Emily stood up.

'See! You have turned my child against me.'

Marianne began to cry, and Martin took her in his arms.

'That's all right, you can take *your* child. You have always shown partiality from the very first. I don't mind, but at least you can leave me my little boy.'

Andy edged close to his father and touched his leg. 'Daddy,' he wailed.

Martin took the children to the foot of the stairs. 'Andy, you take up Marianne and Daddy will follow you in a minute.'

'But Mama?' the child asked, whispering.

'Mama will be all right. Don't worry.'

Emily was sobbing at the kitchen table, her face buried in the crook of her arm. Martin poured a cup of soup and set it before her. Her rasping sobs unnerved him; the vehemence of her emotion, irrespective of the source, touched in him a strain of tenderness. Unwillingly her laid his hand on her dark hair. 'Sit up and drink the soup.' Her face as she looked up at him was chastened and imploring. The boy's withdrawal or the touch of Martin's hand had turned the tenor of her mood.

'Ma-Martin,' she sobbed. 'I'm so ashamed.'

'Drink the soup.'

Obeying him, she drank between gasping breaths. After a second cup she allowed him to lead her up to their room. She was docile now and more restrained. He laid her nightgown on the bed and was about to leave the room when a fresh round of grief, the alcoholic tumult, came again.

'He turned away. My Andy looked at me and turned away.'

Impatience and fatigue hardened his voice, but he spoke warily. 'You forget that Andy is still a little child—he can't comprehend the meaning of such scenes.'

'Did I make a scene? Oh, Martin, did I make a scene before the children?'

Her horrified face touched and amused him against his will. 'Forget it. Put on your nightgown and go to sleep.'

'My child turned away from me. Andy looked at his mother and turned away. The children———'

She was caught in the rhythmic sorrow of alcohol. Martin withdrew from the room saying: 'For God's sake go to sleep. The children will forget by tomorrow.'

As he said this he wondered if it was true. Would the scene glide so easily from memory—or would it root in the unconscious to fester in the after-years? Martin did not know, and the last alternative sickened him. He thought of Emily, foresaw the morning-after humiliation: the shards of memory, the lucidities that glared from the obliterating darkness of shame. She would call the New York office twice—possibly three or four times. Martin anticipated his own embarrassment, wondering if the others at the office could possibly suspect. He felt that his secretary had divined the trouble long ago and that she pitied him. He suffered a moment of rebellion against his fate; he hated his wife.

Once in the children's room he closed the door and felt secure for the first time that evening. Marianne fell down on the floor, picked herself up and calling: 'Daddy, watch me,' fell again, got up, and continued the falling-calling routine. Andy sat in the child's low chair, wobbling the tooth. Martin ran the water in the tub, washed his own hands in the lavatory, and called the boy into the bathroom.

'Let's have another look at that tooth.' Martin sat on the toilet, holding Andy between his knees. The child's mouth

gaped and Martin grasped the tooth. A wobble, a quick twist
and the nacreous milk tooth was free. Andy's face was for the
first moment split between terror, astonishment, and delight.
He mouthed a swallow of water and spat into the lavatory.

'Look, Daddy! It's blood. Marianne!'

Martin loved to bathe his children, loved inexpressibly the
tender, naked bodies as they stood in the water so exposed. It
was not fair of Emily to say that he showed partiality. As Martin
soaped the delicate boy-body of his son he felt that further love
would be impossible. Yet he admitted the difference in the quality of his emotions for the two children. His love for his daughter
was graver, touched with a strain of melancholy, a gentleness
that was akin to pain. His pet names for the little boy were the
absurdities of daily inspiration—he called the little girl always
Marianne, and his voice as he spoke it was a caress. Martin patted
dry the fat baby stomach and the sweet little genital fold. The
washed child faces were radiant as flower petals, equally loved.

'I'm putting the tooth under my pillow. I'm supposed to get
a quarter.'

'What for?'

'*You* know, Daddy. Johnny got a quarter for his tooth.'

'Who puts the quarter there?' asked Martin. 'I used to think
the fairies left it in the night. It was a dime in my day, though.'

'That's what they say in kindergarden.'

'Who does put it there?'

'Your parents.' Andy said. 'You!'

Martin was pinning the cover on Marianne's bed. His daughter was already asleep. Scarcely breathing, Martin bent over and
kissed her forehead, kissed again the tiny hand that lay palm-
upward, flung in slumber beside her head.

'Good night, Andy-man.'

The answer was only a dowsy murmur. After a minute
Martin took out his change and slid a quarter underneath the
pillow. He left a night light in the room.

As Martin prowled about the kitchen making a late meal,
it occurred to him that the children had not once mentioned

their mother or the scene that must have seemed to them incomprehensible. Absorbed in the instant—the tooth, the bath, the quarter—the fluid passage of child-time had borne these weightless episodes like leaves in the swift current of a shallow stream while the adult enigma was beached and forgotten on the shore. Martin thanked the Lord for that.

But his own anger, repressed and lurking, arose again. His youth was being frittered by a drunkard's waste, his very manhood subtly undermined. And the children, once the immunity of incomprehension passed—what would it be like in a year or so? With his elbows on the table he ate his food brutishly, untasting. There was no hiding the truth—soon there would be gossip in the office and in the town; his wife was a dissolute woman. Dissolute. And he and his children were bound to a future of degradation and slow ruin.

Martin pushed away from the table and stalked into the living room. He followed the lines of a book with his eyes but his mind conjured miserable images: he saw his children drowned in the river, his wife a disgrace on the public street. By bedtime the dull, hard anger was like a weight upon his chest and his feet dragged as he climbed the stairs.

The room was dark except for the shafting light from the half-opened bathroom door. Martin undressed quietly. Little by little, mysteriously, there came in him a change. His wife was asleep, her peaceful respiration sounding gently in the room. Her high-heeled shoes with the carelessly dropped stockings made to him a mute appeal. Her underclothes were flung in disorder on the chair. Martin picked up the girdle and the soft, silk brassière and stood for a moment with them in his hands. For the first time that evening he looked at his wife. His eyes rested on the sweet forehead, the arch of the fine brow. The brow had descended to Marianne, and the tilt at the end of the delicate nose. In his son he could trace the high cheekbones and pointed chin. Her body was full-bosomed, slender and undulant. As Martin watched the tranquil slumber of his wife the ghost of the old anger vanished. All thoughts of blame or blemish were distant from him now. Martin put out the bathroom light and raised the window. Careful not to awaken Emily he slid into the bed. By moonlight he watched his wife for the last time. His hand sought the adjacent flesh and sorrow paralleled desire in the immense complexity of love.

RAYMOND CARVER

Will You Please Be Quiet, Please?

18 - Ralph Wyman

1.

When he was 18 and left home for the first time, in the fall, Ralph Wyman had been advised by his father, principal of Jefferson Elementary School in Weaverville and trumpet-player in the Elks' Club Auxiliary Band, that life today was a serious matter; something that required strength and direction in a young person just setting out. A difficult journey, everyone knew that, but nevertheless a comprehensible one, he believed.

But in college Ralph's goals were still hazy and undefined. He first thought he wanted to be a doctor, or a lawyer, and he took pre-medical courses and courses in history of jurisprudence and business-law before he decided he had neither the emotional detachment necessary for medicine, nor the ability for sustained reading and memorization in the *Corpus Iuris Civilis,* as well as the more modern texts on property and inheritance. Though he continued to take classes here and there in the sciences and in the Department of Business, he also took some lower-division classes in history and philosophy and English. He continually felt he was on the brink of some kind of momentous discovery about himself. But it never came. It was during this time, his lowest ebb, as he jokingly referred back to it later, that he believed he almost became an alcoholic; he was in a fraternity and he used to get drunk every night. He drank so much, in fact, that he even acquired something of a reputation; guys called him Jackson, after the bartender at The Keg, and he sat every day in the cafeteria with a deck of cards playing poker, solitaire, or bridge, if someone happened along. His grades were down and he was thinking of dropping out of school entirely and joining the air force.

Then, in his third year, he came under the influence of a particularly fascinating and persuasive literature teacher. Dr. Maxwell was his name; Ralph would never forget him. He was a handsome, graceful man in his early forties, with exquisite manners and with just the trace of a slight southern drawl to his voice. He had been educated at Vanderbilt, had studied in Europe, and later had had something to do with one or two literary magazines in New York. Almost overnight, it seemed to him, Ralph decided on teaching as a career. He stopped drinking so much and began to bear down on his studies. Within a year he was elected to Omega Psi, the national journalism fraternity; he became a member of the English Club; was invited to come with his cello, which he hadn't played in three years, and join in a student chamber music group just forming; and he ran successfully for Secretary of the Senior Class. He also started going out with Marian Ross that year; a pale, slender girl he had become acquainted with in a Chaucer class.

She wore her hair long and liked high-necked sweaters in the winter; and summer and winter she always went around with a leather purse on a long strap swinging from her shoulder. Her eyes were large and seemed to take in everything at a glance; if she got excited over something, they flashed and widened even more. He liked going out with her in the evenings. They went to The Keg, and a few other nightspots where everyone else went, but they never let their going together, or

their subsequent engagement that next summer, interfere with
their studies. They were serious students, and both sets of parents eventually gave their approval of the match. They did their
student-teaching at the same high school in Chico the next
spring, and went through graduation exercises together in June.
They married in St. James Episcopal Church two weeks later.
Both of them held hands the night before their wedding and
pledged solemnly to preserve forever the excitement and the
mystery of marriage.

For their honeymoon they drove to Guadalajara; and while
they both enjoyed visiting the old decayed churches and the
poorly lighted museums, and the several afternoons they spent
shopping and exploring in the marketplace (which swarmed
with flies), Ralph secretly felt a little appalled and at the same
time let down by the squalor and promiscuity of the people; he
was only too glad to get back to more civilized California. Even
so, Marian had seemed to enjoy it, and he would always remember one scene in particular. It was late afternoon, almost evening, and Marian was leaning motionless on her arms over the
iron-worked balustrade of their rented, second-floor *casa* as he
came up the dusty road below. Her hair was long and hung
down in front over her shoulders, and she was looking away
from him, staring at something toward the horizon. She wore
a white blouse with a bright red scarf at the throat, and he
could see her breasts pushing against her front. He had a bottle
of dark, unlabeled wine under his arm, and the whole incident
reminded him of something from a play, or a movie. Thinking
back on it later, it was always a little vaguely disturbing for
some reason.

Before they had left for their six-week honeymoon, they had
accepted teaching positions at a high school in Eureka, in the
northern part of the state near the ocean. They waited a year
to make certain that the school and the weather, and the people
themselves were exactly what they wanted to settle down to,
and then made a substantial down-payment on a house in the
Fire Hill district. He felt, without really thinking about it, that

they understood each other perfectly; as well, anyway, as any two people could understand one another. More, he understood himself; his capacities, his limitations. He knew where he was going and how to get there.

In eight years they had two children, Dorothea and Robert, who were now five and four years old. A few months after Robert, Marian had accepted at mid-term a part-time position as a French and English teacher at Harris Junior College, at the edge of town. The position had become full-time and permanent that next fall, and Ralph had stayed on, happily, at the high school. In the time they had been married, they had had only one serious disturbance, and that was long ago: two years ago that winter to be exact. It was something they had never talked about since it happened, but, try as he might, Ralph couldn't help thinking about it sometimes. On occasion, and then when he was least prepared, the whole ghastly scene leaped into his mind. Looked at rationally and in its proper, historical perspective, it seemed impossible and monstrous; an event of such personal magnitude for Ralph that he still couldn't entirely accept it as something that had once happened to Marian and himself: he had taken it into his head one night at a party that Marian had betrayed him with Mitchell Anderson, a friend. In a fit of uncontrollable rage, he had struck Marian with his fist, knocking her sideways against the kitchen table and onto the floor.

It was a Sunday night in November. The children were in bed. Ralph was sleepy, and he still had a dozen themes from his twelfth-grade class in accelerated English to correct before tomorrow morning. He sat on the edge of the couch, leaning forward with his red pencil over a space he'd cleared on the coffee table. He had the papers separated into two stacks, and one of the papers folded open in front of him. He caught himself blinking his eyes, and again felt irritated with the Franklins. Harold and Sarah Franklin. They'd stopped over early in the afternoon for cocktails and stayed on into the evening. Otherwise, Ralph would have finished hours ago, as he'd planned.

He'd been sleepy, too, he remembered, the whole time they were here. He'd sat in the big leather chair by the fireplace and once he recalled letting his head sink back against the warm leather of the chair and starting to close his eyes when Franklin had cleared his throat loudly. Too loudly. He didn't feel comfortable with Franklin anymore. Harold Franklin was a big, forthright man with bushy eyebrows who caught you and held you with his eyes when he spoke. He looked like he never combed his hair, his suits were always baggy, and Ralph thought his ties hideous, but he was one of the few men on the staff at Harris Junior College who had his Ph.D. At 35 he was head of the combined History and Social Science Departments. Two years ago he and Sarah had been witness to a large part of Ralph's humiliation. That occasion had never later been brought up by any of them, of course, and in a few weeks, the next time they'd seen one another, it was as though nothing had happened. Still, since then, Ralph couldn't help feeling a little uneasy when he was around them.

He could hear the radio playing softly in the kitchen, where Marian was ironing. He stared a while longer at the papers in front of him, then gathered up all the papers, turned off the lamp, and walked out to the kitchen.

"Finished, love?" Marian said with a smile. She was sitting on a tall stool, ironing one of Robert's shirts. She sat the iron up on its end as if she'd been waiting for him.

"Damn it, no," he said with an exaggerated grimace, tossing the papers on the table. "What the hell the Franklins come by here for anyway?"

She laughed; bright, pleasant. It made him feel better. She held up her face to be kissed, and he gave her a little peck on the cheek. He pulled out a chair from the table and sat down, leaned back on the legs and looked at her. She smiled again, and then lowered her eyes.

"I'm already half-asleep," he said.

"Coffee," she said, reaching over and laying the back of her hand against the electric percolator.

He nodded.

She took a long drag from the cigarette she'd had burning in the ashtray, smoked it a minute while she stared at the floor, and then put it back in the ashtray. She looked up at him, and a smile started at the corners of her mouth. She was tall and limber, with a good bust, narrow hips, and wide, gleaming eyes.

"Ralph, do you remember that party?" she asked, still looking at him.

He shifted in the chair and said, "Which party? You mean that one two or three years ago?"

She nodded.

He waited a minute and asked, when she didn't say anything else, "What about it? Now that you brought it up, honey, what about it?" Then: "He kissed you after all, that night, didn't he? . . . Did he try to kiss you, or didn't he?"

"I didn't say that," she said. "I was just thinking about it and I asked you; that's all."

"Well, he did, didn't he? Come on, Marian, we're just talking, aren't we?"

"I'm afraid it'd make you angry, Ralph."

"It won't make me angry, Marian. It was a long time ago, wasn't it? I won't be angry . . . Well?"

"Well, yes," she said slowly, "he did kiss me a few times." She smiled tentatively, gauging his reaction.

His first impulse was to return her smile, and then he felt himself blushing and said defensively, "You told me before he didn't. You said he only put his arm around you while he was driving."

He stared at her. It all came back to him again; the way she looked coming in the back door that night; eyes bright, trying to tell him . . . something, he didn't hear. He hit her in the mouth, at the last instant pulling to avoid her nose, knocked her against the table where she sat down hard on the floor. "What did you do that for?" she'd asked dreamily, her eyes still bright, and her mouth dripping blood. "Where were you all night?" he'd yelled, teetering over her, his legs watery and trembling.

He'd drawn back his fist again but already sorry for the first blow, the blood he'd caused. "I wasn't gone all night," she'd said, turning her head back and forth heavily. "I didn't do anything. Why did you hit me?"

Ralph passed his open hand over his forehead, shut his eyes for a minute. "I guess I lost my head that night, all right. We were both in the wrong. You for leaving the party with Mitchell Anderson, and I for losing my head. I'm sorry."

"I'm sorry, too," she said. "Even so," she grinned, "you didn't have to knock hell out of me."

"I don't know—maybe I should've done more." He looked at her, and then they both had to laugh.

"How did we ever get onto this?" she asked.

"You brought it up," he said.

She shook her head. "The Franklins being here made me think of it, I guess." She pulled in her upper lip and stared at the floor. In a minute she straightened her shoulders and looked up. "If you'll move this ironing board for me, love, I'll make us a hot drink. A buttered rum: now how does that sound?"

"Good."

She went into the living room and turned on the lamp, bent to pick up a magazine by the endtable. He watched her hips under the plaid woolen skirt. She moved in front of the window by the large dining room table and stood looking out at the street light. She smoothed her palm down over her right hip, then began tucking in her blouse with the fingers of her right hand. He wondered what she was thinking. A car went by outside, and she continued to stand in front of the window.

After he stood the ironing board in its alcove on the porch, he sat down again and said, when she came into the room, "Well, what else went on between you and Mitchell Anderson that night? It's all right to talk about it now."

Anderson had left Harris less than two years ago to accept a position as Associate Professor of Speech and Drama at a new, four-year college the state was getting underway in southwestern California. He was in his early thirties, like everyone else they knew; a slender, moustached man with a rough, slightly pocked face; he was a casual, eccentric dresser and sometimes, Marian had told Ralph, laughing, he wore a green velvet smoking jacket to school. The girls in his classes were crazy about him, she said. He had thin, dark hair which he combed forward to cover the balding spot on the top of his head. Both he and his wife, Emily, a costume designer, had done a lot of acting and directing in Little Theater in the Bay Area before coming to Eureka. As a person, though, someone he liked to be around, it was something different as far as Ralph was concerned. Thinking about it, he decided he hadn't liked him from the beginning, and he was glad he was gone.

"What else?" he asked.

"Nothing," she said. "I'd rather not talk about it now, Ralph, if you don't mind. I was thinking about something else."

"What?"

"Oh . . . about the children, the dress I want Dorothea to have for next Easter; that sort of thing. Silly, unrelated things. And about the class I'm going to have tomorrow. Walt Whitman. Some of the kids didn't approve when I told them there was a, a bit of speculation Whitman was—how should I say it? —attracted to certain men." She laughed. "Really, Ralph, nothing else happened. I'm sorry I ever said anything about it."

"Okay."

He got up and went to the bathroom to wash cold water over his face. When he came out he leaned against the wall by the refrigerator and watched her measure out the sugar into the two cups and then stir in the rum. The water was boiling on the stove. The clock on the wall behind the table said 9:45.

"Look, honey, it's been brought up now," he said. "It was two or three years ago; there's no reason at all I can think of we can't talk about it if we want to, is there?"

"There's really nothing to talk about, Ralph."

"I'd like to know," he said vaguely.

"Know what?"

"Whatever else he did beside kiss you. We're adults. We haven't seen the Andersons in . . . a year at least. We'll probably never see them again. It happened a long time ago; as I see it, there's no reason whatever we can't talk about it." He was a little surprised at the level, reasoning quality in his voice. He sat down and looked at the tablecloth, and then looked up at her again. "Well?"

"Well," she said, laughing a little, tilting her head to one side, remembering. "No, Ralph, really; I'm not trying to be coy about it either: I'd just rather not."

"For Christ's sake, Marian! Now I mean it," he said, "if you don't tell me, it will make me angry."

She turned off the gas under the water and put her hand out on the stool; then sat down again, hooking her heels over the bottom step. She leaned forward, resting her arms across her knees. She picked at something on her skirt and then looked up.

"You remember Emily'd already gone home with the Beattys, and for some reason Mitchell had stayed on. He looked a little out of sorts that night to begin with. I don't know, maybe they weren't getting along . . . But I don't know that. But there were you and I, the Franklins, and Mitchell Anderson left. All of us a little drunk, if I remember rightly. I'm not sure how it happened, Ralph, but Mitchell and I just happened to find ourselves alone together in the kitchen for a minute. There was no whiskey left, only two or three bottles of that white wine we had. It must've been close to one o'clock because Mitchell said, 'If we hurry we can make it before the liquor store closes.' You know how he can be so theatrical when he wants? Softshoe stuff, facial expressions . . . ? Anyway, he was very witty about it all. At least it seemed that way at the time. And very drunk, too, I might add. So was I, for that matter . . . It was an impulse, Ralph, I swear. I don't know why I did it, don't ask me, but when he said, 'Let's go'—I agreed. We went out the back, where his car was parked. We went just like we were: we didn't even get our coats out of the closet. We thought we'd just be gone a

few minutes. I guess we thought no one would miss us . . . I
don't know what we thought . . . I don't know *why* I went,
Ralph. It was an impulse, that's all that I can say. It was a wrong
impulse." She paused. "It was my fault that night, Ralph, and
I'm sorry. I shouldn't have done anything like that, I know that."

"Christ!" the word leaped out. "But you've always been that
way, Marian!"

"That isn't true!"

His mind filled with a swarm of tiny accusations, and he tried
to focus on one in particular. He looked down at his hands and
noticed they had the same lifeless feeling as they did when he
woke up mornings. He picked up the red pencil lying on the
table, and then put it down again.

"I'm listening," he said.

"You're angry," she said. "You're swearing and getting all
upset, Ralph. For nothing, nothing, honey! . . . There's nothing else."

"Go on."

"*What* is the matter with us anyway? How did we ever get
onto this subject?"

"Go on, Marian."

"That's all, Ralph. I've told you. We went for a ride . . .
We talked. He kissed me. I still don't see how we could've been
gone three hours; whatever it was you said."

He remembered again the waiting, the unbearable weakness
that spread down through his legs when they'd been gone an
hour, two hours. It made him lean weakly against the corner
of the house after he'd gone outside; for a breath of air he said
vaguely, pulling into his coat, but really so that the embarrassed
Franklins could themselves leave without any more embarrassment; without having to take leave of the absent host, or the
vanished hostess. From the corner of the house, standing behind
the rose trellis in the soft, crumbly dirt, he watched the Franklins get into their car and drive away. Anger and frustration
clogged inside him, then separated into little units of humiliation
that jumped against his stomach. He waited. Gradually the hor-

ror drained away as he stood there, until finally nothing was left
but a vast, empty realization of betrayal. He went into the house
and sat at this same table, and he remembered his shoulder began
to twitch and he couldn't stop it even when he squeezed it with
his fingers. An hour later, or two hours—what difference did it
make then?—she'd come in.

"Tell me the rest, Marian." And he knew there was more
now. He felt a slight fluttering start up in his stomach, and suddenly he didn't want to know any more. "No. Do whatever you
want. If you don't want to talk about it, Marian, that's all right.
Do whatever you want to, Marian. Actually, I guess I'd just as
soon leave it at that."

He worked his shoulders against the smooth, solid chairback,
then balanced unsteadily on the two back legs. He thought
fleetingly that he would have been someplace else tonight, doing something else at this very moment, if he hadn't married.
He glanced around the kitchen. He began to perspire and leaned
forward, setting all the legs on the floor. He took one of her
cigarettes from the pack on the table. His hands were trembling
as he struck the match.

"Ralph. You won't be angry, will you? Ralph? We're just
talking. You won't, will you?" She had moved over to a chair
at the table.

"I won't."

"Promise?"

"Promise."

She lit a cigarette. He had suddenly a great desire to see
Robert and Dorothea; to get them up out of bed, heavy and
turning in their sleep, and hold each of them on a knee, jiggle
them until they woke up and began to laugh. He absently began
to trace with his finger the outline of one of the tiny black
coaches in the beige tablecloth. There were four miniature white
prancing horses pulling each of the tiny coaches. The figure
driving the horses had his arm up and was wearing a tall hat.
Suitcases were strapped down on top of the coach, and what
looked like a kerosene lamp hung from the side.

"We went straight to the liquor store, and I waited in the car till he came out. He had a sack in one hand and one of those plastic bags of ice in the other. He weaved a little getting into the car. I hadn't realized he was so drunk until we started driving again, and I noticed the way he was driving; terribly slow, and all hunched over the wheel with his eyes staring. We were talking about a lot of things that didn't make sense . . . I can't remember . . . Nietzsche . . . and Strindberg; he was directing *Miss Julie* second semester, you know, and something about Norman Mailer stabbing his wife in the breast a long time ago, and how he thought Mailer was going downhill anyway—a lot of crazy things like that. Then, I'll swear before God it was an accident, Ralph, he didn't know what he was doing, he made a wrong turn and we somehow wound up out by the golf course, right near Jane Van Eaton's. In fact, we pulled into her driveway to turn around and when we did Mitchell said to me, 'We might as well open one of these bottles.' He did, he opened it, and then he drove a little farther on down the road that goes around the green, you know, and comes out by the park? Actually, not too far from the Franklins . . . And then he stopped for a minute in the middle of the road with his lights on, and we each took a drink out of the bottle. Then he said, said he'd hate to think of me being stabbed in the breast. I guess he was still thinking about Mailer's wife. And then . . . I can't say it, Ralph . . . I know you'd get angry."

"I won't get angry, Marian," he said slowly. His thoughts seemed to move lazily, as if he were in a dream, and he was able to take in only one thing at a time she was telling him. At the same time he noticed a peculiar alertness taking hold of his body.

"Go on. Then what, Marian?"

"You aren't angry, are you? Ralph?"

"No. But I'm getting interested, though."

They both had to laugh, and for a minute everything was all right. He leaned across the table to light another cigarette for her, and they smiled at each other; just like any other night. He struck another match, held it a while, and then brought the

match, almost to burn his fingers, up under the end of the cigarette that protruded at an angle from his lips. He dropped the
burned match into the ashtray and stared at it before looking up.

"Go on."

"I don't know . . . things seemed to happen fast after that.
He drove up the road a little and turned off someplace, I don't
know, maybe right onto the green . . . and started kissing me.
Then he said, said he'd like to kiss my breast. I said I didn't
think we should. I said, 'What about Emily?' He said I didn't
know her. He got the car going again, and then he stopped again
and just sort of slumped over and put his head on my lap. God!
It sounds so vulgar now, I know, but it didn't seem that way at
all then. I felt like, like I was losing my innocence somehow,
Ralph. For the first time—that night I realized I was really, really
doing something wrong, something I wasn't supposed to do and
that might hurt people. I shouldn't be there, I felt. And I felt . . .
like it was the first time in my life I'd ever *intentionally* done
anything wrong or hurtful and gone on doing it, knowing I
shouldn't be. Do you know what I mean, Ralph? Like some of
the characters in Henry James? I felt that way. Like . . . for
the first time . . . my innocence . . . something was happening."

"You can dispense with that shit," he cut in. "Get off it,
Marian! Go on! Then what? Did he caress you? Did he? Tell
me!"

And then she hurried on, trying to get over the hard spots
quickly, and he sat with his hands folded on the table and
watched her lips out of which dropped the frightful words.
His eyes skipped around the kitchen—stove, cupboards, toaster,
radio, coffeepot, window, curtains, refrigerator, breadbox, nap-
kin holder, stove, cupboards, toaster . . . back to her face. Her
dark eyes glistened under the overhead light. He felt a peculiar
desire for her flicker through his thighs at what she was leading
up to, and at the same time he had to check an urge to stand up
yelling, smash his fist into her face.

" 'Shall we have a go at it?' he said."

"Shall we have a go at it?" Ralph repeated.

"I'm to blame. If anyone should, should be blamed for it, I'm to blame. He said he'd leave it all up to me, I could . . . could do . . . whatever I wanted." Tears welled out of her eyes, started down her cheeks. She looked down at the table, blinked rapidly.

He shut his eyes. He saw a barren field under a heavy, gray sky; a fog moving in across the far end. He shook his head, tried to admit other possibilities, other conclusions. He tried to bring back that night two years ago, imagine himself coming into the kitchen just as she and Mitchell were at the door, hear himself telling her in a hearty voice, Oh no, no; you're not going out for liquor with that Mitchell Anderson! He's drunk, and he isn't a good driver to boot. You've got to go to bed now and get up with little Robert and Dorothea in the morning . . . Stop! Stop where you are.

He opened his eyes, raised his eyebrows as if he were just waking up. She had a hand up over her face and was crying silently, her shoulders rounded and moving in little jerks.

"Why did you go with him, Marian?" he asked desperately. She shook her head without looking up.

Then, suddenly, he knew. His mind buckled. *Cuckold.* For a minute he could only stare helplessly at his hands. Then he wanted to pass it off somehow, say it was all right, it was two years ago, adults, etc. He wanted to forgive: *I forgive you.* But he could not forgive. He couldn't forgive her this. His thoughts skittered around the Middle Ages, touched on Arthur and Guinevere, surged on to the outraged husbandry of the eighteenth-century dramatists, came to a sullen halt with Karenin. But what had any of them to do with him? What were they? They were nothing. Nothing. Figments. They did not exist. Their discoveries, their disintegrations, adjustments, did not all relate to him. No relation. What then? What did it all mean? What is the nature of a book? his mind roared.

"Christ!" he said, springing up from the table. "*Jesus Christ.* Christ, no, Marian!"

"No, no," she said, throwing her head back.

"You let him!"

"No, no, Ralph."

"You let him! Didn't you? Didn't you? Answer me!" he yelled. "That s-s-swine," he said, his teeth chattering. "That bastard."

"Listen, listen to me, Ralph. I swear to you he didn't." She rocked from side to side in the chair, shaking her head.

"You wouldn't let him! That's it, isn't it? Yes, yes, you had your scruples. Oh God! God *damn* you!"

"God!" she said, getting up, holding out her hands. "Are we crazy, Ralph? Have we lost our minds? Ralph? Forgive me, Ralph. Forgive—"

"Don't touch me! Get away from me, Marian."

"In God's name, Ralph! Ralph! Please, Ralph. For the children's sake, Ralph. Don't go, Ralph. Please don't go, Ralph!" Her eyes were white and large, and she began to pant in her fright. She tried to head him off, but he took her by the shoulder and pushed her out of the way.

"Forgive me, Ralph! *Please.* Ralph!"

He slammed the kitchen door, started across the porch. Behind him, she jerked open the door, clattered over the dustpan as she rushed onto the porch. She took his arm at the porch door, but he shook her loose. "Ralph!" But he jumped down the steps onto the walk.

When he was across the driveway and walking rapidly down the sidewalk, he could hear her at the door yelling for him. Her voice seemed to be coming through a kind of murk. He looked back: she was still calling, limned against the doorway. My God, he thought, what a sideshow it was. Fat men and bearded ladies.

2.

He had to stop and lean against a car for a few minutes before going on. But two well-dressed couples were coming down the sidewalk toward him, and the man on the outside, near the curb, was telling a story in a loud voice. The others were already laughing. Ralph pushed off from the car and crossed the street.

In a few minutes he came to Blake's, where he stopped some afternoons for a beer with Dick Koenig before picking up the children from nursery school.

It was dark inside. The air was warm and heavy with the odor of beer and seemed to catch at the top of his throat and make it hard for him to swallow. Candles flickered dimly in long-necked wine bottles at some of the tables along the left wall when he closed the door. He glimpsed shadowy figures of men and women talking with their heads close together. One of the couples, near the door, stopped talking and looked up at him. A box-like fixture in the ceiling revolved overhead, throwing out pale red and green lights. Two men sat at the end of the bar, and a dark cutout of a man leaned over the jukebox in the corner, his hands splayed out on each side of the glass.

The man is going to play something. Ralph stands in the center of the floor, watches him. He sways, rubs his wrist against his forehead, and starts out.

"Ralph!—Mr. Wyman, sir!"

He stopped, looked around. David Parks was calling to him from behind the bar. Ralph walked over, leaned heavily against the bar before sliding onto a stool.

"Should I draw one, Mr. Wyman?" He had the glass in his hand, smiling.

He worked evenings and weekends for Charley Blake. He was 26, married, had two children, babies. He attended Harris Junior College on a football scholarship, and worked besides. He had three mouths to feed now, along with his own. Four mouths altogether. Not like it used to be. David Parks. He had a white bar towel slung over his shoulder.

Ralph nodded, watched him fill the glass.

He held the glass at an angle under the tap, slowly straightened it as the glass filled, closed the tap, and cut off the head with a smooth, professional air. He wiped the towel across the gleaming surface of the bar and set the glass in front of Ralph, still smiling.

"How's it going, Mr. Wyman? Didn't hear you come in." He put his foot up on a shelf under the bar. "Who's going to win the game next week, Mr. Wyman?"

Ralph shook his head, brought the beer to his lips. His shoulders ached with fatigue from being held rigid the last hour.

David Parks coughed faintly. "I'll buy you one, Mr. Wyman. This one's on me." He put his leg down, nodded assurance, and reached under his apron into his pocket.

"Here. I have it right here." Ralph pulled out some change, examined it in his hand from the light cast by a bare bulb on a stand next to the cash register. A quarter, nickel, two dimes, pennies. He laid down the quarter and stood up, pushing the change back into his pocket. The man was still in front of the jukebox, leaning his weight on one leg. The phone rang.

Ralph opened the door.

"Mr. Wyman! Mr. Wyman, for you, sir."

Outside he turned around, trying to decide what to do. He wanted to be alone, but at the same time he thought he'd feel better if other people were around. Not here though. His heart was fluttering, as if he'd been running. The door opened behind him and a man and woman came out. Ralph stepped out of the way and they got into a car parked at the curb. He recognized the woman as the receptionist at the children's dentist. He started off walking.

He walked to the end of the block, crossed the street, and walked another block before he decided to head downtown. It was eight or ten blocks and he walked hurriedly, his hands balled into his pockets, his shoes smacking the pavement. He kept blinking his eyes and thought it incredible he could still feel tired and fogged after all that had happened. He shook his head. He would have liked to sit someplace for a while and think about it, but he knew he could not sit, could not yet think about it. He remembered a man he saw once sitting on a curb in Arcata: an old man with a growth of beard and a brown wool cap who just sat there with his arms between his legs. But a minute later it snapped into his mind, and for the first time he tried to get a clear look at it; himself, Marian, the children—his world. But it was impossible. He wondered if anyone could ever stand back far enough from life to see it whole, all in one piece. He thought of an enormous French tapestry they'd seen two or three years ago that took up one wall of a room in the De Young Museum. He tried to imagine how all this would seem twenty years from now, but there was nothing. He couldn't picture the children any older, and when he tried to think about Marian and himself, there was only a blank space. Then, for a minute, he felt profoundly indifferent, somehow above it, as if it did not concern him. He thought of Marian without any emotion at all. He remembered her as he had seen her a little while ago; face crumpled, tears running off her nose. Then Marian on the floor, holding onto the chair, blood on her teeth: "Why did you hit me?" . . . Marian reaching under her dress to unfasten her garter belt . . . She raises her dress slowly as she leans back in the seat.

He stopped and thought he was going to be sick. He moved off onto the edge of a lawn. He cleared his throat several times and kept swallowing, looked up as a car of yelling teenagers went by and gave him a long blast on their musical horn. Yes, there was a vast amount of evil loose in the world, he thought, and it only awaited an opportunity, the propitious moment to manifest itself . . . But that was an academic notion. A kind of retreat. He spat ahead of him on the walk and put his heel on it. He mustn't let himself find solace in that kind of thinking. Not now. Not anymore, if he could help it. This he *knew* was evil: he felt it in his bones.

He came to Second Street, the part of town people called Two Street. It started here at Shelton, under the street light where the old rooming houses ended, and ran for four or five blocks on down to the pier, where fishing boats tied up. He'd been down here once, two years ago, to a second-hand store to look through the dusty shelves of old books. There was a liquor store across the street, and he could see a man standing outside in front of the glass door, looking at a newspaper.

Ralph crossed under the street light, read the headlines on the newspaper the man had been looking at, and went inside. A bell over the door tinkled. He hadn't noticed a bell that tinkled over a door since he was a child. He bought some cigarettes and went out again.

He walked down the street, looking in the windows. All the places were closed for the night, or vacated. Some of the windows had signs taped inside: a dance, a Shrine Circus that had come and gone last summer, an election—Vote For Fred C. Walters, Councilman. One of the windows he looked through had sinks and pipe-joints scattered around on a table. Everything dark. He came to a Vic Tanny Gym where he could see light coming under the curtains pulled across a big window. He could hear water splashing in the pool inside, and the hollow echo of voices calling across the water.

There was more light now, coming from the bars and cafés on both sides of the street. More people, groups of three or four but now and then a man by himself, or a woman in slacks walking rapidly. He stopped in front of the window of one place and watched some Negroes shooting pool. Gray cigarette smoke drifted around the lights over the table. One of the Negroes, who was chalking his cue, had his hat on and a cigarette in his mouth. He said something to another Negro, looked intently at the balls, and slowly leaned over the table.

He walked on, stopped in front of Jim's Oyster House. He had never been here before, had never been to any of these places before. Over the door the name was in yellow light bulbs: JIM's OYSTER HOUSE. Above the lights, fixed to an iron grill, a huge neon-lighted clam shell with a man's legs sticking out. The torso was hidden in the shell and the legs flashed red, on and off. Ralph lit another cigarette from the one he had, and pushed open the door.

It was crowded. A lot of people were bunched on the floor, their arms wrapped around each other or hanging loosely on someone's shoulders. The men in the band were just getting up from their chairs for an intermission. He had to excuse himself several times trying to get to the bar, and once a drunken woman took hold of his coat. There were no stools and he had to stand at the end of the bar between a coast guardsman and a shrunken-faced man in denims. Neither of them spoke. The coast guardsman had his white cap off and his elbows propped out in front of him, a hand on each side of his face. He stared at his glass without looking up. The other man shook his head and then pointed with his narrow chin two or three times at the coast guardsman. Ralph put his arm up and signaled the bartender. Once, Ralph thought he heard the shrunken-faced man say something, but he didn't answer.

His life was changed from tonight on. Were there many other men, he wondered drunkenly, who could look at one singular event in their lives and perceive the workings of the catastrophe that hereinafter sets their lives on a different course? Are there many who can perceive the necessary changes and adjustments that must necessarily and inevitably follow? Probably so, he decided after a minute's reflection.

Outside, in the alley, he took out his wallet again, let his fingers number the bills he had left: two dollars, and some change in his pocket. Enough for something to eat. Ham and eggs, perhaps. But he wasn't hungry. He leaned back against the damp brick wall of the building, trying to think. A car turned into the alley, stopped, and backed out again. He started walking. He went past the front of the Oyster House again, going back the way he'd come. He stayed close to the buildings, out of the way of the loud groups of men and women streaming up and down the sidewalk. He heard a woman in a long coat say to the man she was with, "It isn't that way at all, Bruce. You don't understand."

He stopped when he came to the liquor store. Inside he moved up to the counter and stared at the long, orderly rows of bottles. He bought a half-pint of rum and some more cigarettes. The palm tree on the label of the bottle, the drooping fronds with the lagoon in the background, had caught his eye. The clerk, a thin, bald man wearing suspenders, put the rum in a paper sack without a word and rang up the sale. Ralph could feel the man's eyes on him as he stood in front of the magazine rack, swaying a little and looking at the covers. Once he glanced up in the mirror over his head and caught the man staring at him from behind the counter; his arms were folded over his chest and his bald head gleamed in the reflected light. Finally the man turned off one of the lights in the back of the store and said, "Closing it up, buddy."

Outside again, Ralph turned around once and started down another street, toward the pier; he thought he'd like to see the water with the lights reflected on it. He wondered how far he would drop tonight before he began to level off. He opened the sack as he walked, broke the seal on the little bottle, and stopped in a doorway to take a long drink. He could hardly taste it. He crossed some old streetcar tracks and turned onto another, darker street. He could already hear the waves splashing under the pier.

3.

Birds darted overhead in the graying mist. He still couldn't see them, but he could hear their sharp *jueet-jueet*. He stopped and looked up, kept his eyes fixed in one place; then he saw them, no larger than his hand, dozens of them, wheeling and darting just under the heavy overcast. He wondered if they were sea-birds, birds that only came in off the ocean this time of morning. He'd never seen any birds around Eureka in the winter except now and then a big, lumbering seagull. He remembered once, a long time ago, walking into an old abandoned house—the Marshall place, near Uncle Jack's in Springfield, Oregon—how the sparrows kept flying in and out of the broken windows, flying around the rafters where they had their nests, and then flying out the windows again, trying to lead him away.

It was getting light. The overcast seemed to be lifting and was turning light-gray with patches of white clouds showing through here and there. The street was black with the mist that was still falling, and he had to be careful not to step on the snails that trailed across the damp sidewalk.

A car with its lights on slowed down as it went past, but he didn't look up. Another car passed. In a minute, another. He looked: four men, two in front, two in the back. One of the men in the back seat, wearing a hat, turned around and looked at him through the back window. Mill workers. The first shift of plywood mill workers going to work at Georgia-Pacific. It was Monday morning. He turned the corner, walked past Blake's; dark, the venetian blinds pulled over the windows and two empty beer bottles someone had left standing like sentinels beside the door. It was cold, and he walked slowly, crossing his arms now and then and rubbing his shoulders.

He came up the street to his house. He could see his front porch light on, but the rest of the house was dark. He crossed the lawn and went around to the back. He turned the knob, and the door opened quietly. He stepped onto the porch and shut the door. He waited a moment, then opened the kitchen door.

The house was quiet. There was the tall stool beside the draining board. There was the table where they'd sat. How long ago? He remembered he'd just gotten up off the couch, where he'd been working, and come into the kitchen and sat down . . . He looked at the clock over the stove: 7:00 a.m. He could see the dining room table with the lace cloth, the heavy glass centerpiece of red flamingos, their wings opened. The draperies behind the table were open. Had she stood at that window watching for him? He moved over to the door and stepped onto the living room carpet. Her coat was thrown over the couch, and in the pale light he could make out a large ashtray full of her cork cigarette ends on one of the cushions. He noticed the phone directory open on the coffee table as he went by. He stopped at the partially open door to their bedroom. For an instant he resisted the impulse to look in on her, and then with his finger he pushed open the door a few inches. She was sleeping, her head off the pillow, turned toward the wall, and her hair black against the sheet. The covers were bunched around her shoulders and had pulled up from the foot of the bed. She was on her side, her secret body slightly bent at the hips, her thighs closed together protectively. He stared for a minute. What, after all, should he do? Pack his things, now, and leave? Go to a hotel room until he can make other arrangements? Sleep on the extra bed in the little storage room upstairs? How should a man act, given the circumstances? The things that had been said last night. There was no undoing that—nor the other. There was no going back, but what course was he to follow now?

In the kitchen he laid his head down on his arms over the table. How should a man act? *How should a man act?* It kept repeating itself. Not just now, in this situation, for today and tomorrow, but every day on this earth. He felt suddenly there was an answer, that he somehow held the answer himself and that it was very nearly out if only he could think about it a little longer. Then he heard Robert and Dorothea stirring. He sat up slowly and tried to smile as they came into the kitchen.

"Daddy, daddy," they both said, running over to him in their pajamas.

"Tell us a story, daddy," Robert said, getting onto his lap.

"He can't tell us a story now," Dorothea said. "It's *too* early in the morning, isn't it, daddy?"

Ralph stepped into the bathroom and locked the door.

"Is your father here?" he heard Marian ask the children. "Where is he, in the bathroom? Ralph?"

"Ralph," she turned the knob. "Ralph, let me in, please, darling. Ralph? Please let me in, darling. I want to see you. Ralph? Please?"

"Go away, Marian. Just let me alone a while, all right?"

"Please, Ralph, open the door for a minute, darling. I just want to see you, Ralph. Ralph? What's wrong, darling? . . . Ralph?"

"Will you please be quiet, please?"

She waited at the door for a minute, turned the knob again,
and then he could hear her moving around the kitchen, getting
the children breakfast, trying to answer their questions.

He turned away from the mirror and sat down heavily on
the edge of the bathtub, began to unlace his shoes. No cowardly
Aegisthus waiting for him here, no Clytemnestra. He sat there
with a shoe in his hand and looked at the white, streamlined
clipper ships making their way across the pale blue of the plastic
shower curtain. He unbuttoned his shirt, leaned over the bathtub
with a sigh, and dropped in the plug. He opened the hot water
handle, and the steam rose.

As he stood naked a minute on the smooth tile before getting
into the water, he gathered in his fingers the slack flesh over his
ribs, looked at himself again in the clouded mirror. He started
when Marian called his name.

"Ralph. The children are in their room playing . . . I called
Von Williams and said you wouldn't be in today, and I'm going
to stay home." She waited and then said, "I have a nice breakfast
on the stove for you, darling, when you're through with your
bath . . . Ralph?"

"It's all right, Marian. I'm not hungry."

"Ralph . . . Come out, darling."

He stayed in the bathroom until he heard her upstairs over
the bathroom in the children's room. She was telling them: settle
down and get dressed; didn't they want to play with Warren
and Jeannie?

He went through the house and into the bedroom where he
shut the door. He looked at the bed before he crawled in. He
lay on his back and stared at the ceiling. *How should a man act?*
It had assumed immense importance in his mind, was far more
crucial and requiring of an answer than the other thing, the event
two years ago . . . He remembered he'd just gotten up off the
couch in the living room where he'd been working, and come
into the kitchen and sat down . . . The light ornament in the
ceiling began to sway. He snapped open his eyes and turned
onto his side as Marian came into the room.

She took off her robe and sat down on the edge of the bed. She put her hand under the covers and began gently stroking the lower part of his back. "Ralph," she murmured.

He tensed at her cold fingers, and then, gradually, he relaxed. He imagined he was floating on his back in the heavy, milky water of Juniper Lake, where he'd spent one summer years ago, and someone was calling to him, Come in, Ralph, Come in. But he kept on floating and didn't answer, and the soft rising waves laved his body.

He woke again as her hand moved over his hip. Then it traced his groin before flattening itself against his stomach. She was in bed now, pressing the length of her body against his and moving gently back and forth with him. He waited a minute, and then he turned to her and their eyes met.

Her eyes were filled and seemed to contain layer upon layer of shimmering color and reflection, thicker and more opaque farther in, and almost transparent at the lustrous surface. Then, as he gazed even deeper, he glimpsed in first one pupil and then the other, the cameo-like, perfect reflection of his own strange and familiar face. He continued to stare, marveling at the changes he dimly felt taking place inside him.

WILLIAM SHAKESPEARE

Excerpts from Romeo and Juliet

FROM ACT I, SCENE 3

LADY CAPULET. Marry, that 'marry' is the very theme
   I came to talk of. Tell me, daughter Juliet,
   How stands your disposition to be married?
JULIET. It is an honor that I dream not of.
NURSE. An honor! were not I thine only nurse,
   I would say thou hadst suck'd wisdom from thy teat.
LADY CAPULET. Well, think of marriage now; younger than you
   Here in Verona, ladies of esteem,
   Are made already mothers. By my count,
   I was your mother much upon these years
   That you are now a maid. Thus then in brief;
   The valiant Paris seeks you for his love.
NURSE. A man, young lady! lady, such a man
   As all the world—why, he's a man of wax.
LADY CAPULET. Verona's summer hath not such a flower.
NURSE. Nay, he's a flower; in faith, a very flower
LADY CAPULET. What say you? can you love the gentleman?
   This night you shall behold him at our feast:

Read o'er the volume of young Paris' face,
And find delight writ there with beauty's pen;
Examine every married lineament,
And see how one another lends content;
And what obscured in this fair volume lies
Find written in the margent of his eyes.
This precious book of love, this unbound lover,
To beautify him, only lacks a cover:
The fish lives in the sea; and 'tis much pride
For fair without the fair within to hide:
That book in many's eyes doth share the glory,
That in gold clasps locks in the golden story:
So shall you share all that he doth possess,
By having him making yourself no less.
NURSE. No less! nay, bigger: women grow by men.
LADY CAPULET. Speak briefly, can you like of Paris' love?
JULIET. I'll look to like, if looking liking move:
But no more deep will I endart mine eye
Than your consent gives strength to make it fly.

FROM ACT II, SCENE 2

ROMEO. O, wilt thou leave me so unsatisfied?
JULIET. What satisfaction canst thou have to-night?
ROMEO. The exchange of thy love's faithful vow for mine.
JULIET. I gave thee mine before thou didst request it:
And yet I would it were to give again.
ROMEO. Wouldst thou withdraw it? for what purpose, love?
JULIET. But to be frank, and give it thee again.
And yet I wish but for the thing I have:
My bounty is as boundless as the sea,
My love as deep; the more I give to thee,
The more I have, for both are infinite.

FROM ACT III, SCENE 2

JULIET. What storm is this that blows so contrary?
Is Romeo slaughter'd, and is Tybalt dead?

My dear-loved cousin, and my dearer lord?
Then, dreadful trumpet, sound the general doom!
For who is living, if those two are gone?
NURSE. Tybalt is gone, and Romeo banished;
  Romeo that kill'd him, he is banished.
JULIET. O God! did Romeo's hand shed Tybalt's blood?
NURSE. It did, it did; alas the day, it did!
JULIET. O serpent heart, hid with a flowering face!
  Did ever dragon keep so fair a cave?
  Beautiful tyrant! fiend angelical!
  Dove-feather'd raven! wolvish-ravening lamb!
  Despised substance of divinest show!
  Just opposite to what thou justly seem'st,
  A damned saint, an honorable villain!
  O nature, what hadst thou to do in hell,
  When thou didst bower the spirit of a fiend
  In mortal paradise of such sweet flesh?
  Was ever book containing such vile matter
  So fairly bound? O, that deceit should dwell
  In such a gorgeous palace!
NURSE.   There's no trust,
  No faith, no honesty in men; all perjured,
  All forsworn, all naught, all dissemblers.
    Ah, where's my man? give me some aqua vitæ:
  These griefs, these woes, these sorrows make me old.
  Shame come to Romeo!
JULIET. Blister'd be thy tongue
  For such a wish! he was not born to shame:
  Upon his brow shame is ashamed to sit;
  For 'tis a throne where honor may be crown'd
  Sole monarch of the universal earth.
  O, what a beast was I to chide at him!
NURSE. Will you speak well of him that kill'd your cousin?
JULIET. Shall I speak ill of him that is my husband?
  Ah, poor my lord, what tongue shall smooth thy name,
  When I, thy three-hours wife, have mangled it?

But wherefore, villain, didst thou kill my cousin?
That villain cousin would have kill'd my husband:
Back, foolish tears, back to your native spring;
Your tributary drops belong to woe,
Which you mistaking offer up to joy.
My husband lives, that Tybalt would have slain;
And Tybalt's dead, that would have slain my husband:
All this is comfort; wherefore weep I then?

FROM ACT IV, SCENE 3

JULIET. What if it be a poison, which the friar
  Subtly hath minister'd to have me dead,
  Lest in this marriage he should be dishonor'd,
  Because he married me before to Romeo?
  I fear it is; and yet, methinks, it should not,
  For he hath still been tried a holy man.
  How if, when I am laid into the tomb,
  I wake before the time that Romeo
  Come to redeem me? there's a fearful point.
  Shall I not then be stifled in the vault,
  To whose foul mouth no healthsome air breathes in,
  And there die strangled ere my Romeo comes?
  Or, if I live, is it not very like,
  The horrible conceit of death and night,
  Together with the terror of the place,
  As in a vault, an ancient receptacle,
  Where for these many hundred years the bones
  Of all my buried ancestors are pack'd;
  Where bloody Tybalt, yet but green in earth,
  Lies festering in his shroud; where, as they say,
  At some hours in the night spirits resort;
  Alack, alack, is it not like that I
  So early waking, what with loathsome smells
  And shrieks like mandrakes' torn out of the earth,
  That living mortals hearing them run mad:
  Or, if I wake, shall I not be distraught,

Environed with all these hideous fears?
And madly play with my forefathers' joints?
And pluck the mangled Tybalt from his shroud?
And, in this rage, with some great kinsman's bone,
As with a club, dash out my desperate brains?
O, look! methinks I see my cousin's ghost
Seeking out Romeo, that did spit his body
Upon a rapier's point: stay, Tybalt, stay!
Romeo, I come! this do I drink to thee.

SARA TEASDALE

The Lamp

If I can bear your love like a lamp before me,
When I go down the long steep Road of Darkness,
I shall not fear the everlasting shadows,
    Nor cry in terror.
If I can find out God, then I shall find Him,
If none can find Him, then I shall sleep soundly,
Knowing how well on earth your love sufficed me,
    A lamp in darkness.

Quote from the Bible

ECCLESIASTES 4:9-12

Two are better than one,
because they have a good reward for their toil.
For if they fall, one will lift up his fellow;
but woe to him who is alone when he falls and
    has not another to lift him up.
Again, if two lie together, they are warm;
but how can one be warm alone?
And though a man might prevail against one who is alone,
two will withstand him.
A threefold cord is not quickly broken.

HOBERT SKIDMORE

O My Lovely Caroline

Claude Hanson stood on the upper deck of the showboat Starlight and watched the hillmen hang lanterns from the trees on
the river's bank. As each lantern was lighted, more and more hill
people appeared suddenly, like apparitions, out of the darkness.
To Claude they were eager mourners come to watch him perish.

Though still erect, still large and handsome at sixty, Claude
lowered his head. But he understood that prayers could not
change the inevitable. Never before in his life had he broken a
promise to his beloved Caroline, but now he knew he was going
to be forced to forsake her.

His arms hung loosely at his sides, the fiddle in his left hand
and the bow in his right. As each lantern was lighted, throwing
a sterner glow on the wooden lacework of the showboat's decks,
each one seemed to highlight a different moment of his life with
Caroline. He saw again the astonishing way they had met, the
immediacy of their love, the patient weeks and months during
which she had taught him to read music and to learn the lines in
the plays, the joyous years on the river, the night he had saved
the Starlight from sinking, and Caroline's pride in him. He could

hardly believe they had had twenty-five years together—forty, really, for though she had been gone fifteen years, he had never once felt she had left him.

The last picture appeared clearly before his eyes, stronger than memory, sharper and more immediate.

The Starlight, tied up at Charleroi on the Monongahela, squatted grandly in the moonlight and though the spring night was balmy, their little room behind the stage held a fearful coldness.

"I've always loved you, Carrie," Claude said, holding his wife close to him, smiling a reassurance he did not feel, for the doctor had said she would never survive the diphtheria.

Lifting her hands, she placed them on his cheeks. Though she was forty, she seemed almost a child, an eager child forever impetuous and hopeful, as though the days and years were too brief. Her eyes passed around the tiny room, seeing each memento, every small and personal reminder of their years together: tintypes, bits of costume tinsel, sheet music hung about the mirror, souvenirs from hundreds of towns along the rivers. "You love the river, don't you, Claude?"

"Yes, Carrie, honey, just like I love you."

"How many rivers there are. The Wabash and Tennessee, Kentucky, Green, Ohio, Kanawha and Arkansas. And the Mississippi. Floating down them, playing the shows—oh, it's a special kind of life. The years have passed like magic. It's gone so quickly I don't even feel like I am a woman yet."

"You are my girl."

As though she did not hear him, Caroline continued, "It's a private world. The shores separate us from other people. And inside there's another world. A world we create on the stage. It is magic. It is!"

"Of course, Carrie."

Suddenly, frenzied, she grabbed him, her eyes looking at him with desperate beseeching. "Don't ever leave the river, Claudie. Promise me. Whatever happens, I'll always be on the river. Don't leave me, Claudie—don't leave me alone on the river."

"Never, my darling. Never."

And then, as simply as footlights go out, she was gone from him.

From beneath the flickering lanterns on the bank someone shouted, "Bring your fiddler! Old John's here! Your fiddler scared, or something?"

Only now did Claude become aware of the shouting and taunting around him. The entire company and crew of the Starlight were lined along the deck in front of the hand-painted pictures of wild animals, acrobats and characters from the plays of Shakespeare, shouting at the hill people. On the shore, the women were silent, but the men, fortified with whisky, yelled defiantly, "Old John can outfiddle any man can lift a bow!"

Claude started slowly down the deck toward the gangplank. When he passed the new captain, the younger man did not speak, but only nodded, saying silently, *You had better win, Claude Hanson.*

For years he had outfiddled anyone who challenged him—anyone from Minnesota to the bayous of the Atchafalaya. Caroline had taught him theatrical runs and trills, double-stops and quick changes of tempo, and even when he knew he was being bested, he had always been able to overwhelm his opponent and the audience by a fiery display of style. But it was not going to work tonight. Glancing ashore, he saw the aged, stooped man known as Old John of Ravens' Glen, and known, too, as the best fiddler who ever lived. Claude's heart sank. He could not remember how many fiddlers along the rivers had said to him, "The best of 'em all, the fairest fiddler of all is Old John of Ravens' Glen."

At the gangplank, Emil Hausner, the temperamental cook and female impersonator, reached out and touched his arm. "You'll win, Claude. You'll win. I just know it."

Claude tried to smile thankfully, but he knew the captain would fire him if he lost the contest. And there would not be another job on the river, not for a man passing sixty, a fair fiddler, but a poor player of villains. No, there wouldn't be another job.

I'll have to leave the river and desert my Caroline, he told himself as he walked down the gangplank, his shoulders thrown back and the fiddle swinging at his side as though it were an extension of his arm, a part of his body.

The hill people moved back as Claude strode slowly up the bank. Someone had brought two empty nail kegs, and Old John sat on one of them, his left arm bent and the base of his fiddle resting in the crotch of his elbow. He looked up and nodded, saying, "Howdy."

Claude spoke, bowing slightly, but as he took his place on the other keg he studied the aged man's face in the flickering light. Old John was small, wizened, and his cheeks were sunken inward between his toothless gums. His face was expressionless, except for his astonishingly hazel eyes, which sparkled with mischievous anticipation.

Glancing around, Claude saw the women were standing far back in the darkness, but the men were edging closer, speaking directly to Old John, but speaking words which Claude knew were aimed at his ears, "Play him right down the river, Old John. Play all the different kinds of tunes you know to mind."

Claude looked at the hillmen. They were angry and resentful. Not merely because he was going to play against Old John. No, it was something else, something he had seen happen hundreds of times. Not more than an hour before, the hill people had sat in the theater, entranced with the play, removed from their own world into a life so rich and vivid with emotion that they resented the sudden ending of the play which plunged them back into their toil-filled lives. It wasn't simply that he was the villain in The Red Dagger and during the performance the men in the audience, carried away by the play, had loudly threatened to kill him if he kidnaped the heroine. They had felt every emotion the actors portrayed and they were indignant that the performance had transported them into a dazzling world, and then, abruptly, abandoned them, making them appear foolish. Now they were determined that Old John should put him to shame and defeat.

"You play Rippytoe Ray!" a gaunt hillman shouted. He had his hands folded beneath the bib of his overalls, and when he spoke, it was like a command. "You hear me, Old John! Play Rippytoe Ray!"

Old John did not look up. "I got to discord my fiddle to play that," he said, as though there was no tune or style of playing which he did not know. He quickly tuned his fiddle so the bow could be drawn across two strings at a time and a rush of notes flew upward from the open strings.

Claude sat quietly.

The gaunt hillman began to shout out the words as the bow sawed out the three-eighths time:

> *"And a damn good fiddler was he!*
> *But all the tune he could play*
> *Was Rippytoe Ray, oh, Rippytoe Ray!*
> *Oh, Rippytoe Ray, oh, ree-e-e!"*

Closing his eyes, Claude thought of all the contests in which he had played. In the early days, his beloved had always stood beside him, smiling confidence and pride, and ever since her death he had sensed her presence. But tonight there was something angry and violent in the air, and it seemed, as Old John's bow sped across the strings, that he was alone for the first time since he had met Caroline. He wondered, as he sat with his head lowered and his eyes closed, if, with the passing of the years, his mind had become strange. He wondered if it was only his imagination which had made him feel she was near him. It was a thing that could happen when a man was heartsick with loneliness.

Old John's foot was going now, beating out the rhythm on the ground. It reminded Claude of Caroline's dancing, the quick, light tapping of her feet in the Highland fling. Even up to her death she had been billed as The Singing and Dancing Wonder. He imagined her whirling before him, wearing her short, full skirt, the bespangled bodice dazzling in the light. For a moment she seemed almost near him, smiling as she spun, and he lost himself in the reverie, remembering that always at the end of the number, when the curtain rolled down to the floor, she hurried to him, kissing him happily and crying, "Oh, Claudie, Claudie, I love to dance to your music!"

"Well, mister, you aimin' to play?"

"Maybe he's done give up already."

Claude roused himself. He had hardly been aware that Old John had finished his tune.

Awkwardly, fumbling, he tuned his violin, wondering what discorded tune he could play. The only one which came to his mind was Lost Indian. Testing the bow on the strings, he recalled the day Caroline first began teaching him the tune. It was a haunting song, filled with eerie sounds, but it was a song of river people. It was the story of a showboat tied up at a landing because the swollen river was filled with logs and driftwood. To while away the time, the company danced to a fiddler's tunes, but in the middle of the dance they heard weird shouts and looked out on the raging water to see an Indian on a large log. As they watched, the current caught the log, whirled it violently, and with a wild wail the Indian disappeared in the angry water. The fiddler became almost demented by the frightful scene, and forever after, it was said, he could play only the tune he was playing when the Indian drowned.

Caroline had asked him to play it often, for she felt there was joy and sorrow, life and death, in the haunting tune, and something of the awful cruelty which can come even to the innocent.

Catching his bow near the center because the tune was very fast and fine, Claude began to play, but each time he tried to imitate the wails and shrieks of the Indian, his bow only grated against the strings. Over and over he played the chorus, but it had neither life nor style and it revealed nothing of what he wanted to say, nothing of the awareness that life must end, violently or peacefully, but it must end.

Finally he dropped the fiddle from his shoulder and waited.

Old John began at once. He played Sally Goodin, and the hillmen shouted out the verse:

> *"A sheep and a cow*
> *Awalkin' in the pasture.*
> *The sheep said, 'Cow,*
> *Can't you walk a little faster?'* "

Claude knew that Old John and the men were taunting him because he had not played fast enough. He looked at the aged fiddler, but Old John appeared lost in his music, unaware of anything about him. Briefly he glanced at Claude, and his startlingly colored eyes were indifferent, almost defiant and scoffing.

The words of the song ran through Claude's mind: *I had a piece of pie, and I had a piece of puddin', and I gave it all away for to see my Sally Goodin.*

What had there been in life, what would there ever be, he wondered, that he wouldn't give to see his Caroline? From the day they had met, he had wanted to possess nothing except that which would give her pleasure and happiness. Now there was no reason to possess anything, except the pride and joy she had given him.

He had been twenty when they met, tall and raw and unlearned. He had come down from the hills and stood along the banks of the Arkansas River, entranced with the beauty of the boat, waiting for the show, for it was rumored that the show was for men only. He had never seen such a show and he was young, almost trembling with eagerness. But when the manager saw that the audience was made up solely of men, he told them they had the wrong idea and that all the women on the boat were ladies. "Go to the box office and get your money back," he had said from the stage.

The last to leave, Claude looked once more at the ornate tier of box seats. The acetylene-gas footlights were still glowing and the white, pale green and rust colors of the auditorium were like white clouds reflected in the water, the green of shoals and the burnished sunset on the river. As he stood, entranced and awed with the beauty, the curtain was rolled up and the prettiest girl he had ever seen walked onto the stage. Her beautiful red dress hardly reached to her knees and some pretty in her blond hair gleamed and glistened until a man could hardly believe it. Seeing him, she stopped suddenly, and then, as though she had no shame, she came down from the stage and walked up the aisle to him.

Claude was so frightened he wanted to run.

"I'm sorry there isn't going to be a show," she said in a soft, sweet voice.

"I am, too, ma'am. Sorrier than I can speak."

"You live here?"

"No, 'm. I live back in the hills. A ridge farmer is my life, but I'm alone and it ain't what you'd rightly call a real life. I thought seein' a showboat show"—he paused, blushing at what he had thought to see—"I'd have somethin' to call to mind durin' the wintertime."

Looking him directly in the eyes, she laid her hand on his arm. Claude felt that he was going over backward. The touch of her hand sent his heart to pounding so loudly he was afraid she would hear it.

"I like to ask people their names. Names interest me. What's yours?"

"Claude. Claude Hanson," he managed.

"And you're a handsome man, Claude. Now I'll never forget it. Claude Hanson."

His breath stopped. There was nothing wicked or forward in the way she talked. It was a thing she felt, and she said it honestly. And it was a thing a man could hardly bear to hear from a beautiful girl. Blushing, almost terrified, Claude turned and stumbled outside.

"Maybe next year!" she called after him. "Maybe next year, Claude Hanson!"

Next year! How could a man live so long? Reaching the bank, he leaned against a tree, hidden in the dark, and stood there for hours and hours, unable to believe what had happened to him. Inside the boat, he knew, there was such beauty and ease and joy that no other world seemed real to him. Any other life was only a burden, a thing to be endured.

Near midnight he heard the voices. Hillmen with their wives and sweethearts walked along the road and down to the gangplank, shouting happily that they had their women now and they wanted to see the show.

When the performance was over, Claude sat silently, unable to applaud or smile or shout. All his life, even before his parents died, he had been starved for beauty, and now he had found it. But it was in another world, a world which floated effortlessly through time, and he did not think he could bear to leave it.

At the top of the gangplank the beautiful girl was selling pictures of herself. He could not read well, but he saw her name, Caroline, written across the bottom of the pictures. "Car-o-line," he pronounced slowly. "It couldn't 'a' been any other name in the whole world."

And then they looked into each other's eyes. Though he was shy, even backward, he did not take his eyes from hers, for she seemed to command him. Suddenly she grabbed his broad hands and pressed them to her cheeks.

"Where do you go tomorrow?" he asked. "Where could I see the show again?"

"Moss Landing."

"I'll be there. I couldn't stand it not to see you again."

"I know, Claude. I know. I never danced as I did tonight."

Before he realized it, he was saying, "You got a work-job, here, for a man?"

"There'll be something!" she cried. "We'll find something!"

And then she embraced him.

Suddenly an older man spoke, "Caroline. Caroline, you'd better go inside."

"Yes, father," she said softly, almost like an obedient child, but she turned, and pulling Claude's head down, she gave him the first kiss he had ever had from anyone. "I'll be waiting for you."

Near dawn Claude reached his ridge farm. He gave his cow and his horse and chickens to a neighbor to keep, and started the forty-mile walk across the mountains to Moss Landing, carrying only his cash money—twenty-two dollars—and the suit he had bought when his mother had been buried at the clapboard church in Thunder Hollow.

He had never returned, but, looking at the hillmen about him, he thought it strange that they did not realize that he had been born one of them. It gave him a feeling of being stranded, of being neither a hillman nor a riverman, with no way ahead and no way back.

Old John had changed tunes and tempos and was playing Mississippi Sawyer. It was an old tune, a favorite with fiddlers everywhere. But as he listened, caught in the memory of his empty youth, Claude knew he had never heard the song played so beautifully. Through Old John's tricky bowing there could be heard the faint sound of anvils, the clinking of horseshoes and the sawing sound, drawn and easy, of sickles and scythes being whetted. It was a square-dance tune and the people began to clap hands to its rhythm.

Claude sat silently trying to recall the dreamless days of his boyhood, but his youth seemed so empty that he could hardly remember living before he met Caroline.

Living on the solitary ridge, he had grown to manhood knowing only loneliness and work, but from the moment he walked aboard the Starlight at Moss Landing, there had never been another moment of loneliness. His first job had been general handy man and bouncer, hustling ashore the drunken, pistol-waving coal miners and migrants who drifted along the rivers in shanty boats. Even at the beginning, Caroline, impetuous and determined, began to train him to become a member of the company. When she learned he had taught himself some simple fiddle tunes during the long winter evenings on the ridge, she began teaching him to read music, to play from the notes. She helped him to memorize lines from the plays and to speak them as if he were some other individual than himself. For weeks on end, drifting down the rivers or being towed up them, they sat alone on the upper deck.

Though he had been slow to learn, he recalled, she had never lost patience with him.

"Don't try to hurry so," she always said, but every day she led him onto the deck and sat with him while he practiced, urging him on. And she constantly corrected his speech, showing him how to enunciate clearly, erasing from his vocabulary the words and phrases which marked him as a hillman.

"Why are you so patient with me, Caroline?" he asked.

She looked off toward the bank of the river, toward the hills, but not seeing them. He knew she was looking into the future, and it made her strangely thoughtful.

"Because I am proud of you." She turned to him, smiling intimately. "Because I love you."

"Why? I can't fathom why you do."

"I'll tell you, Claude. I'll tell you as truly as I can. I just can't help it. I guess I was made to love you."

"I couldn't ever love anybody else," he told her. "I'd be ashamed was I ever to try."

Now, sitting silently as Old John played, he knew that life on the showboat, on the river, had changed them both. Or had it been the river and the boat? Hadn't it been love, a love so total and complete that no other life existed? Had this not been the quality which made the audience adore them, and which was now missing when he stepped alone onto the stage? He remembered with happiness the first night he had been allowed to play for Caroline while she danced. It had been far down in Louisiana, far from home, but as he played both a waltz and a Highland fling, never missing a note, he felt he had found the home which life had never given him before.

He recalled, tormented by the heartbreaking reverie, the entry in the boat's log the captain had made the next day: "Stopped at Le Grand to get Caroline and Claude married. Warm rain tonight." And now it was coming to an end. He knew he could never outfiddle the aged man next to him, and since his only value to the company was playing the fiddle contests to attract people to the boat, there was no doubt the captain would discharge him. He wondered what he could do and where he could go. What was there for a man of sixty, no longer able to make a living in the hills and rejected by the life he had always held dear?

Lifting the fiddle to his chin, he wondered at the peculiar treachery of life. The one thing which had given him joy and happiness, which had caused the years to rush by like autumn leaves on the river, had left him helpless to face the desolate loneliness of the longest years.

He looked out across his fiddle at the showboat company lined along the rail of the upper deck. They were silent and distant, quiet. Already they appeared to be drifting away.

The hurt was deep in him, and yet it was not a personal hurt. That kind of hurt had long since passed from him, assuaged by his memories. The pain he felt now was a sorrow, a grief, a sense of bewilderment and loss and estrangement, as if he had lived beyond his time and was left to wander alone.

Turning slightly, he peered at Old John, trying to tell him that he knew he was beaten and that from here in he would play only the tunes which filled his heart, evoking for the last time the happiness he had known. Old John returned his gaze, and even in the pale light the aged man's oddly colored eyes seemed to change, to turn a deeper color, as though he looked inward on some ancient knowledge. Resting his arms on his crossed legs, John nodded slightly.

There was a waltz Caroline had loved: I'll Be All Smiles Tonight. While Claude played the song, unmindful of anyone about him, the words came to him in Caroline's sweet, clear voice.

> *I'll deck my brow with roses,*
> *The loved one will be there.*

It had not been only for a night that she had been all smiles, he knew. Throughout the years he had shared with her she had been gay and happy, creating an aura of joy, a sense that love could never end.

> *And even them that know me*
> *Will think my heart is light,*
> *Though my heart may break tomorrow,*
> *I'll be all smiles tonight.*

For the first time Claude wondered if Caroline knew she would die young. Perhaps she had known she must leave him and had tried to tell him that he must not mourn. But loneliness and heartbreak are different from mourning, he told himself.

Without Claude being aware of it, Old John had begun to play. Claude could not be sure whether he had just let the bow become idle on the strings or whether Old John, in a wild flourish of sound, was banishing him, subjecting him to shameful defeat.

The fiddler from Ravens' Glen was playing Bonaparte's Retreat, producing an overwhelming barrage of sounds, drumming the strings with the back of his bow, plucking them, simulating musket fire and the din of battle, and then suddenly shifting to a long and continuous use of the bow until the sound of bagpipes and fifes could be heard. Even the hillmen were suddenly silenced and a woman, taking a steel comb from her hair, stepped beside Old John and struck the strings along the fingerboard, producing a sound of drumming.

Claude could not believe any man could re-create so much of life with a fiddle and he knew there was no use to compete. Yet he could not get up and walk away like a whipped dog. There was something he had to say—say to himself and the night—he had to speak his farewell to the river.

When Old John had finished, Claude began to play, and he could not stop. One tune after another rushed through his mind like leaves whirling brightly in an eddy. He wanted to play every tune he had ever known, every song he had shared with Caroline. He wanted to play them all and regain for a brief while the life they had known together. He no longer played to be heard, but with deep longing, with yearning and with a shattering anguish, for he wondered if it would have been more fortunate if he had never loved. In his youth he had been able to bear aloneness, but now, aged and lost, he was lonely for someone, for his love, and he found that the loneliness was terrifying.

Without pausing, he began Sandy River. He did not know whether he was playing well or not, for he believed Caroline was near him and he played only for her.

Sandy River always reminded her of the time he had saved the Starlight. It had been November, almost a quarter of a century ago. They were floating down below St. Louis when suddenly the Starlight rocked and shuddered. Screaming, the actors fled to the decks, ready to abandon the boat. Claude, grabbing a lamp, ran below. The boat had struck a piling and ripped a hole in her bottom as big as his body. He stood staring at the water rushing in through the rupture. Most of the crew were asleep and his shouting would not be heard above the swift swishing of the river. The hole had to be plugged quickly, he knew, and there was only one way a single man could do it.

Bounding up the stairs, he grabbed a thick blanket from the bed he shared with Caroline and ran back below. He knew the water was freezing, but he quickly wrapped the blanket around his body and lowered himself into the hole, pushing and shoving his weight against the inrushing water until he was waist deep. His own thick body, wrapped in the blanket, plugged the hole. His outspread arms supported him upright, but his freezing body caused him to shake and he feared he would be unable to hold on.

Finally the captain appeared. Bellowing profanely, shouting for the crew as the Starlight drifted on in the dark water, he ordered them to build a box.

"Get some boards!" he shouted. "Build a box around him! Build a box to hold that hellish water out or we'll sink before morning!"

Claude had hardly been aware when Caroline came to his side. His teeth were chattering and his eyes were clenched against the icy cold.

"Here, darling. Sip this, Claudie," she urged, holding to his lips a cup of hot coffee laced with whisky. "Oh, Claudie, you're the greatest trouper on the river."

It took almost an hour for the men to build the box around the hole, and in that time she never took her free arm from around his shoulders. And never once did she weep or speak a word of idle sympathy. Instead she smiled to him, teased him for his love, laughing as though it were a lark, but there passed from her to him such a feeling of pride and love that it carried him through the following week when he lay shivering and feverish.

Days later, the captain had come to him, telling him he would always have a place on the Starlight. But as he finished Sandy River and, without pausing, started the lively Go to the Devil and Shake Yourself, Claude reminded himself that that captain was long dead. A new captain owned the boat now, and he had no regard for old promises.

All those years—the whole of his life really—seemed suddenly unreal and improbable. And yet he knew they had happened. He ached to recapture them, to live those times once more before the night was over, before the hopeless wandering began.

But he was lost and confused. He could find no talisman to lead his thoughts backward. His bow hand dropped to his side and he stared about, helpless and lost. Old John was peering at him, quietly, barely smiling. He nodded his head very slowly, almost reverently, and Claude knew the fiddler was saying, "Go ahead; I will follow."

Lifting his fiddle to his chin, Claude felt a surging strength in his arms. Through The Devil in the Canebrake and Sugar Betty Ann, Old John followed, filling in the background, giving strength and fullness to the remembered music.

Claude knew he was playing better than he ever had before. He felt as though a gentle hand guided his bowing arm and it no longer mattered about the hills and the people. It was something coming through the music, not his or John's, but the music they played together, a kind of conformation John was giving him.

Once when he hesitated, wondering what tune to play, Old John took the lead, playing Darling Cory—playing it slowly, the way it sounded best. To Claude's amazement, Old John sang, flat and nasally, but directly and warmly:

> *"Don't you hear the bluebirds asingin'?*
> *Don't you hear that mournful sound?"*

And then he understood that through the music Old John of Ravens' Glen was telling him he understood—understood the heartbreak of life, the loneliness that is youth and age, understood that a man could give his life to the woman he loved, only to find that he had to remain long after she had gone.

Claude nodded to him, almost shaking with gratitude. Old John only smiled, his hazel eyes twinkling, telling him that life is not a thing that begins and ends, like a day, but flows on forever, like the river, flowing through all the days of a man's life, even the lonely and bitter ones. When the tune was finished, Old John waited.

Only Caroline had ever understood how he felt, Claude knew, but now an aged fiddler with hazel eyes had come down from the hills, smiling as Caroline had smiled, to tell him that if a man knows real love in his lifetime, it is enough to help him endure whatever else remains.

Why didn't I think of it before? Claude wondered, recalling the words he had written long years before, a kind of poem, and the music Caroline had composed to go with them. It was *O My Lovely Caroline*, and while he had been unable to play it since her death, he lifted his bow and began.

Though he couldn't have heard the tune before, Old John followed, playing the music as if he had known it all his life, discording it, pulling the deep and trembling notes from the strings. Claude looked at him, astonished. Old John appeared ageless, quiet as a spirit in the night.

Turning back, Claude looked at the showboat and the surging river beyond. His heart rose with joy, for he was neither lonely nor fearful. Out on the river, waiting, was all the love he had

ever known, and the fairest fiddler of all, Old John of Ravens'
Glen, by following him, by giving him the lead, was sending him
back to the river.

Now they played together. The night throbbed and hummed
with their music as it spread across the river and the hills, vanish-
ing upward. The hill people, who had been curiously quiet, as
though they sensed, but did not understand what was happening,
started to clap their hands, and then, hurrying to the level ground
above the trees, they began to dance, whirling and spinning and
stomping in the pale light, shouting joyously.

One by one, the show people came down the gangplank and
joined them. Again the lives of the hill people were joined with
magic as they danced with the heroine, the soubrette, the come-
dian and the imposter—all the characters from the play—throwing themselves into a world where happiness always won out.

Claude paused a moment, as the captain came up the bank,
but Old John urged him on, "Go ahead. Take the lead, young
feller. Tonight you're acallin' the tunes."

It wasn't that Old John was implying he was the best fiddler,
Claude knew. He was saying that love is a thing no man can conceal, not from a man who learned a headful of tunes by playing
them a thousand times—tunes of sorrow and joy and happiness
and love and loneliness, tunes learned by playing them alone in
the woods, where music seems a thing caught out of the air.

The two bows began to move, darting and shooting across
the strings, calling up music which first was played a hundred
lifetimes ago.